The Big Society Deb

The Big Society Debate

A New Agenda for Social Welfare?

Edited by

Armine Ishkanian

Lecturer in NGOs and Development, London School of Economics, UK

Simon Szreter

Professor of History and Public Policy, University of Cambridge Fellow, St John's College, Cambridge, UK

HISTORY & POLICY
Connecting historians, policymakers and the media

www.historyandpolicy.org

Edward Elgar
Cheltenham, UK • Northampton, MA, USA

Published by
Edward Elgar Publishing Limited
The Lypiatts
15 Lansdown Road
Cheltenham
Glos GL50 2JA
UK

Edward Elgar Publishing, Inc.
William Pratt House
9 Dewey Court
Northampton
Massachusetts 01060
USA

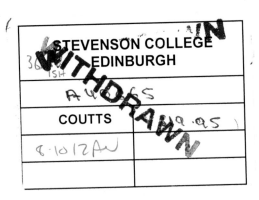

A catalogue record for this book
is available from the British Library

Library of Congress Control Number: 2012930614

MIX
Paper from
responsible sources
FSC FSC® C018575
www.fsc.org

ISBN 978 1 78100 207 0 (cased)
ISBN 978 1 78100 222 3 (paperback)

Typeset by Sparks, Gloucestershire, UK – www.sparkspublishing.com
Printed and bound by MPG Books Group, UK

Contents

Contributors

Martin Albrow, Senior Research Associate at the 'China in Comparative Perspective Network', LSE and Emeritus Professor, University of Wales, UK

Kate Bradley, Lecturer in Social History and Social Policy, School of Social Policy, University of Kent, UK

Lorie Charlesworth, Reader in Law and History, Law School, Liverpool John Moores University, UK

Richard Fries, Chief Charity Commissioner 1992–99 and Visiting Fellow Centre for Civil Society LSE 2000–2006, UK

Jose Harris, Emeritus Professor of Modern History, St Catherine's College, Oxford University, UK

Matthew Hill, Senior Research Officer, Institute for Volunteering Research, UK

Matthew Hilton, Professor of Social History, University of Birmingham, UK

Jane Holgate, Senior Lecturer in Work and Employment Relations, Work and Employment Relations Division, Leeds University Business School, UK

Armine Ishkanian, Lecturer in NGOs and Development, Department of Social Policy, London School of Economics, UK

Markus Ketola, Tutorial Fellow, Department of Social Policy, London School of Economics, UK

Diana Leat, Visiting Professor, Cass Business School, UK

David Lewis, Professor of Social Policy and Development, Department of Social Policy, London School of Economics, UK

Rachael McGill, National Coordinator, National Coalition for Independent Action, UK

Nick Ockenden, Director, Institute for Volunteering Research, UK

John Page, Secretary at Hackney Unites, UK

Cathy Pharoah, Professor of Charity Funding and Co-Director, ESRC Centre for Charitable Giving and Philanthropy, Cass Business School, UK

Liz Richardson, Research Fellow, School of Social Science, University of Manchester, UK

Joanna Stuart, Head of Research, Institute for Volunteering Research, UK

Simon Szreter, Professor of History and Public Policy, Cambridge University and Fellow of St John's College, Cambridge, UK

Daniel Weinbren, Research Fellow at The Open University, UK

Abbreviations

ACEVO	Association of Chief Executives of Voluntary Organisations
BBC	British Broadcasting Corporation
BSC	Big Society Capital
CDFI	Community Development Finance Institutions
CGAP	Consultative Group to Assist the Poor
CIC	Community Interest Company
CITR	Community Interest Tax Relief
CMPO	Centre for Market and Public Organisation
DCMS	Department for Culture, Media and Sport
EBRD	European Bank for Reconstruction and Development
EU	European Union
GNP	Gross national product
GP	General Practitioner
GWP	*Giving White Paper*
HM	Her Majesty's
IMF	International Monetary Fund
IVR	Institute for Volunteering Research
LEA	Local education authority
NCIA	National Coalition for Independent Action
NCS	National Citizen Service
NCVO	The National Council for Voluntary Organisations
NGO	Non-governmental organisation
NHS	National Health Service
OBE	Order of the British Empire
PASC	Public Administration Select Committee
PRSP	Poverty Reduction Strategy Paper
SAP	Structural Adjustment Programme
TUC	Trades Union Congress
UNFPA	United Nations Fund for Population Activities (The UN Population Fund)
USAID	United States Agency for International Development

Acknowledgements

The editors would like to thank the Suntory and Toyota International Centres for Economics and Related Disciplines (STICERD) at the London School of Economics (LSE) for funding the one-day workshop which was held on 23 March 2011. Others present at that workshop, whose participation and contribution was much appreciated, were: Faiza Chaudary, Professor Nicholas Deakin, Professor Bernard Harris, Daniel Stevens, Karen Weisblatt and Kate Spieglehalter. STICERD also co-funded a panel debate titled 'Big Society and Social Policy in Britain', which was held at the LSE on 27 January 2011 and which itself inspired the workshop. The panel debate was also supported by funds from the LSE Department of Social Policy and for that we are grateful to Professor Tim Newburn, Convenor, for his support and encouragement. Further information and a podcast of the panel debate is available on the LSE website http://www2.lse.ac.uk/socialPolicy/newsandevents/Home.aspx

We would additionally like to thank Professor Pat Thane, and Fiona Holland and Douglas Dowell of the Public Affairs Office of History and Policy at The Institute of Contemporary British History, King's College London, for their roles in supporting the 23 March workshop and in convening workshops at the Cabinet Office Strategy Unit on 15 June 2010 on civic society and at the Office for Civil Society on 28 February 2011 on local government, at which several of the contributions from the historians in this volume were first presented.

We are particularly grateful to Maria Schlegel, Programme Administrator at the LSE Department of Social Policy, for her support in organising the initial public lecture and seminar as well as for her overall project management duties, which included liaising with contributors, formatting the manuscript, etc. She has done a wonderful job and for that we would like to express our great thanks and gratitude.

We would also like to thank Dr Hakan Seckinelgin for his work on the book. Hakan was initially one of the editors of the volume but withdrew mid-way through the project for personal reasons. We missed his input in the later stages of the project, but were grateful to benefit from his participation at the beginning. We would like to extend this thanks also to the other participants at both the LSE and H&P organised workshops in 2010 and 2011, whose contributions at those workshops assisted with the discussions leading to this book. Finally, thanks to Hilary Cooper for providing editorial advice on the last draft of the editors' Introduction.

Introduction: what is Big Society? Contemporary social policy in a historical and comparative perspective

Simon Szreter and Armine Ishkanian

1 INTRODUCTION: POLICY AND RHETORIC

There can be no sensible commentary or meaningful debate about Big Society without full recognition that it 'is a deeply historical concept', to cite Matthew Hilton's opening sentence in his chapter below. The aim of this volume is to create a dialogue between history, policy and practice, and to provide readers with a historically grounded, internationally informed, multidisciplinary answer to the question we pose in the title – *The Big Society Debate: A New Agenda for Social Welfare?*

The idea for the volume came about following a one-day workshop held in March 2011 at the London School of Economics titled 'Thinking Critically about the Big Society'. The workshop brought together academics from different disciplines, practitioners from the voluntary and public sectors, and historians from the History and Policy network to discuss the underpinnings of the 'Big Society' agenda, the historical context from which this idea emerged, the effects of the Big Society in practice, its implications longer term for civil society, relations between state and non-state actors, and what lessons can be drawn from international experience. This volume continues that discussion and begins with the historical. The chapters in Part I provide the archivally researched contributions of professional historians, which are vital to critically inform and complement the chapters in Part II that focus on social policy and examine the challenges of operationalising the three key components of the Big Society agenda as defined by the Cabinet Office: community empowerment; opening up public services; and social action (Office for Civil Society, 2011a). Various chapters in this volume raise questions and problematise these stated aims. They examine the limitations and consider the challenges involved in translating these ideas into practice.

The opening chapter of Part I by Jose Harris is a crucial starting point for anyone who wants to know something of this term's historical provenance. As Harris makes clear, Big Society, whether its chief proponents such as Phillip Blond and Jesse Norman know it or not, is a term with longstanding, reverberating, transatlantic and cross-Channel historical echoes down the generations AS 'great society'. While classical forebears can be summoned, Harris chooses to focus on the modern ancestry of the term since the founding discussion in Adam Smith's *Theory of Moral Sentiments* of 1759. She explores how this immediately bequeathed a formative ambivalence to the discussion, since Smith propounded, by turns, both the planned and organised great society and the free market alternative. Most frequently the precise term invoked has been 'great society' and theorists and politicians as unalike as August Comte and Graham Wallas before the First World War, Friedrich Hayek and Lyndon Johnson since the Second World War, have each laid claim to it as a term expressing the ideal society they aspired to create. However, Harris argues, notions of a great society were not explicitly invoked when the welfare state was designed and implemented during the 1940s. Perhaps, if Martin Albrow (in this volume) is right, philosophers, politicians and their advisors in Britain have only spent their efforts envisaging and exhorting the creation of a great or big society when they felt it was a desirable but unattainable dream, a safe exhortation. Uniquely, between 1939 and 1948 a variant of the planned version of the great society became practical politics and an implemented policy in Britain.

In the first chapter of Part II, Martin Albrow cogently argues that, as well as having a historical pedigree, albeit of a mongrel character, it is also the case that Big Society today 'has to be understood in the first instance as a rhetorical intervention'. It is a slogan for communicating with the general public and as such, he argues, we can be sure that David Cameron and his advisors, including the marketing and media professionals who dominate the new Big Society Network, will have decided on it only after the most rigorous consideration, since 'slogans in politics are as important as brand names for businesses' (Albrow).

Ever since David Cameron first introduced the idea of Big Society for the 2010 election campaign, he has had to defend and relaunch it a number of times. In spite of this, and contrary to what critics expected in 2010, the concept has had extraordinary staying power. It remains at the very heart of the government's agenda – rhetorically if not always in practice. Thus, if we accept the proposition that much forethought went into the decision of the naming of this idea, then why choose such an ambiguous, elusive and polysemic slogan? In focusing on its value as political rhetoric, Albrow argues that this is precisely one of its key functions: deliberate vagueness allows for flexibility in application so that Big Society can simultaneously signify different things to different groups including, as we discuss later in this chapter, between the two partners in the governing Coalition.

This ambiguity was evident in the aftermath of the August 2011 riots, when pundits and policymakers proffered contradictory interpretations of how the riots and vigilantism were the 'embodiment of "big society"' (Williams, 2011) or that Big Society is exemplified by the post-riot, community led clean-ups (Ashton, 2011). Recognising the flexibility and elusive nature of this concept, rather than attempting to define Big Society with a pithy sentence or two here at the beginning of this volume, we believe it is more important to pose, in this opening introduction to the volume, a set of five key questions.

First, as it is informing government policy, we can ask what aspects of the British polity, in its broadest sense, does Big Society refer to? What does it seek to engage with and foster, or to disengage with, alter and shun? Second, as rhetoric, what political work does Big Society do for the Tory dominant partner in the Coalition, whose leader, the Prime Minister, has coined the term and continued to argue that advancing the Big Society is his 'mission' (BBC, 2011)? Third, we ask the question that always has to be asked of rhetoric – what of reality? How does the general viewpoint and vision projected by Big Society match up to the historical and contemporary realities which it invokes to justify its proposals? Fourth, we ask, what lessons can be learned from international experience? Since many of the policies advanced in the Big Society agenda have been implemented in other countries over the past two decades – and indeed, in some instances, with funding from the UK Department for International Development – we believe it is important to examine the implications of that experience in the context of the Big Society policy agenda in the UK. Finally, in view of the nature of the gap that is always there between rhetoric and reality, what are the chances of either the rhetorical or the policy success of this agenda? It could prove to be ineffective, even counterproductive policy, yet still count as a rhetorical success for the Tory-led Coalition government, notably, for instance, if Big Society succeeds with the electorate as a communication device, in masking its own policy failure, should that occur.

In this Introduction we integrate the discussion of the various chapters with reference to these five key questions to demonstrate the linkages between the individual chapters of the two sections on cross-cutting themes and issues related to the Big Society agenda. In addition to discussing the chapters produced by academics, we have also included two boxes in this Introduction that were written by practitioners as a way of enhancing our dialogue between history, policy and practice. The two boxes illustrate the issues 'front-line'[1] practitioners from charities and campaigning organisations encounter when attempting to translate Big Society rhetoric and policies into practice.

2 THE UNIVERSE OF BIG SOCIETY: WHAT'S IN AND WHAT'S OUT?

To address the first of these five questions, Big Society, in principle, gestures to and invokes the importance for the nation's future of the entire gamut of institutions, associations and activities that lie between those of the tax-funded central state, the market and the elementary social unit of the family household (which sometimes – in a gradually increasing proportion of cases today – refers to a solitary individual). However, within that vast and diverse ecological social space, whose very name is contested (civil society, third sector, voluntary sector, non-profit sector etc.), there dwell many species and genera. These can be generalised into a set of phyla of institutional types each embracing a number of sub-variants, such as charities; pressure groups; leisure groups; mutual support associations; social networks. These phyla and genera contain many individual species, some of which have the characteristics of more than one of the more general categories. They range in size, scope, level of formality and professionalisation, etc. Some, but tellingly not all, of these organisational species are favoured by Big Society proponents, whose work and efforts they seek to support and promote.

Mr Cameron's speeches, drawing from the ideas of the main protagonists of Big Society, such as Phillip Blond, Jesse Norman, and Lord Nat Wei, have preferred to focus on the agency of individuals in their communities, the 'army of volunteers' in the locality, 'community' action and, of course, individual responsibility and empowerment. Among the preferred species of organisations, which include registered charities, non-governmental organisations (NGOs), social enterprises and self-help groups, Big Society proponents favour, above all, individual citizen-volunteers doing good in their community, organising themselves and taking responsibility for sorting out their locality's needs. Just as the free market of neo-liberal, micro-economic theory throws up spontaneous order in the form of the optimal allocation of resources – because each buying and each selling agent knows their requirements better than a government planner – so, too, the defenders of Big Society contend that it is important to unleash the freedom of the individual citizens and 'unshackle' them from the 'unnecessary bureaucracy – red tape' and 'countless forms' so that they can 'make a real difference in their communities' (Lord Hodgson of Astley Abbotts, 2011; Office for Civil Society, 2011b). Although Phillip Blond, for instance, would no doubt protest that his version of Big Society would seek to empower the local as well as the individual, it is Mr Cameron's interpretation that counts, so far as policy is concerned.

There are several kinds of intermediary associations which also occupy that space between state, family and market, which Big Society is *not* seeking to invoke or support, notably the political organisations representing the sectional interests of industry, employers and parts of the business community, the trade unions and the professional associations; while quangos are another such intermediary institution not intended to be included, as they are too close to Big Government, which is one of the key rhetorical antitheses of Big Society in Tory rhetoric. Finally, there is the most difficult phylum of all for Big Society, democratically elected local government. By definition, local government is not the Big Government of 'the central state'. However, the Big Society speeches of David Cameron so far have no place for elected local government in them, but proponents of the concept cannot continue to ignore the elephant in the room for much longer – sooner or later Mr Cameron will have to spell out where he and his government stand on the relationship between Big Society and elected, representative local government.

This is because, as Szreter's chapter shows, throughout British history during the last half-millennium, local government, while continuously evolving, has been experienced and understood as a chief bulwark of the local against overbearing central state interference and, frequently, as the single most important expression of local community and participatory citizenship. When it has worked effectively, responsive and respectful local government has provided the institutional basis for linking social capital (see box below) which, Szreter and Woolcock (2004) have argued, is critical for socially inclusive participation and civic activism in those many real-life communities where differences of power, authority and resources between individuals are commonplace and salient.

BOX I.1   SOCIAL CAPITAL

Social capital is itself a term with a complex conceptual history (Farr, 2004). It has been most vigorously promoted by Robert Putnam (2000), who defined social capital as inhering in networks and norms of reciprocity and trust. Putnam (2000, pp. 22–4) also adopted the distinctions between 'bonding' and 'bridging' social capital originally proposed by Gittell and Vidal (1998). Bonding social capital refers to trusting and cooperative relations between members of a network who see themselves as being similar, in terms of their shared social identity. Bridging social capital, by contrast, comprises relations of respect and mutuality between people who know that they are not alike. Szreter (2002) and Szreter and Woolcock (2004) critiqued Putnam's formulation, arguing that it failed to address structures and inequalities of power and authority in both national societies and communities and that therefore a third category of 'linking' social capital was required, without which the concept was theoretically incomplete. Linking social capital refers to the possibility of relationships of trust between members of a network who know themselves not only to be different in terms of social identity (bridging social capital) but also in terms of their institutionalised endowments of power and resources.

This is supposedly what the Big Society is all about in its claims that a 'broken society' now needs to be regenerated by voluntary participation and leadership in such fractured communities at the local level. Proposing that this should be done while ignoring local government makes little sense; proposing that it be done in place of elected and accountable local government begins to look like some form of vigilante alternative to democratic structures

A type of vigilantism emerged during the August 2011 riots when groups of men, armed in some cases with baseball bats, defended their shops, homes and neighbourhoods from looters. Journalists across the political spectrum lauded the Turkish men in Dalston and the Sikh men in Birmingham who defended their shops with baseball bats; one journalist even called them 'turbaned avatars of Cameron's Big Society come to stop the burning' (Kain, 2011). They were far less enthusiastic about the group of white men, who called themselves the Enfield Defence League, who marched in Enfield wearing white T-shirts and chanting 'England' and 'EDL' (one presumes that in this instance they were referring to the Enfield Defence League and not the English Defence League).

One could play devil's advocate and argue that these two groups, however different they may be, were in some way filling in the gap or picking up where the state was overextended. Whether we wish to cheer or denigrate these instances as examples of self-organised defence or dangerous vigilantism, one thing remains clear: these groups were based on narrow ethnic, religious or racial identities. As such, they are examples of bonding social capital rather than bridging social capital (Putnam, 2000, pp. 22–4). Big Society proponents, such as Lord Wei, would probably want to support only the latter (Ramesh, 2010). Not only was the social capital of these self-defence actions exclusive, in that it was constructed along narrow categories of identification and belonging, but moreover, it excluded others within the same community who did not belong to that specified group. Yet, if communities are to organise in their own collective interests, as is desired by Big Society proponents, then it is absolutely essential that connections are made not only within groups but more importantly *between* groups in a community (or indeed between communities); and also, Szreter and Woolcock (2004) would insist, between citizens and those in positions of power and authority within and from outside the communities. But it is no secret that such bridging and linking social capital is the most difficult to build and, indeed, sustain; and the least likely to emerge spontaneously in the manner apparently envisaged by Big Society proponents. The recent experience of Hackney Unites provides an example of a community going beyond mere bonding social capital, but it also demonstrates how building such bridging and linking social capital in this locality required directed political self-organisation and a genuinely felt local common cause.

Hackney Unites works in one of the areas that was greatly affected by the riots in August 2011. Recognising and celebrating the diversity in Hackney, the organisation operates on the premise that the diverse communities in Hackney will achieve more working together than separately. Their work, which is described below, is to find the 'cement that can bind a community together'. They attempt to find creative and constructive solutions to the social and economic problems in their community by finding ways to connect its diverse members. Since Hackney Unites is a 'front line organisation', we asked Jane Holgate and John Page what they thought of Big Society and how the policies underlying the Big Society agenda were affecting their work.

BOX I.2   HACKNEY UNITES: A 'BIG SOCIETY' INITIATIVE?

By Jane Holgate and John Page, Hackney Unites

In one of his many speeches attempting to launch the Big Society, David Cameron posed an unresolved question: 'The Big Society demands mass engagement: a broad culture of responsibility, mutuality and obligation. But how do we bring this about?' Hackney, East London, is perhaps not the place where you would instinctively look for a community organisation that might provide a model for the Big Society. Hackney has a history of dysfunctional local politics. It is a multicultural borough, with a significant gay and lesbian community. It is a borough of both 'haves' and 'have nots', where the median average income is above the national average, but it is the second most deprived Local Authority in England which has amongst the worst unemployment rates in the country, high levels of transience in the population (making stable communities more difficult to sustain) and, lastly, it is a borough where sections of our youth belong to a violent gang subculture. Today, in Hackney, culture is marked by its sheer diversity as people of different ethnic backgrounds, faiths, languages, histories of migration, incomes, jobs and hopes live side by side. What does the graduate, working in the City and living in Hackney until their children are school age, have in common with the office cleaner, who may live 100 yards away and even clean the building in which the graduate works, but whose lives and opportunities are vastly different? Hackney Unites celebrates this diversity and operates on the simple premise that the diverse communities in Hackney will achieve more working together than separately. We ask, where is the cement that can bind a community together? The organisation has built an ethnically diverse leadership, worked in coalition with dozens of local groups, and mobilised hundreds of residents around specific issues. In short we have taken key steps towards developing a local culture of 'responsibility, mutuality and obligation'. More recently, and following the disturbances in London and elsewhere in the UK in the summer of 2011, we have redirected our activities to ensure that young people are more included in community organising and we have developed a training programme to provide the skills necessary to organise other young people around issues that are important to them.

Hackney Unites was founded in conflict and it is largely sustained by conflict. A collective sense of injustice, of threat and of isolation from the political process drives our work. Hackney Unites began life as 'Hackney Unites against the BNP', an initiative launched by local trade unionists seeking to encourage voter participation in the 2008 mayoral elections. The British National Party (BNP) had not tried to run candidates in the borough for many years and when their national membership list was leaked they had just 12 members in the borough. With less than a week's notice, the group was informed that the local paper had accepted an advert for the BNP. This was seen as a gross provocation as Hackney viewed itself as BNP-free. Eventually the group hit upon a novel and powerful plan. By using 'critical path analysis' and 'power mapping' techniques, we identified that the people with the power to stop this advert were the newsagents. The vast majority of newsagents in Hackney are from ethnic minority backgrounds who need no convincing of the poison that would be spread by the inclusion of an advert for the BNP in the local paper. We drafted a fax on behalf of newsagents which said in effect: I am a retailer upon whom you rely to sell your paper. If you run the advert for the BNP, then I am cancelling my order for your paper. The result was that many dozens of newsagents faxed the statement to the *Hackney Gazette*'s publishers and they withdrew the advert. Not only did they do that, but for all the other titles in their portfolio, they donated any money received to charity and stated they would not in future run the adverts. This was an early and powerful success for the coalition. Coming out of this two-year, anti-BNP campaign, the informal core of the group reached a consensus that the coalition was too valuable to be decommissioned and so the group was reconfigured as 'Hackney Unites' coalition.

This anti-racist work, which had been the conception of Hackney Unites, brought an eclectic mix of people together, including two employment lawyers, and a number of active trade unionists. Together they realised that they had the potential to do something along the lines of the American 'Workers Centres' where professionals provided free advice to vulnerable workers in sectors of the economy where trade unions were virtually non-existent. In exchange the workers agreed to participate in the organisation and to spread understanding of employment rights to their colleagues. In many ways this is Hackney Unites' key 'outreach' project. It has held surgeries in community halls, tenant halls, churches and for ethnic minority community groups.

Post-riots Hackney Unites is an example of how local activists, working together and utilising community organising strategies, can begin to create the solidarity that is inherent in the concept of a Big Society. Lauded by the TUC, by Searchlight educational trust and by the local Council for Voluntary Services, and working with over 40 local groups from across the political and cultural spectrum (including the local rugby club), Hackney Unites is a success story.

However, its very success perhaps underlines the contradiction in Cameron's Big Society. If community organising works because marginalised communities can be taught the skills necessary to exert ever-increasing power over their circumstances, then they will, inevitably, challenge the current government's agenda of rolling back the welfare state, deregulating industry and abandoning the social safety net. Hackney Unites shows not only what can be achieved, but also that, for community organising to work, it needs a target and an injustice that is deeply felt and widely felt. For communities like those in Hackney the widely felt and deeply felt injustice will be Cameron's attempts to redistribute wealth and power towards the already wealthy. The target will be Cameron's own policies. The only question is, when will he recognise that his Big Society will see the chickens coming home to roost?

3 STRATEGIC AIMS OF THE BIG SOCIETY RHETORIC

To move on to our second question, Big Society as rhetoric serves at least three strategic political purposes for the Conservatives in the Coalition government. First, it offers to the right and centre of the Conservative Party considerable continuity with the touchstone ideology of Thatcherism, in being against Big Government and the tax-hungry state; and in favour of the heroic, autonomous individual and their liberty to act economically and socially as they see fit. Second, it diverts attention away from government and towards the responsibilities of others during a programme of deep cuts to the public sector, which the Coalition adopted as its preferred policy choice (the alternative policy option being more gradual cuts combined with more steeply progressive tax rises on the financial elite and the financial services sector in order to pay for the deficit caused by those working in that sector of the economy). Third, in positively evoking 'society' it helps to keep the Lib Dems on board, creating the impression that the Conservative Party has truly changed, to the extent that it now discusses the mythic banned entity of Mrs Thatcher, for whom 'society' was a term altogether too close to the great enemy, 'social-ism'.

The rhetoric of Big Society is all about empowering individuals, communities and organisations, promoting greater responsibility, and access to information. But this assumes that every community and organisation is on a level playing field and that they have equal access to information, skills and resources with which to take over the running of services and programmes. This is hardly the case. On the contrary, asymmetries of power and of information affect how communities and associations mobilise, organise and even compete for funding. In an effort to address these asymmetries and to build local capacity, the government provided funding in February 2011 for the Community Organisers programme. The aim of the programme is to catalyse community action by 'igniting the impulse to act'. The goal is for the five thousand community organisers working for this programme to build capacity and empower local communities, by identifying local leaders, projects and opportunities. The assumption is that, once empowered and supported, the communities will be able to take advantage of Big Society initiatives, such as the right to bid to run public services (Office for Civil Society, 2011c).

Despite the Big Society rhetoric of 'unshackling' charities and 'igniting' people's impulse to act, the evidence shows that the spending cuts have often negatively impacted charities and, indeed, led to the curtailment of services and closure of many organisations (False Economy, 2011). Moreover, there is a big difference between participating in a local initiative, as opposed to bidding for a contract to provide a service. Many people working in the voluntary and community sector are angry and dismissive of the Big Society proposals and initiatives, including the Community Organisers programme. They are angry not only because they are experiencing funding cuts, but also because of the emphasis on volunteerism within the Big Society agenda, which is presented as a strategy by which charities can compensate for the loss of paid staff. Many professionals working in charities argue that the assumption that volunteers can simply step in and take over the running of services or programmes devalues and belittles the skills, experience and knowledge of professionals. But, as Rachael McGill from the National Coalition for Independent Action (NCIA) discusses below, despite their anger, in the current political climate third sector professionals and charities often feel compelled to buy into the rhetoric and to engage 'as if they think it is a workable concept'. McGill argues that the strategy of saying one thing in public and another in private – and declining to openly challenge the ideology behind Big Society – means that many voluntary organisations are 'colluding in their own demise, allowing the government to turn all activity that used to be called "charity," "voluntary" or "civil society" into business' – the alternative is that voluntary action simply disappears.

BOX I.3   THE IDEOLOGY BEHIND THE BIG SOCIETY: THE DESTRUCTION OF VOLUNTARY ACTION

By Rachael McGill, NCIA

The National Coalition for Independent Action (NCIA) is a network of individuals and organisations who give their time on either a paid or voluntary basis to the professionalised 'voluntary sector', the more informal 'community sector', and/or activism and campaigning.

People get involved with NCIA because they believe there is a need to unite to celebrate, support and defend independent voluntary and community activity. They see our ability to challenge and change the world about us as increasingly constrained. Unless confronted, this threat to independent action will undermine our civil society, our political health, and the capacity of communities to get what they need for themselves.

This analysis of 'big society' is an edited extract from our policy paper 'Voluntary action under threat' (available to download on our website at www.independentaction.net). The paper gathers together evidence and arguments about the role of 'big society' in the government's wider agenda: privatisation and the destruction of the welfare state and of voluntary and community activity as we know them. In place of any big commitment to supporting the individuals and groups doing work for the good of 'society', we have documented big cuts, big attacks on the voluntary and community sectors, a big market, big government, big contradictions, big bigotry, big inequalities, big demands on ordinary people and big control: all big danger signals for those of us who care about community and social action to improve our world.

The 'big society' proposals are dismissed by nearly everyone you meet in the voluntary and community sector when they are talking off the record. In public, some organisations engage with the 'big society' as if they think it is a workable concept, lining up to help 'deliver' it, in the hope that they can grab a piece of the ever-diminishing funding pie. By declining to highlight the ideologically noxious thinking behind the 'big society', voluntary organisations are colluding in their own demise, allowing the government to turn all activity that used to be called 'charity', 'voluntary' or 'civil society' into business. NCIA urges those in voluntary sector organisations to voice their concerns openly, not to say one thing in private and another in public.

Much has been made of the possibility of services coming under community control through the government's Localism Bill. However, the 'right to challenge' included in the bill is specifically intended to open up the 'public service market'. In the absence of any genuine 'enabling and encouraging' of communities to take on services (in fact the reverse is happening as local charities and community provision are being decimated by cuts), it is the large corporate charities and the private sector which are taking on this role. The *Independent* reports that 'LSSI, an American firm which manages 13 public libraries across the US, has set itself a target to manage libraries in eight British local authorities by the end of the year and to capture 15 per cent of the market within five years.'

The government wants to institutionalise the idea that the preferred way to fund traditionally charitable activity is through social enterprise methods: loans and income generation through contracts, charging or trading, rather than grants or other public subsidies. These are the first steps towards ending government support for voluntary action completely. In the gap between what the state won't provide – determined by the cuts, and what the private or voluntary sector can't make money from, or raise money for – people will be left to make their own arrangements. Instead of being a public service that complements our welfare state, services like support to refugees will become something that happens only in some areas because people do it for free. A return to the values of Victorian-style philanthropy will allow those with money to decide which resources are needed, to do what, according to their measure of what is most deserving.

Most community groups have no interest in delivering public services. Their vision of what is needed may not fit that of the government. A Third Sector Research Centre working paper found that most grass-roots community groups saw themselves as an 'important response to needs that were currently unmet either due to lack of resources, or the failure of the state and other agencies to identify or address need.' Getting involved in a local group to improve your community is different from taking responsibility for a social enterprise and bidding for contracts. Matt Scott, of the Community Sector Coalition, says: 'real devolution of power by communities would go beyond the opportunity to ... take over the running of a building ... if localism were to happen from the grass roots upwards we would see a rich diversity of informal community action, which inevitably takes years and costs money. The more likely scenario is that local community action will continue to decline, as always happens at times of economic hardship because the rational choice is to use one's time to seek paid work, not to volunteer.'

The 2008 Conservative Party green paper, *A Stronger Society*, quoted the architect of the welfare state, William Beveridge: 'people and organisations are ... more "vigorous and abundant" when given the freedom to act on their own initiative rather than when ordered from above.' It is difficult to see how cuts to their independent sources of funding and the exhortation to deliver services determined by the government will help community groups and organisations to do this. The Carnegie Commission said: 'Civil society associations can never be just providers of services ... their energy comes from values – of justice, equality and mutuality ... civil society thrives best when it has an independent and confident spirit, when it is not beholden to the state or funders, and when it is not afraid to make trouble.'

The 'big society' is certainly lazy and cynical policymaking (if good things happen the government will claim credit for having 'enabled' people to do things for themselves, if they don't it will be the fault of people for not being enterprising enough), but it is also much worse than that. Matt Scott says: 'if someone wanted to set the sector back not just decades but into the Victorian era they could not do better.'

> Community groups that emerge for other reasons than to de-
> liver services are a way for people with less power in society (most
> of us) to look out for each other and represent ourselves. If we
> feel we have no voice, the result is increased social strife in com-
> munities. This is why, historically, more enlightened governments
> and charitable trusts have given informal, needs-led local groups
> money and support which did not compromise their independ-
> ence. If these groups are left out of the picture there is more space
> for those with the most money, time and influence to further their
> interests at the expense of everyone else's.
>
> It is not just individual groups and services which are in danger
> of disappearing as part of the 'big society', privatisation and cuts.
> It is the recognition of, and support for, a whole sphere of human
> activity: the space in which people are free to do things, large or
> small, not because the government promotes them or because
> they will generate profit, but to try to change the world.

Kate Bradley's chapter provides a historical perspective on this in the area of youth work. Bradley finds that the invention of bespoke Big Society volunteer groups by central government and its supporters, such as the new National Citizens' Service, may already be doing positive damage by draining limited resources in a sector – youth work – where there is a long history of well-established, professional non-governmental activity. This dates back to the late Victorian East End settlement movement. Bradley is concerned that some of the established and experienced organisations in this important and complex sphere of social work, where tact and local knowledge are important and require much experience to build up, are now being replaced by well-meaning novice amateurs. Such volunteers have no professional accountability for their young clients – when mistakes occur, as they inevitably do with this vulnerable section of society, volunteers can simply walk away. In an era of cuts these new and untried Big Society initiatives may actually be crowding out, not complementing, established players in the voluntary sector.

As public sector funding shrinks, charities are being forced to seek alternative sources of funding including from charitable foundations, trusts and corporations. The funding decisions of these alternative sources are driven by and shaped by their own interests, conditions and objectives. As such, funding programmes for public benefit is not always their main priority. Cathy Pharoah's chapter outlines the emerging debates and discusses the proposed models for financing social ventures in the context of Big Society (e.g. Big Society Capital, etc.). She identifies some of the issues and implications that arise for funding social welfare through the Big Society approach. The government's concept, she states, is that a successful Big Society is one where communities generate their own local solutions to meeting service needs rather than merely asking for more funding. The Coalition's vision, Pharoah writes, is that 'alternative models of financing will emerge as part of a cultural shift to stronger local empowerment and engagement in service delivery.' Yet, it is unclear whether these alternative financing models can be effective and sustainable in the long term. Not all organisations will survive, let alone thrive, in the new funding context. Small organisations in particular will be negatively affected by the loss or decline in statutory funding and will find it difficult to access alternative sources, including corporate funding. The latter, Pharoah demonstrates, are generally concentrated in particular areas of concern, such as cancer or animal welfare, or issues of concern to religious organisations and faith-groups, which can leave organisations that work on other and unfashionable problems, such as social welfare and special needs, in a precarious position.

Diana Leat's chapter grapples with a related topic – the role of philanthropic foundations in the context of Big Society. Leat questions how much the Coalition government really understands the philanthropic foundations they are trying to woo. She considers the role of philanthropy and foundations both in the UK and the US. Her chapter demonstrates how foundations tend to fiercely guard their independence and autonomy in decision making. Leat argues that although government may hope that foundations will provide funding for the programmes or services that will be affected by public spending cuts, the reality is that foundations often choose to fund in a range of rather different spheres, some of which include giving to their pet projects which may be of little policy relevance. Leat suggests that policymakers need to recognise that foundations have functions that are different from government and that they can do things that government cannot or should not do. Foundations are not – and show no signs of wishing to be – a substitute, supplement, or back pocket for the provision of public services.

Thus, even in its most basic aims and assumptions, there appears to be a major disjuncture between the rhetoric of how Big Society works and the reality of what is already happening on the ground.

4 HISTORICAL AND CONTEMPORARY REALITIES

Thus, as we move from rhetoric, politics and professed aims on to our third question – of the historical and contemporary reality, against which to judge the concept of Big Society and its claims about a broken past, and its capacity to fix this and to engender a golden future of civic activism – we begin to encounter very significant issues and problems. As the chapters collected here in both Parts I and II attest, there is such a yawning gap between the rhetoric and the reality in so very many respects that, if 'Big Society' was ever to be taken at all seriously by our legislators as a guide or talisman for divining the optimal social policies and service delivery pattern for Britain, it would likely have catastrophic consequences, so demonstrably does it fly in the face of both the recent and the long-term history of this country and, indeed, of many others (see chapters by Ketola and Ishkanian).

Big Society as policy proposition rests on two eminently empirically testable assertions about British society and its recent history. First, that Britain today is a broken society in which civic-minded participation is petering out and volunteering has come to an end. Second, that this is because of the growth of the overweening central state, particularly the welfare state and its bureaucratic social security budget, which has robbed British citizenry of its capacity for responsible independence. In the most simple rhetorical formulations it is claimed that philanthropy and voluntary associational activity have been 'crowded out' by 'Big Government', which appears to subscribe to a crude notion of a finite fund of 'altruistic' behaviour, which will disappear from civil society if 'monopolised' by the central state.

The historical chapters by Szreter, Charlesworth, Weinbren, Bradley and Hilton, and the comparative chapters by Ketola and Ishkanian, each demonstrate that this is the exact opposite of the reality of the way in which British society and many others have functioned and continue to do so. In fact, a high level or a dynamic trend of rising provision of tax-funded public goods and services mandated by the state tends typically to be associated with high or rising levels of citizens' participatory activity in the life of their communities. In part this is because all citizens have before them the practical lesson, embodied in both national and local governments' policies, that caring collectively for the whole community is a high cultural priority of this society and that all are expected to participate fully, with the greatest contribution necessarily coming from the wealthiest citizens through their taxes. The truth of this proposition is supported by a particularly long history in England (see chapter by Szreter).

The chapters by Charlesworth and by Fries each foreground the importance of two foundational Acts of Elizabeth I in 1601, one of which set out a mandatory framework of rate-funded local parish government for administering individual universal entitlements to welfare, while the other specified the proper purposes of charity trusts, which were also thereby directed to the relief of poverty and education of the poor. Thus, Tudor England was a global pioneer in creating an extraordinarily far-sighted legal framework, which sought to encourage the wealthy elites of all parishes to engage fully in their responsibilities toward the less fortunate in a growing market economy. The Elizabethan state both endowed the poor with inalienable legal rights to relief, to be paid for by a mandatory tax on the wealthy (rates levied on the value of land occupied), while at the same time, and alongside this, directing and facilitating elites to use their surplus personal wealth for noble and charitable purposes. This policy is clearly premised on the opposite assumption to that of 'crowding out'. The fact that it worked so effectively for centuries was due to the cogency of the incentive structure it thereby created for the wealthy: genuinely effective and well-designed charitable acts would not only bring honour to the wealthy but would also, to the extent that they relieved poverty, reduce the mandatory costs they incurred as the main financial contributors to the parish Poor Law fund.

The other testable assertion behind Big Society, the 'declinist' thesis – that since some point in the 1950s, 1960s or 1970s volunteering in British society has been falling away – is derivative from the influential 'Bowling Alone' thesis of Robert Putnam (2000), concerning the decline of 'community' or 'social capital' in the US since the 1970s. As Matthew Hilton's chapter, reporting on his team's important research programme shows, as far as post-war British history is concerned such a thesis is dependent on an anachronistic, a-historical and selective mis-reading of the course of civic activism since the early 1970s. There has been a decline in some face-to-face forms, as practised by traditional associations such as the Mothers' Union, but there has also been massive quantum growth in new forms of citizen activism, demonstrating a trend of much increased trust in highly professional, media-savvy campaigning NGOs, which individuals are prepared to join, donate their financial resources to and attend their cultural and publicity events, in return for proven effectiveness, even on a global scale, in getting laws changed and their desired policies implemented. The internet and social media are only likely to boost this trend further.

The historical and comparative evidence assembled in these chapters indicates that what Big Society proponents castigate as Big Government, the enemy of civic participation, is often, in the context of a functioning democratic society like post-war Britain (or Sweden – see below), in fact the key facilitating framework for volunteering to flourish and to play its most valuable role – in independence from the parties in power in the central state – as innovator of complementary and supplemental goods and services to the state-provided, tax-funded universal basics. Hilton's research indicates that in Britain since the 1970s its activist and participatory citizenry have become increasingly disenchanted, not with their own 'broken society', but with an increasingly broken state, which no longer provides the facilitating framework. Mrs Thatcher's government declared war on local government in Britain, reducing its powers and funding so that it became largely a transmission mechanism for centrally planned government policies – a great irony from the administration that promised to roll back the state. Weinbren's chapter documents a twentieth-century precedent: the distortion of the mutual Friendly Societies into the 'approved societies' of the central state, used after 1911 to deliver a national insurance policy on the cheap in the interwar decades of cuts and then recession. He shows that when central government uses its power to co-opt localist, voluntary institutions as its hand-servants for carrying out unpopular tax-saving policies, this can have disastrous consequences for the institutions so used. For these same reasons, local government, the proud and independent bastion of localism for centuries in British history, has been in a parlous state for three decades since the Thatcher onslaught; and while New Labour fed town halls more resources for their last eight years in office, they did little to increase elected councils' autonomy over how this was spent.

Thus, Hilton documents how charities and NGOs have become ever more highly valued by citizens during the last three decades as their main hope to achieve their activist goals and to change society for the better, as they see it. They are valued for their independence from the Westminster governing establishment and its tarnished institutions, for their professionalism and disinterested vocational commitment to the cause in question, and for their capacity to extract change out of the lumbering political establishment, which to many in Britain seems only to serve the interests of a corporate oligarchy of tax exiles, personified by Lord Ashcroft of Belize, the chief funder of the Tory Party's election campaign. By contrast to these new organisations, Hilton sees local volunteers, which Mr Cameron wants to promote with the rhetoric of Big Society, as historical throwbacks not fit for purpose: apolitical, part-time do-gooders in the local community are of no interest to these participatory, increasingly virtually connected communities of networked citizens who want to voice their concerns and see them acted on. Yet NGOs, and other voluntary organisations, are not all-purpose 'magic bullets'. Their strength lies in campaigning for change and addressing gaps in provision, not in the routine delivery of social welfare services.

Having first, during the twentieth century, co-opted the Friendly Societies and then local government to do its bidding in difficult times, Richard Fries' chapter argues that it will be very difficult for government simply to co-opt the charitable sector to act on its behalf, as perhaps the most ambitious version of Big Society might aspire to do. There is not much scope for Parliament to bend charities to the executive's bidding through law and that leaves the purse strings as the only method. While this has been an effective strategy in relation to the approved societies and local government in the recent past – and Fries notes a worrying development in a recent trend, which has seen government increase subventions for charities to a historic high level of one-third of their funding – this is also a figure which will inevitably decrease over the next decade or so of government cuts, so that this form of leverage is likely to weaken not strengthen, at least in the short and medium terms.

In her chapter, Liz Richardson discusses how and why some policymakers, frustrated by the limitations of the traditional tools of exhortation and legislation, are turning to 'nudge' techniques, by which is meant the paternalist attempt to influence choices people make through the ploys of behavioural psychology, such as placing healthy foods at eye-level, unhealthy ones on the less accessible shelves. Richardson examines the ethical and moral debates about the legitimacy of the use of 'nudge' and concludes that it is not yet apparent whether nudging has the capacity to deliver on the objectives of the Big Society agenda, which requires sustained behaviour change. She argues that while 'nudge' techniques can work in certain instances, the Big Society type activities, which require long-term volunteering, regular giving to charity and consistent engagement in the running of community services, need significant and sustained efforts on the part of those involved and therefore are unlikely to be achieved in this way.

Nick Ockenden, Matthew Hill and Joanna Stuart draw on the vast amount of research undertaken by the Institute for Volunteering Research since 1997 on recent patterns of volunteering in the UK to point out that the current government is certainly not the first to encourage enthusiastically an increase in volunteering. However, their evidence renders them sceptical of the expectation that volunteering will 'deliver everything expected of it by the Big Society'. Volunteers will not automatically fill the gap left by a retreating state and a financially reduced local government. Moreover, evidence of stagnant rates of traditional volunteering suggests that the government's aims to increase dramatically such volunteering are, at best, overly ambitious and may even exacerbate current inequalities amongst those who volunteer. They conclude that perhaps too much has been placed at the door of volunteering, which may have the potential to change some individuals' lives, but is far from being a panacea for all of society's ills.

Together, the historical and contemporary chapters assembled here to review the evidence on volunteering and civic activism fundamentally challenge the evidential basis for the two key assertions that underpin the Big Society's diagnosis of Britain's ills and how to remedy them. They also counsel great prudence, lest the established charities and voluntary associations of Britain see Big Society as an opportunity to deliver government welfare priorities in this era of public funding cuts, a move which, history suggests, may ultimately undermine their independence and *raison d'être*.

5 INTERNATIONAL EXPERIENCE AND LESSONS

For anyone familiar with international development, the policies of the Big Society agenda are eerily, some may even say frighteningly, familiar. Big Society policies are aimed at building social capital, empowering individuals and communities, enhancing civic or collective action and substituting for rolled-back state services. All of these policies have been implemented – but rarely with

much success – in many parts of the world, including in sub-Saharan Africa, Latin America, South Asia, as well as in the countries of the former Soviet Union. The first similarity between Big Society and development policies of the recent past is in the withdrawal and the shrinking of state-funded services. Throughout the late 1980s and early 1990s, the rollback of the state was part of the anti-statist, neo-liberal sentiment that led to the implementation of structural adjustment policies (SAPs) by international donor agencies throughout developing countries. While donors hailed the potential of SAPs to stimulate economic growth and development, as Jude Howell and Jenny Pearce demonstrate, not only did the SAPs fail to stimulate growth but they also aggravated inequalities and diminished access for the poor to basic needs such as education and health (Howell and Pearce, 2001, p. 90). In the UK, the austerity measures and cuts to public spending are also being implemented in an effort, we are repeatedly told, to stimulate economic growth. Yet, after two years of cuts, the economy continues to stagnate as access to services also continues to shrink (e.g. the closure of Sure Start centres, etc.).

In her chapter, Ishkanian argues that the neo-liberal rhetoric of Big Society tends to valorise non-governmental activism and initiatives as a form of empowerment. While community-based self-organising can be empowering and rewarding, she contends that there are also instances where the curtailment or withdrawal of state services and support can have negative consequences, particularly for deprived communities and vulnerable groups. Ishkanian discusses how the neo-liberal reforms and 'shock therapy' policies implemented in the former Soviet countries left much suffering in their wake. Rates of poverty, unemployment, social inequality and social exclusion rose, while the cuts led to many people being left without services and support.

The second and related similarity between Big Society policies and those implemented in developing and transition countries is the emphasis on civil society and civic participation. Since the late 1980s, very large sums of money were spent by international development agencies on strengthening, building, and supporting the institutions of civil society, training civil society activists, and funding their projects as a means of promoting democracy, good governance, poverty reduction and development. This focus on civil society subsequently led to the 'explosive' growth of local NGOs (USAID, 1999, p. 3) because, while donors have recently broadened their definition of civil society, in the early 1990s civil society often came to be equated with NGOs (Howell et al., 2008).

Within the context of development, NGOs were expected to step in and fill the gap left by the receding state by delivering services more affordably, efficiently and accountably. They were also expected simultaneously to 'scale up' their work (Korten, 1990) by campaigning on behalf of their beneficiaries and promoting civic participation and activism. These are somewhat contradictory

aims and neither can be said to have been successfully met. First, time and again, NGO service provision in developing countries has been criticised for being characterised by problems of quality control, poor coordination and general amateurism (Lewis and Kanji, 2009, p. 92; Robinson, 1997a). Second, beginning in the 2000s, many social movements and grassroots organisations began to criticise NGOs for having become too distant from their beneficiaries and their specific needs and problems, de-radicalised and co-opted by donors and their well-meaning but often rigidly 'western' values (Howell et al., 2008, p. 83). This has meant that, while NGOs might be implementing projects intended to be socially beneficial, their work has become fragmentary, 'apolitical', and insufficiently responsive and adapted to local communities and cultures. The technicisation and depoliticisation of development aid has long been noted, and critiqued, by scholars who have demonstrated the short-sightedness of such approaches, which tackle the outward manifestations of a problem without addressing the underlying causes and structural factors (Escobar, 1995; Ferguson, 1994; Kabeer, 1994). Fear of losing funding leads NGOs to focus increasingly on narrow, technical projects and to avoid mobilising or criticising the broader social, structural or political inequalities that lie at the root of the problems they address (Ishkanian, 2007).

Finally, there are similarities between the Big Society agenda and international development in the area of social capital. Social capital has long attracted policymakers and donor agencies working in international development. One senior economist from the World Bank even identified it as the 'missing link' in development (Grooteart, 1997). One of its attractions lies in the promise it holds for filling in the gap left by the shrinking of government provision due to SAPs. The expectation, at least in the context of development, was that if international agencies and NGOs could support and foster the development of civil society and social capital, then we would witness a rise in local organisation and self-help. In other words, if social capital could be enhanced, then the poor and disadvantaged would be able to 'pull themselves up by their own boot straps' which, John Harriss argues, 'is remarkably convenient for those who wish to implement large-scale public expenditure cuts' (Harriss, 2002, p. 7). The idea that these empowered and networked individuals would have the 'capacity to organise in their own collective interests, cooperate to perform collective tasks and achieve mutual benefits' (Babajanian, 2008, p. 1299) led to the implementation of projects such as the World Bank's Community Driven Development (CDD) programmes throughout developing countries in sub-Saharan Africa, Asia, Latin America, the Middle East and also in the former socialist countries in Eastern Europe and the former Soviet Union in the 2000s. These projects, however, have yet to bear fruit. For example, in the countries of the former Soviet Union, despite investment in CDD programmes and other social capital enhancement projects, institutional and generalised trust, which are essential for social capital, remain very low (Dudwick et al., 2003; EBRD, 2011).

Ketola's comparative chapter, which examines the experience of continental European and Scandinavian countries, provides a very important contrasting perspective for discussion of the relationship between public spending/taxation and volunteering. He demonstrates that Sweden, the high taxing big state, has also consistently been the 'big society', with highest levels of participatory volunteering. This is a direct empirical contradiction of the untested policy propositions of Big Society proponents. Against the counter argument that this might represent something unique about Sweden that can't be applied to Britain, Szreter's historical chapter demonstrates that civic society and local activism have been at their most effective during periods when communities taxed themselves most progressively for their collective needs, paying particular attention to ensuring the wealthiest could not evade paying their full, progressive share, through taxation on land and urban property values. As Fries' and Charlesworth's chapters also indicate, only if linking social capital is facilitated by careful legal and institutional design by the central state can bridging social capital flourish in those many and typical communities where there are significant social inequalities.

6 CHANCES OF SUCCESS

Although it may be premised on a misleading representation of the reality of both modern and early modern British history, and therefore constitute a poor guide for future social and welfare policy, can Big Society nevertheless perform satisfactorily as political rhetoric? That would seem to depend partly on whether it proves adept for the Coalition government in both satisfying the right of the Conservative Party whilst simultaneously continuing to bind in the Lib Dems. But it may also be subject to intolerable pressures, in the discrepancy between the cosy world of do-gooding citizens, which it invokes, and the reality of a Britain becoming ever more unequal by the year.

In the UK, Big Society proponents also have high hopes for social capital but it is unclear whether initiatives such as the Community Organisers and the National Citizen Service will, indeed, inspire and ignite bridging social capital, collective action and volunteering. If trust in the state and the larger collectivity is absent, bridging and linking social capital will diminish, as witnessed during the August 2011 riots in Britain. Instead, we will see emerging in Britain, as has happened already in parts of the US, only what Szreter calls 'segregated encampments of bonding social capital' (Szreter, 2002, p. 613). This happens when diverse and mutually distrustful sections of society huddle together for mutual support, while the elites absent themselves fiscally, protesting the disbenefits of higher taxation on the wealthy and engaging in institutionalised tax avoidance, which for some slips also into evasion and non-compliance. Indeed, this has now reached such a point that some mavericks among the wealthy elite, such as Warren Buffett, have broken ranks to join the calls of such civic society manifestations as the Tax Justice Network, in demanding more and better-enforced taxation on the wealthiest citizens in countries like the US and the UK. Even key opinion formers on the right, such as the *Telegraph* columnists Peter Oborne (2011) and Charles Moore (2011), the official biographer of Margaret Thatcher, have issued high-profile articles essentially endorsing the line of the Opposition leader of the Labour Party, Ed Miliband, that it is time for personal and fiscal responsibilities to be imposed on the new financial elites (Miliband, 2011b).

Governments around the globe are being confronted by angry citizens, who criticise politicians for imposing austerity measures and public spending cuts while continuing to subsidise and bail out the banks and corporations whose tangibly irresponsible behaviour led to the crisis in the first place. The Occupy Wall Street movement rapidly expanded and other protest movements have emerged, such as the St Paul's encampment in London; and already comparisons have been made between the methods used by this movement and those of the Arab Spring, which became an inspiration for many movements emerging around the globe. In this recent upsurge of protest activity the 'occupation' model was in fact first adopted by students in Britain in November 2010, protesting at the Coalition government's tripling of university fees, before – more successfully and momentously – it became the symbol of protest in Cairo's Tahrir Square from January 2011. Activists now use social media, including Facebook, Twitter, and BlackBerry Messenger, as well as YouTube, to organise, mobilise, connect and communicate with supporters locally and across the globe. And, as Matthew Hilton's research demonstrates, these movements of self-organised political protest, such as 38 Degrees and Avaaz, are becoming increasingly professional in their use of new technology. From the student movement led by 'Commander Camilla' in Chile to the *Indignados* in Spain and the strikes in Greece, each of these movements is challenging the status quo and arguing that the great majority – 99 per cent in some countries – is suffering due to the greed and folly of the 1 per cent of wealthy corporations and individuals. Their robust critique of the capitalist system is not unprecedented, but it certainly signals the end of the triumphalist discourse that began with the collapse of the Soviet Union and the other socialist systems in Central and Eastern Europe.

Profound changes are also emerging in Britain's political landscape. British citizens – particularly those most educated, from among whom all the evidence shows volunteers are most likely to be drawn – have lost confidence in local government to act independently for their communities because they know it has so little discretion; they have lost trust in central government and national political parties to represent their interests, while the most recent revelations of the triple scandal of the bankers, MPs' expenses and the methods of the Murdoch media empire have only compounded that systemic distrust of all the formal institutions of central political power in Britain. However, it remains to be seen how the democratic and participatory forces of the real 'big society' of citizen social networks will develop. They are clearly something quite different from Mr Cameron's Big Society of politically safe, and anodyne, amateurish do-gooding; a misplaced nostalgia for an age of volunteering that never existed in the form that some proponents of the Big Society fondly imagine to have been the case. To ask amateur volunteers to take increasing responsibility for a range of serious social problems which, Mr Cameron must fully know, can only be exacerbated, both by rapidly rising unemployment and falling real incomes and by the withdrawal of government support for professional service deliverers, looks like an extraordinarily politically audacious attempt to place responsibility for the consequences of his own Big Government's policy choices on the shoulders of others. To answer the question posed in this book's title: if, beyond its function as political rhetoric, Big Society is supposed to be taken seriously as an agenda for the delivery of social welfare, it is a bid for the continuation and expansion of failed neo-liberal polices by other means, Canute-like in its refusal to learn from the past or to comprehend the present.

NOTE

1. A report commissioned by the Calouste Gulbenkian Foundation, titled *The Big Society: A View from the Frontline*, highlighted the difficulties faced by 'frontline workers' and concluded that 'Government must work with civil society'. For the full report see http://www.gulbenkian.org.uk/news/news/147-The-Big-Society--A-View-from-the-Frontline.html.

PART I

History

1. 'Big Society' and 'Great Society': a problem in the history of ideas

Jose Harris

1 INTRODUCTION

Everybody uses the word 'society', but nobody is quite sure what it means. Over many centuries, great philosophers and religious teachers, economists and sociologists, sublime poets and ordinary folk have all pondered the nature of this mysterious entity. Against this background, how are we to interpret the currently fashionable term 'Big Society'? Is it a variant of the much older term 'Great Society', or a smaller version of the same thing (and, if so, how much smaller?), or is it something quite different? And how does 'Big Society' relate to other similar-sounding historical antecedents, such as the 'Great Community', the 'Great Republic', the 'Great Commonwealth', the 'Good Society', the 'Civic Society' as conjured up by Gordon Brown (Brown, 2000), or simply 'Society' *tout court*, as the arithmetical sum of 'individuals and families', famously envisaged by Margaret Thatcher (Thatcher, 1987)? Contributors to the 'Big Society' debate, both enthusiasts and critics, often assume quite recklessly that it is closely akin to, or even identical with, such terms as the 'Great Society' or 'Civil Society'.[1] But history suggests that ideas and concepts can subtly, or even dramatically, change their meanings in different cultural and historical settings. This paper explores a few of the historical antecedents of the current debate, and suggests that over many generations human understanding of both 'Great Society' and 'Big Society' has been more variable, complex and unpredictable than initially meets the eye.

2 THE HISTORICAL EMERGENCE OF 'SOCIETY'

Contested views about the virtues of large-scale versus small-scale 'societies' had a long, tumultuous and often violent history in pre-modern and early-modern Europe. In origin they were closely linked to controversies within and about the Catholic Church, its authority over 'national' churches, and its relation to emperors, territorial kingdoms, small groups and individual human beings. Indeed, the very word 'society' (*societas*) invited such controversies, since it was a term in Roman law that had originally applied to small-scale private associations, partnerships, and corporations, and only later came also to be applied to much larger entities (including even the Roman Empire and the Church). Such debates were to supply important intellectual precedents for many later ideas about nationhood, religious pluralism, charities, self-governing fraternities, relations between rulers and subjects, and the eventual emergence of 'modern' secular states (Stein, 1988; Nichols, 1975).

England was unusual in early-modern Europe, in its successful resistance both to foreign domination and to the widespread continental revival of Roman law. Nonetheless, over the course of the seventeenth and eighteenth centuries, ideas selectively adapted from Roman legal thought began to penetrate many aspects of English commercial, social, and religious life – including the multipurpose term 'society' (Innes, 2009; Harris, 2003). The English constitutional settlement of 1689, and the union with Scotland in 1707, helped to foster a growing diversity of sociable, religious, scientific and commercial organisations – many small and local, but some national or even international in outlook. Some of these became legally incorporated as 'societies' or 'partnerships', whilst others remained wholly informal. But the developments in local, provincial and national culture that they embodied gradually came to be seen as an important part of a much larger conception of 'society', as a vehicle of wider national identity in its own right, that was quite distinct from the formal organs of government.

Both the miniscule and the more enlarged conceptions of society were to be transmitted to British settlements in North America, where residents continued to develop their own particular style of associational thought and behaviour, that was to be graphically depicted during the 1830s and 1840s in the writings of Alexis de Tocqueville (Tocqueville, 1835 and 1840 [1968], pp. 58–71, 241–8, 304–14, 342–412). And both traditional and newer understandings of 'society' have continued to evolve and mutate down to the present time, in both academic writings and the language and practice of everyday life. Indeed, as presaged by Emile Durkheim, the very idea of 'society' has come to subsume the totality of human experience. It ranges promiscuously over private relationships, work, leisure, culture, public opinion and the mass media, through to activities that would once have been classed as generically distinct from the 'social' sphere, such as human subjectivity, high politics, and transcendental beliefs (Durkheim, 1912 [2001], pp. 310–43; Stedman Jones, 2001, pp. 201–7).

3 RIVAL CONCEPTIONS OF A 'GREAT SOCIETY'

How did this ever-more-elastic perception of society relate to the evolution of ideas about 'society', as an analytical and/or normative concept in social, political and economic theory? A useful starting point is Adam Smith's discussion of a 'great society' in *The Theory of Moral Sentiments*. Smith's account carefully distinguished between what a 'great society' might mean when directed by a 'man of system', as opposed to a 'man of public spirit'. Under a 'man of system', the inhabitants of a 'great society' could be organised and shifted around 'with as much ease as the hand that arranges the different pieces on a chessboard', with little regard to freedom, personal initiative, or individual wishes. By contrast, in Smith's preferred model, the 'man of public spirit' would understand that 'in the great chessboard of human society', the chessmen themselves had their own private goals and desires which the legislator 'cannot annihilate without great violence'. In this latter vision, the 'great society' involved mutual respect, assistance, and cooperation between citizens and rulers, chessmen and players. And it also involved self-restraint, with the wise ruler aiming not for 'the best system of laws', but for 'the best that the people can bear'; while the virtuous citizen would 'at all times be willing that his own private interest should be sacrificed to the public interest of his own particular order or society'. And he would also acknowledge the higher claims of 'the greater interest of the universe ... the interest of that great society of all sensible and intelligent beings, of which God himself is the immediate administrator and director'.

Nonetheless, even within this divinely ordered scheme of things, Smith appeared to envisage a strictly limited role for private charity and beneficence, other than for the totally helpless. In a feudal or caste society, the poor had had no choice but to be dependent on their overlords; but in a 'great society', even beggars swapped and traded with the free gifts of the charitable; while 'benevolence', however intrinsically virtuous, 'does not give us our dinner'. Moreover, 'benevolence' was less essential to human flourishing than strict 'justice', without which 'the immense fabric of human society ... must in a moment crumble into atoms' (Smith, 1759 [1979], pp. 85–6, 232–7; Smith, 1776 [1976], vol. I, pp. 18–19, 497).

Although the terminology of a 'great society' was not to be widely employed until a much later date, Smith's image of an ever-expanding process of social and economic exchange was to be taken up and deployed by many different theorists and social movements over the next two centuries. In early Victorian Scotland, many of Smith's ideas about a market economy, tamed and civilised by extensive voluntary benevolence, could be seen in the 'godly commonwealth' system promoted by Dr Thomas Chalmers (Brown, 1992, pp. 61–80). And Smith's vision of a 'great society' organised by the 'man of system' was to find a powerful echo during the mid-nineteenth century in the writings of the French positivist philosophers, Henri Saint-Simon and August Comte (Pickering, 1993, pp. 128–9, 158, 306–10, 674). Comte set out a model for what he called 'the Great Republic of the West', closely based on Smith's account of an international exchange economy, but led and managed by a technocratic planning elite who would impose 'systematic discipline' (i.e. Smith's 'man of system'), rather than by the spontaneous interaction of a mass of private individuals. This 'positivist' version of a 'great society' was to be closely reflected in the policies of 'L'Etat-Providence', promoted by the elite polytechnics of the French Third Republic. And it was also to become widely pervasive in late nineteenth- and early twentieth-century Britain among Fabian socialists, 'new liberals' and managerial conservatives (Ewald, 1986; Freeden, 1978; Hill, 1993, pp. 591–622; Bevir, 2002, pp. 217–52).

On the brink of the First World War, such themes were to be explored in detail by Graham Wallas in *The Great Society: a Psychological Analysis*. Wallas was a founding member of the Fabian Society, an admirer of the French positivist school and first Professor of Political Science at the London School of Economics. Despite his 'positivist' background, Wallas was increasingly concerned that the sheer scale and pace of mass production and global commerce were far outstripping the reach of public regulation of any kind (whether by a liberal market regime or a more collectivist and authoritarian one). Such forces appeared to be transforming not just the international economy, but the fundamental character of human life, including democratic politics, small-scale self-help organisations and intimate human sociability: all of which Wallas himself cherished no less fervently than had Adam Smith.[2] To counteract these trends, Wallas advocated the guidance and channelling of 'instinct' and 'custom' by greatly increased public 'intelligence' – the latter to be expressed through the 'organisation of thought', the 'organisation of will' and the 'organisation of happiness'. These seemingly rather vague terms nevertheless referred to three very specific goals: first, the systematic deployment of new scientific knowledge at all levels of social life (ranging from health, childcare and nutrition, through to education and industrial management); second, reform of political institutions at all levels so as to engage the 'popular will'; and, third, making work for all classes of society more 'human', productive and rewarding (Wallas, 1914, pp. 249–394). Wallas's account of a 'great society' thus appeared (like Comte's) to be the direct antithesis of Adam Smith's, which had emphasised not deliberate 'policy', but the spontaneous cohesion of a multitude of private initiatives. But this contrast was in some ways deceptive, since – despite his emphasis on conscious 'organisation' – Wallas himself was highly critical of what he saw as the bureaucratic and 'impersonal' tendencies of recent social legislation in Britain. He disliked the incorporation of self-governing voluntary bodies, such as friendly societies and trade union welfare schemes, into the routine administration of state social insurance (see Chapter 4, Mutual aid and the Big Society). And he was repelled by the 'inhuman scale' of many new municipal housing estates, which were being built with the 'best of intentions', but were nevertheless better suited to the 'needs of giants and not men' (Wallas, 1908, pp. 27–38, 273–81; Wallas, 1914, pp. 254–5, 378–80, 391–3).

Wallas's *The Great Society* was initially less influential in Britain than in the US, where his ideas were popularised by the American social theorist and management consultant, Mary Follett (1918). And the philosopher, John Dewey, was to pursue very similar themes during the 1920s, through a series of inquiries into how the ever-more-gigantic scale of modern corporate capitalism could be contained and made answerable to north American traditions of localism, micro-democracy, personal autonomy and self-help. Dewey's answer was the nationwide conversion of the 'Great Society' into the 'Great Community'. By this he meant the revival of older traditions of small-scale civic life (now largely moribund) by promotion of new forms of democratic mass communication – the latter to be mediated not by giant commercial organisations, but by schools and colleges, trade unions and professional bodies, local and voluntary civic and cultural associations. Such schemes were to be designed not just as a counterweight to economic corporatism, but as a way of enabling local groups of citizens to promote their own civic schemes and to contribute *in advance* to both local and federal public policy formation (Dewey, 1927 [1991]). Dewey's schemes were to be thwarted by the 1929 crash and the onset of the Great Depression; and his vision of a publicly planned 'private pluralism' was to be publicly denounced by the celebrated liberal journalist Walter Lippmann, as requiring civic virtues that were 'superhuman; they are the attributes of Providence and not of mortal men' (Lippmann, 1927; Lippmann, 1937 [2005], p. 362). Lippmann himself earlier in life had studied under Graham Wallas at Harvard, and at that time had favoured a highly regulatory system of government inspired by Plato's 'guardians'; but by the late 1920s he had rejected 'collectivism' in favour of what he called the 'Good Society', based on free competition restrained and humanised by private generosity, as set out by Adam Smith. What Lippmann now derided as 'the Providential State' (which he identified with the programmes of John Dewey) required a knowledge of social facts and contingencies that he claimed lay wholly outside the range of human comprehension. 'It is not merely that we do not have today enough factual knowledge of the social order, enough statistics, censuses, reports. The difficulty is deeper than that. We do not possess the indispensable logical equipment – the knowledge of the grammar and syntax of society as a whole – to understand the data available or to know what other data to look for' (Lippmann, 1937 [1943], pp. 29–34).

4 THE ERA OF THE STATE

Such 'Great Society' perspectives found little echo, however, in the controversies about public/private provision in the field of social welfare that took
place in 1930s Britain, reaching a crescendo during and after the Second World
War. In these British debates, there was extensive discussion of the roles of
the state, the individual, voluntary action and big business, and endemic conflict between rival social groups, but surprisingly little explicit reference to the
intermediate role of something identifiable as 'society'. The Beveridge Plan
on Social Insurance in 1942 assumed that a partnership between the state, the
individual, and a wide range of intermediate voluntary organisations would
continue after the war. In fact, the welfare state legislation of 1946–48 wholly
excluded voluntary insurance schemes from provision of state welfare, while
voluntary hospitals were almost entirely absorbed into the new NHS. Notions
of a 'Great Society' or 'Good Society' cropped up scarcely at all in the extensive debates about post-war reconstruction. Indeed, 'society' in any of it modes
appeared to play a diminishing and even discredited role in public awareness of
the period, as Beveridge himself was to find when he carried out his post-war
enquiry into the future of 'voluntary action' (Oppenheimer and Deakin, 2011).
In political thought the turn towards linguistic positivism in British philosophy
made the very concept of 'society' seem spurious and outmoded; while treating
'human duties as if they were dependent on membership of some great society'
was dismissed as having 'its rise in a false analogy' (Mabbott, 1947, pp. 82–5).
Instead, planners and citizens alike looked back on the pre-war epoch as an era
of mass poverty and forward to the hopes and promises of a much more centralised and interventionist 'command economy' and 'welfare state'. Nor did
the concept of 'society' *per se* (as opposed to the claims of individuals, states
and ethnic groups) figure at all prominently in the international movements of
the 1940s for the settlement of displaced persons and the promotion of human
rights (Simpson, 2004; Judt, 2005).

5 THE REVIVAL OF 'GREAT SOCIETY'

The later 1950s and early 1960s, however, brought a gradual re-emergence of
the theme of a 'Great Society' in Britain and elsewhere: a theme once again
expressed through a variety of seemingly contradictory channels – statist and
anti-statist, large- and small-scale, secular and religious. An early example
came in the mid-1950s from a widely respected English Dominican priest, in
writings that re-asserted the role of the Catholic Church as 'the largest of voluntary societies' and as a 'constituent body of the Great Society', whose distinctive mission was to embody upon earth the second Person of the Trinity and

thus to 'complete the intellectual structure of man' (Foster, 1958, pp. 51–90). These works, though largely written for a confessional audience, may nonetheless be seen as a dawning reaffirmation of the view that the collective life of mankind was not to be wholly expressed through the medium of 'the state', however law-abiding, redistributive and democratic.

In the secular sphere, renewed British discussion of a 'Great Society' was in part triggered in the early 1960s by the burgeoning civil rights movement in the US; but it was also a response to economic stagnation and conflict within Britain itself and to contemporary political developments in Europe. In 1963, after General de Gaulle's veto on Britain's first application to join the Treaty of Rome, an informal 'Great Society' group came together within and on the fringes of the British Labour party. It was supported by a collection of academics, journalists, social scientists and independent writers who favoured radical social and educational change, but were opposed to those elements in the Labour party who refused to address the problems of Britain's bad industrial relations, monetary inflation, low levels of productivity and stagnating public services. The aim of the Great Society group was to foster a mixed economy, based not on large-scale extensions of public ownership, but on managerial, structural and cultural reforms, designed both to ward off pressures for further 'nationalisation' and to prepare Britain for a renewed attempt to join the European Common Market. Its leading figure was the economist Thomas Balogh, a close adviser to Harold Wilson; while other prominent members included the future Labour MPs Gerald Kaufman and Roy Hattersley, the pioneer of the social survey movement Mark Abrams, and the historian Hugh Thomas.[3] The group laid great stress on 'technological union' between the different nations of Europe as the basis for a successful 'European Great Society' of the future (Calmann, 1967, pp. 64–74). And in domestic policy they favoured an 'unapologetic materialism' in the restructuring of British industry, including extensive reforms in industrial relations. These reforms were to focus on the introduction of much higher, performance-related wage-rates, in return for a restoration of shop-floor discipline under the control of a works foreman, and abandonment of the restrictions on output and other workplace 'taboos' imposed by 'shop-stewards' (Coulter, 1966; Ivens, 1967).

In addition, the group pressed not just for industrial change, but for a 'shake-up' of Britain's social, administrative, cultural and educational institutions (which they portrayed as still 'paralysed' by long-standing and newly emerging social-class divisions). A key policy was reform of the civil service, where bland and amateurish mandarins were to be replaced by 'professionally qualified people', ideally recruited from 'the physical or social sciences' (Balogh, 1968, pp. 11–52; Seers, 1968, pp. 83–109). Selective schools were to be replaced by universal equalisation of educational opportunities, while 'free choice' and 'selection by merit' were condemned as 'spurious and harmful', and as favouring only the children of 'the sleeker middle-class' (Marsden, 1967, p. 51; Windsor, 1967, p. 51). The 'rabid and continuing class mistrust' of the period was to be dissolved by social policies designed to promote 'the class equivalent of a multi-racial society, where ethnic differences are appreciated not obliterated' (Mabey, 1967, p. 16). And there was to be a systematic attempt to transform popular attitudes to the welfare state, which (it was claimed) many people still viewed in largely negative terms, as 'a charge on the well-to-do, and a gift to the poor' (Murray, 1967, p. 81). Instead, a national 'Great Society' programme should promote 'an effort by society as an organic whole to order its affairs for the benefit of society as a whole'; while the mass media should aim to disseminate a totally new model of 'affluence' and well-being, as measured by 'creativity' and 'style and gesture', rather than by 'social class and caste' (Murray, 1967, p. 81; Hall, 1967, pp. 93–114).

The Labour Party's 'Great Society' group was merely one strand among many competing factions that struggled for power within the British left, both inside and outside the Labour Party, over the course of the 1960s. Moreover, although the group had come together a year before the launching of President Lyndon Johnson's 'Great Society' crusade, its role in British public awareness of the period was to be largely eclipsed by the much grander, more heroic scale and character of the programme of the same name, that was to be introduced in the US from 1964. The American 'Great Society' programme went much further than any earlier movement of its kind in asserting the positive virtues of big government and bureaucratic expertise, of 'positive discrimination' on behalf of the poor, and of using federal state power not just to defend but to extend and enforce the legal, constitutional, educational and social rights of disadvantaged minorities (Patterson, 1997; Davies, 1996). And, despite certain apparent similarities in their policies, the underlying goals of the British and American 'Great Society' movements of this period were, in fact, very different. In both countries 'Great Society' enthusiasts of this era favoured using government-inspired policies to combat poverty and to equalise access to education and social services. But the US Great Society programme was a major exercise in federal state power, backed by the president, and (though ultimately disappointing to its most fervid supporters) penetrated deeply into spheres of public policy unprecedented in earlier US history (Levitan, 1969). The British 'Great Society' group, by contrast, was a relatively minor pressure group within the arena of national politics. The position of the two movements in the wider political spectrum was also very different, with the main resistance to a 'Great Society' programme in the US coming from business corporations and right-wing opponents of federal power; whereas in Britain a major objective was to provide a social democratic and libertarian alternative to the much more radical corporatist and state-interventionist demands coming at that time from the Labour party's hard left.

There can be no doubt, however, that the language and aspirations of both movements represented a stark and startling contrast to a yet further vision of a 'Great Society' regime, which was to emerge over the following decade. This was the model of a 'Great Society' set out in the later writings of the liberal economist and philosopher, F.A. Hayek. Hayek had been modestly famous since the later 1930s as a persistent critic of politically orchestrated notions of 'social justice', as opposed to more classic liberal notions of mere 'justice' (in the sense of 'fair procedures' and equal access for all individuals to the common law). And since the mid-1940s Hayek had been even more famous as the author of *The Road to Serfdom,* which had attacked what he saw as the latently 'totalitarian' implications of centralised economic planning, and of all forms of social welfare provision that went beyond a level that could be provided without 'controlling or abolishing the market' (Hayek, 1944, pp. 89–91). But the wider conception of a 'Great Society' had played only a muted role in Hayek's writings of the 1950s and 60s and, even then, mainly with reference to his interpretation of a properly working market economy as set out by Adam Smith. It was not until the 1970s, in his three-volume study of *Law, Legislation and Liberty*, that the 'Great Society' came to figure much more centrally in Hayek's thought, both as a description of how the global economy actually worked and of how it *ought to work* in accordance with correct economic principles.

Hayek's account of the 'Great Society' in his writings of the 1970s, in many important respects, still closely followed the much earlier and more muted conception of Adam Smith. The 'Great Society' was not a communal or corporate or 'command' enterprise, but was the overall sum of the private desires, decisions, inventions, contracts, partnerships and other endeavours engaged in by free individuals pursuing their own multitudinous concerns, regulated only by a common framework of law. Like Smith, Hayek emphasised that the Great Society was not a static phenomenon but was continually evolving through different stages of human history, as its participants progressively advanced in self-awareness and economic understanding, and liberated themselves from the taboos and limited perspectives of earlier times. Moreover, like Adam Smith, Hayek portrayed the Great Society as a system of 'general rules' rather than of 'hard cases'. In other words, it was geared to the interests of the majority who formed the 'general run of mankind', rather than to the weak and unfortunate, whose needs certainly made claims upon their fellow men, but were to be met by personal moral duty on the part of both givers and receivers, rather than by enforced redistribution for its own sake or by more radical forms of systemic political change. Both authors believed that the sum of material wealth generated by a 'Great Society' engaged in international trade would always outweigh what could be produced by an autarchic collective enterprise: and both believed that, under a system of impartial laws, the 'trickling down' of benefits to the poor under a 'Great Society' regime would ultimately far outweigh the benefits derived from a dedicated political regime of either collective production or compulsory redistribution (Hayek, 1973–79, vol. I, pp. 153–7, 160–61; vol. II, pp. 71, 185–6).

There were, nonetheless, some important differences of emphasis in the accounts of a 'Great Society', as set out by Hayek and Smith. In Hayek's account, any deviation from the market order of a 'Great Society', however well-meaning and apparently justified by circumstance, was bound to end in disaster and 'can never be just'. Indeed, 'a Great Society has nothing to do with, and is in fact irreconcilable with "solidarity" in the true sense of unitedness in the pursuit of known common goals' (Hayek, 1973–79, vol. II, p. 111). Far from being the 'little platoons' that held larger societies together, small groups were often simply redundant, if not positively 'anti-social from the point of view of the Great Society'; while in the commercial sphere what controlled giant corporations was other giant corporations: 'Size has thus become the most effective antidote to the power of size' (Hayek, 1973–79, vol. II, pp. 143–4; vol. III, pp. 77–80).

But, as suggested above, these positions did not wholly accord with the views of Adam Smith. Although Smith clearly had not relished the prospect of a Great Society run by 'men of system', he certainly had not ruled it out as an impossible contradiction in terms. Although (as Hayek pointed out) Smith certainly thought that 'strict justice' was compatible with 'sitting still and doing nothing', he had also remarked (which Hayek neglected to mention) that moral life under such circumstances would be like living 'in a great desert'. There were undoubtedly cases 'in the greatest public as well as private disasters' where in Smith's view private enterprise was wholly inadequate; while 'charity' and 'public spirit', under whatever regime, were consistently portrayed by Smith as positive and practical as well as moral virtues. 'Where the necessary assistance is reciprocally afforded from love, from gratitude, from friendship and esteem, the society flourishes and is happy' (Smith, 1775 [1976], pp. 82–5). Moreover, as indicated above, the nineteenth-century 'Solidarist' and 'Positivist' movements (and even some explicitly 'Socialist' ones) had drawn inspiration from Adam Smith's social and moral theories, no less than had market economists like Dr Thomas Chalmers. In Hayek's account, by contrast, 'altruism', however well-intentioned, was always likely to be counterproductive in a process that was intrinsically impersonal and non-moral; while recent history, he claimed, endorsed the view that any advance in the one system of economic thought and policy inexorably led to the erosion and destruction of the other (Hayek, 1983, pp. 29–35) It was this latter perspective that Hayek was to inject so powerfully into much British public policy debate of the 1970s and 1980s.

6 GREAT SOCIETY AND BIG SOCIETY: SOME UNRESOLVED QUESTIONS

How far do these shifting, and often contradictory, perceptions of a 'Great Society' reflect, not just prevailing social and economic ideas at particular historical moments, but general truths about human behaviour? The above discussion suggests that, over several centuries, different theorists and observers veered between two very diverse vantage points. Some portrayed the 'Great Society' as a powerful guideline or slogan with which to address certain concrete public policy problems at a specific moment in time (as in both Britain and the US during the 1960s). Others, by contrast, viewed the 'Great Society' as an abiding, almost Platonic, vision of how human societies would organise themselves, if all perverse obstructions could be removed. This view characterised many nineteenth-century positivists, together with Graham Wallas and Hayek himself (although the latter would have vehemently denied any common ground). The intellectual perspective of Adam Smith, who must surely emerge as the mastermind of this debate, even after two and a half centuries, seemed to hint not at a finite or final solution, but at an ongoing dialectic between the two.

The question remains, however, of how far the classic and much-contested theme of a *'Great* Society' bears any relation to the debate surrounding the notion of a *'Big* Society' at the present time. Practising politicians, from Pericles to the present, have fruitfully borrowed ideas from earlier political theorists and philosophers; and there is nothing at all strange about the fact that the notion of a 'Big Society' should have been taken up and launched by a practising politician. But, nonetheless, the exact intellectual provenance and substantive content of the current 'Big Society' programme seem to invite much further explanation and inquiry. The speech in which the 'Big Society' was launched by David Cameron in September 2010 contained little that any altruistic and public-spirited person could possibly have questioned – other, perhaps, than provoking mild surprise that its sentiments about the convergence of civic, moral, and economic goals were almost identical with those expressed eight years earlier by Gordon Brown in his Arnold Goodman lecture on 'Civic Society' (Brown, 2002). Much more puzzling, however, is the exposition of what the concept of a 'Big Society' is all about, as set out in the writings of its more 'theoretical' exponents and supporters. Phillip Blond, for example, in *Red Tory* (2010), did not disagree with but simply ignored the very powerful tradition of free-market economic thought that had dominated intellectual and political conservatism in Britain throughout the later decades of the twentieth century (a tradition represented not just by Hayek, but by the Institute of Economic Affairs and by a long line of recent Conservative Chancellors of the Exchequer). Instead, Blond suggested the Edwardian 'distributists', G.K. Chesterton and Hilaire Belloc, as theorists whose ideas about small-scale ownership, production and marketing might inspire experiments in social responsibility and cohesion in the future, although how in practice one moves from global capitalism to the post-industrial equivalent of peasant proprietorship is not made clear (Blond, 2010a, pp. 159–279). Likewise Jesse Norman, in *The Big Society; an Anatomy of the New Politics*, tells us that 'British society is not well', and needs to be cured not by disembodied rational calculation, but by 'connectedness' and 'compassion' (Norman 2010a). Norman suggests a range of attractive ideas about decentralisation, cultural renewal, 'empowerment of intermediate institutions' and a revival of 'civic virtue'. But his proposal for a massive 'audit' of all major government agencies skirts around the question of how, and by whom, such an audit could in practice be accomplished, and leaves the classic political-theory dilemma of 'who controls the controllers' unaddressed and unsolved (Norman, 2010b). What is missing from all these discussions, however, is any attempt to explain how the 'Big Society' of the future will relate to the globally encircling presence of the 'Great Society', which in one form another has been with us for several hundred years and seems unlikely to go away.

NOTES

1. For example, discussants of 'Big Society' on the BBC's Radio Four programme *Beyond Belief* (24 July 2011) appeared to assume without question that 'Big Society', 'Great Society' and 'Civil Society' were identical. Contributors included Phillip Blond, whose *Red Tory: How Left and Right Have Broken Britain and How We Can Fix It* has been a major publication of the 'Big Society' campaign.
2. Studies of Wallas's thought have noted in passing his interest in Adam Smith, but have made little or no reference to Smith's explicit discussion of a 'Great Society' (Qualter, 1980).
3. Other contributors include the economist, Roger Opie; the environmentalist, Richard Mabey; the development theorist, Dudley Seers; the author and publisher, John Calmann; and rising young cosmopolitan radicals like Stuart Hall, the author, and Peter Fryer.

2. Britain's social welfare provision in the long run: the importance of accountable, well-financed local government

Simon Szreter

INTRODUCTION

The precise meaning and agencies of the 'Big Society' are unclear. Mr Cameron, its chief political advocate, offers a definition which at times seems close to pure rhetoric, where it serves simply as the opposite to 'the broken society', another ill-defined term first publicly aired, like Big Society, during the 2010 election campaign: 'We do need a social recovery to mend the broken society and to me, that's what the Big Society is all about.'[1]

In terms of the agency envisaged for the 'social recovery', Mr Cameron has talked of individuals volunteering with donations of time and money in their communities and of promoting the activities of non-profit charities.[2] Big Society proponents, such as Cameron's former speechwriter Danny Kruger, also talk of being in favour of a shift of power and resources away from central government social welfare policies and schemes, with a preference instead for the 'voluntary sector' operating at its best in local 'communities'.[3]

But in that case what is the role of local government in all this? There has been no clarity on whether 'Big Society' includes the elected and accountable local governments of communities or whether the latter are seen as part of the problem of too much 'big government', preventing individuals and non-profits from taking local and community responsibility. There are two key pointers in terms of policy, which both seem to suggest that the promotion of 'Big Society' is in fact envisaged as a centrally imposed alternative to a more empowered role for representative local government. First, the Coalition government's scale of cuts in funding to local government which, even by Mr Cameron's own acknowledgement, reduces the overall level of funding for local government back to where it was in 2007 – and, in reality, this is a much greater real cut given the failure of his comparison to take inflation properly into account.[4] Second, the free schools initiative to create more schools outside local education authority supervision, allied to Mr Gove's move to turn 200 poorly performing schools into academies, directly responsible to the Secretary of State and independent from the LEAs and their local electorates. A crucial further pointer will be the government's response to a recent proposal that local councils be allowed to set and keep a greater share of the business rates in their area as a source of revenue independent from central government.[5] This would in theory permit them more incentives to set their own policy priorities within their local authorities.

Thus, there is an apparent tension between the Coalition's Big Society agenda and the parallel localism agenda over the key question of the proposed role for elected, accountable local government. This has been singled out for critical comment in the most recent report on localism by the House of Commons Select Committee on Communities and Local Government (which, like all select committees, is composed of a majority of members from the governing coalition parties). While observing that there is cross-party support for decentralisation and devolution of power to the local level, the report notes that the approach in the government's Localism Bill is 'marked by inconsistency and incoherence' due to the 'infusion' of 'Big Society rhetoric':

> Devolution of power both to local government and to local communities are not always compatible aims and the latter appears to be the Government's priority. The infusion of the Government's pronouncements on localism with 'Big Society' rhetoric implies a diminished, not greater, role for local authorities, and there are differences across government in the level of trust departments appear willing to place in councils. Lacking is any coherent vision for the future role of local authorities. (p. 4)

> The democratic mandate of local authorities is crucial in securing acceptance of greater variation in services between areas. The broad remit and powers of councils will also make them invaluable in facilitating the kind of low-level civic activism that the Government wishes to promote. (p. 4)

> The Government's 'Big Society' already exists in many respects, and so realism is needed about the extent to which it can further expand to take on services and functions shed by statutory bodies. (p. 4)

In particular the Select Committee warns that:

Localism should not be adopted purely as a way to achieve reductions in public sector costs ... Stimulating greater democratic participation and civic activism will carry its own costs if it is to be successful and sustainable. (p. 3)[6]

If the notion of Big Society is to be more than a rhetorical electioneering slogan, then it is in need of a cogent vision of precisely how its community civic activism is to articulate with local government. Though currently unfashionable, the institution of elected, accountable local government remains, both throughout British history and across the world today, the best democratic hope for communities. History indicates that volunteering and charitable activity can only function effectively to improve the social welfare of the poorer sections of society when such volunteers are working in the context of vigorous, responsive local government. History also shows that this, in turn, requires the full financial support and commitment of the wealthier section of society. 'Big Society' will prove to be no more than ephemeral rhetoric – or worse, a misguided irrelevance – if it does not also facilitate a reinvigorated democratic local government and full buy-in by the propertied elite.

SOCIAL WELFARE AND ACCOUNTABLE LOCAL GOVERNMENT OVER THE LONG RUN IN ENGLAND AND WALES

The history of England and Wales over the last half-millennium exhibits two distinct and prolonged episodes during which both social welfare and local civil society – the latter broadly corresponding to Cameron's Big Society – flourished throughout much of the country. Each episode was of course quite different but certain commonalities can be discerned which provide general policy lessons for today.

Something akin to a Big Society of volunteering and charitable-giving flourished and contributed to a genuinely effective social welfare system in the more than 10 000 parish communities of England and Wales served by the Elizabethan Poor Laws during the period c. 1600–1834 (Slack, 1990; Slack, 1998). The Elizabethan or 'Old' Poor Law was created by two statutes 'For the Relief of the Poor' 1598 and 1601. The laws mandated that every single parish create a fund financed by progressive taxation on property proportional to the value of land held by all individuals within the parish. This fund was to support the poor of the parish all the year round, not only in times of harvest dearth or unemployment, but also to sustain the old, ill and disabled, orphans, widows and the illegitimate children of single mothers. It was administered by volunteer church wardens and overseers of the poor. The whole apparatus was overseen by the local justices of the peace, who held their appointments at the pleasure of the Crown and were ultimately legally responsible for ensuring the setting and collecting of the annual rates on all property and providing accessible local justice to ensure that all legitimate claims on the parish fund were met. After half a century's experience of litigation over parishes' liability for particular individuals, the so-called Settlement Acts of the 1660s formalised the various rules (mostly by birth, marriage or a period of employment) by which every subject of the Crown was deemed to have a legal right to relief from the collective funds of his or her 'parish of settlement' (Hindle, 2004; Sokoll, 2001; Charlesworth, 2009, pp. 5, 35).

The Elizabethan Poor Law replaced a long-standing practice of purely voluntary bequests and charitable giving by the rich to religious foundations and to the parish box. Instead it now *required* the parish to levy an adequate poor rate from all its property owners, without exception and in proportion to the value of their landholdings. Thus, an unstable and unreliable previous arrangement of voluntary collective charity, dependent on wealthy individuals' sense of religious obligation – and so subject to personal whim and also to the free-rider problem (letting other rich individuals shoulder the burden) – was superseded by a system of obligatory taxation for all wealth-holders in the parish and applying to every parish in the land. The Crown, through the agency of the Privy Council, bore down relentlessly during the first half of the seventeenth century on parishes where local elites attempted to evade their legal responsibilities by refusing to establish an adequate Poor Law fund (Hindle, 2004).

Abram de Swaan argues that the English Elizabethan Poor Laws were effective because they solved the free-rider problem (which applies to any form of collective action), by replacing an unstable pre-Reformation local equilibrium of merely voluntary collective charity by a system of obligatory taxation (De Swaan 1988, pp. 21–36). This led to the increasing formalisation of the subsequent Settlement Laws which, in turn, accompanied and legitimised the Poor Laws, facilitating the sustained growth in the sums raised and dispensed as shown in Figure 2.1 (Slack 1990, pp. 45–58; Smith, 1996). There is also strong evidence that the unique English system of a universal, but highly devolved, parish social security system worked effectively both in promoting the welfare of the poor and the productivity of the economy, with the English being the first nation in Europe free from famine mortality after the 1620s, while also experiencing the highest rates of both local and long-distance labour mobility in the growing economy (Galloway, 1988).

Furthermore, far from crowding out voluntary initiative and charitable activity, as crude rational choice models might predict, the fact that the wealthy in each community found themselves compelled by statute, Privy Council and magistrate to support the poor, in fact 'crowded in' and enhanced their charitable activity while also ensuring its greater effectiveness, creating, according to Lyn Hollen Lees, a 'welfare society' in England (Lees, 1998). With the social and economic elite in each parish directly financially responsible for alleviating the burden of poverty, illness and human misfortune among fellow

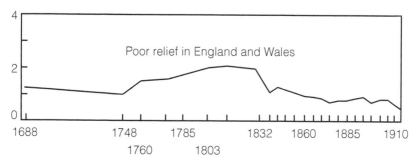

Source: Adapted from Lindert (1994).

Figure 2.1 Poor Law expenditure as percentage of national product 1688–1910

members of their local communities, they had plenty of incentives to use their wealth and ingenuity to attempt to minimise this financial burden by devising various administrative and charitable initiatives which would genuinely allevi-ate the long-term costs of such human problems. Thus, unable to avoid their tax responsibilities for the poor, they deployed their skills and resources instead in more constructive ways than in evading their responsibilities. Successful local merchants founded schools for the poor scholars of the local community (the origins of several of England's oldest grammar schools, many of which have transmuted over time into today's elite private schools patronised by the wealthy again – but now for their own children's education); parishes devised schemes of apprenticeship to equip children of the very poor or orphans with income-earning work skills; alms houses were built to house the infirm elderly so as to rationalise the care and upkeep of this dependent section of the local populace and, in some parishes, salubrious cottages were even built to house more health-ily the poorest families at parish expense (Hindle, 2004; Broad, 2000).

This era in which the Old Poor Law expanded its protective functions in as-sociation with invigorated charitable and voluntary activism was also a period known to historians as one of 'urban renaissance', lasting from the Restora-tion of 1660 to the late eighteenth century. Many towns, with increasing funds from their leading citizens' merchant wealth, were able to invest in their pub-lic amenities and their infrastructure – for instance, widening their streets and building subscription hospitals (Borsay, 1989). However, by the opening dec-ades of the nineteenth century, the prospering towns came up against increas-ingly outdated statutory limits on their corporate borrowing and rating powers, which meant that they could not invest on the scale needed as they rapidly expanded above 50 000 and even above 100 000 inhabitants. Many of the more lucrative urban services, notably supplying water and gas, had to be placed increasingly in the hands of private joint stock companies from the 1810s and 1820s to achieve any expansion. These private companies generally failed to supply services where they could not charge the users commercial rates. They had no legal or commercial responsibility – nor did they want one – for connecting up the poor parts of town, which consequently became unlit, unwatered fever dens, in which the poor, the unenfranchised workers, their families and infants died like – and, indeed, partly from – flies, a major vector of diarrhoea (Hassan, 1985).

Expenditure on the Poor Law had risen to peak levels of 2 per cent of GNP between the 1750s and the 1810s (Figure 2.1). However, new thinking, critical of the Poor Laws and promoting the model of free market relations, had begun to appear with Adam Smith's *Wealth of Nations* from 1776, also supported by Malthus's subsequent writings on the dangers of promoting incipient over-populationism with doles to the poor. By the 1830s, arguments for reform deriving from the new 'sciences' of political economy and Benthamite utilitarianism had achieved ascendancy among a critical section of the governing elite (Brundage, 1978; Mandler, 1987). Consequently, with the passing of the 1834 Poor Law Amendment Act, expenditure was dramatically reduced by almost 50 per cent (Figure 2.1), while its administration was radically rationalised into just 650 'Unions' (groupings of large numbers of parishes), the centrepiece of whose policy was to be the building of deterrent Union workhouses, so that all those now drawing support from the community would first face the 'workhouse test' – proof of their destitution, in that they were prepared to enter the workhouse, where man and wife were segregated to the disgust of many clerics, and a menial work regime enforced in return for gruel.

From the end of the Napoleonic Wars in 1815 all forms of expenditure by the central state fell as a percentage of GNP in Great Britain, in conformity with the new laissez-faire ideology, from a peak of over 20 per cent down to 12 per cent by 1830 and to just 6 per cent by 1870. As Table 2.1 shows, it remained at this low level (with the temporary exception of Boer War spending) until the First World War pushed it back up above the previous peak of the Napoleonic Wars. The overall spend of local government was also held down in the era of laissez-faire despite massively increased needs for spending on the nation's fast-growing towns and their overcrowded, insanitary environments. For instance, not even counting London, the proportion of the nation living in the largest provincial cities of more than 100 000 inhabitants quadrupled from just 1 in 20 in the 1820s to 1 in 5 by the 1870s (Szreter, 2005, Table 6.7). Although some forms of civic activism proliferated, notably working-class friendly and burial societies, nonconformist sects and urban religious missionary work, it was powerless to compensate for the withdrawal of government welfare in the 1830s: child mortality was as high as 500/1000 in some central city districts and the poverty diseases of cholera, typhoid, typhus and tuberculosis were rife (Szreter, 2005, Chapter 6).

However, from the 1870s an entirely new and striking trend is detectable in Table 2.1 in these statistics of local government expenditure. Over the next four decades, while central government activity remained static at a historic low, local government expenditure actually rose very substantially in real terms, more than doubling to over 6 per cent of GNP in 1905. At that point it represented more than 50 per cent of total (local and central) UK government expenditure. This transformation in the character of English municipal local government opened up a second long period of civic activism – the municipal Big Society. Its origins can be dated quite definitely to the late 1860s and 1870s when the young scion of Birmingham's leading screw manufacturing business (Nettlefold and Chamberlain, later G.K.N.), Joseph Chamberlain, along with a network of allies including like-minded industrialist families such as the Kenricks and Martineaus, became enthused with the 'civic gospel' of municipally organised uplift for the poor. Chamberlain proceeded to defeat the incumbent 'dirty party' of 'economy' (i.e. holding down local property rates to the minimum) by standing for mayor on a platform of spending on improvement, using the secret weapon of the local Liberal Party's ward-level 'caucus' system for mobilising the new, urban working-class voters created by the 1867 Second Reform Act and the 1869 Municipal Franchise Act (Hennock, 1973). Chamberlain negotiated large-scale deals to buy up local private monopoly services such as gas and water to use their profits as revenue for the city, hence the soubriquet of 'gas and water socialism' aimed at him (ineffectively) by his opponents. With revenue from these services he sufficiently relieved the burden on the rates of the high costs of transforming the city to avoid an immediate 'ratepayers' revolt'. From the 1870s onwards central government increasingly facilitated this successful Birmingham model by making large-scale Exchequer

Table 2.1   Local government expenditure as a percentage of total government expenditure and as a percentage of GNP

Date	% of total government expenditure	% of GNP
1820	12.5	2.7
1870/71	32.0	3.0
1905	51.1	6.3
1918	5.7	3.0
1925	34.6	8.4
1935	38.8	9.6
1945	9.4	6.2
1950	23.4	9.1
1979	27.9	11.6 (10.7 GDP)
1998/9	23.9	(9.2 GDP)

Sources: For 1820–1955, Peacock and Wiseman (1967), ch.3, esp. Table 1 and p.39, and Appendix, Table A-20; for 1979, HMSO (1979); for 1998/9, HM Treasury (2000), Cmd 4601, Tables 1.11 and 4.1.

loans available to all cities for improvement purposes, resulting in a massive upsurge in their take-up (rising from just £267 000 loaned in 1871 to £2.757 million by 1876 and reaching over twice that level each year by the 1890s). Other cities sought to emulate Birmingham, no longer rivalling each other to charge the lowest property rates to attract business, but now competing to attract with the lowest mortality rates by spending on their environment and social services.

Urban charity and volunteering work did not wither away in the face of this long-term rising commitment by elected local government to ever-increasing, rate-funded improvement in the material environment and basic services of the poor, but it did become much more effective. The bottom line for evaluating whether civic society and local government were having any impact must be the statistics of the urban population's health. These show that the early and mid-Victorian classic age of religious charity and moral philanthropy, which Dickens famously witnessed personally, was one of unparalleled misery and drastic ill-health for the urban masses. Significant and sustained improvement in health, first among adults, then among children and the old, and finally among infants and mothers in childbirth, only occurred once the power of democratic rate-funded, elected local government had been politically harnessed to the task of improvement after 1870, the year of Dickens's death. Without this, mere volunteering and well-meaning charity work was an ineffective sop to the middle-class conscience, as Dickens clear-sightedly depicted it, and as the religious proponents of the 'civic gospel', George Dawson and Robert Dale, also recognised from their long personal experience of ineffective missionary work with Birmingham's urban poor in the decades before the 1870s (Hennock, 1973).

Since its 1905 peak the proportionate share of local government expenditure, relative to central government expenditure, has appeared to shrink back during the twentieth century because of the massive ratcheting up of central government expenditure in each of the two World Wars (by 1943, for instance, the national government was in direct control of about 70 per cent of the whole economy). However, Table 2.1 shows that this eye-catching expansion in the level of central government expenditure during the twentieth century masks the underlying continuity of a trend of substantial continuing real and absolute growth in local government vigour and spending. By 1935, local government expenditure had risen from 6.3 per cent of GNP in 1905 to 9.6 per cent of a much larger GNP; and this in turn had grown again by 1979 to 11.6 per cent of GNP. The familiar story of the twentieth century has supposedly been that of the apparently inexorable growth of central state expenditure in a liberal mass democracy. While this is true, it obscures another important truth about government in a democratic society that is much less widely appreciated. This is the pre-existing *and continuing* trend of very substantial and real growth (i.e. as a proportion of GNP) in the amount and diversity of expenditure and activity of elected local government, lasting continuously for over a century from 1870 until 1979.

Thus, the notion of Victorian Britain as a paradigm era of the small state, with abundant philanthropy, volunteering, self-help and civil associations happily doing much of the work of governance and social welfare after the 1834 withdrawal of the *laissez-faire* state, is only very partially true. It applies, if at all, only to the first half of Victoria's long reign, 1837–1870, when the health statistics show that such volunteering and charity was utterly ineffective in producing social welfare. From the 1870s onwards, it was rate-funded local government that was clearly the most dynamic feature of the civic and social welfare landscape. This was not the kind of central state dynamism and leadership of nation-building seen at that time on the continent of Europe. Instead it was the elected municipal governments of Britain's proudly independent provincial industrial and commercial cities that led the way (governance in the capital city remained far behind the trend until it reformed its vestry system to create the much more dynamic LCC in 1889) (Davis 1988). Large-scale borrowing on the security of the city's rate-base was the key to these town councils' increased vigour and autonomy. This municipal dynamism continued through the interwar and post-war decades until as recently as the 1970s. Not many today know, for instance, that several of the famous new universities of the 1960s like Sussex were, like the provincial red-bricks of an earlier generation such as Birmingham University, also created entirely through local initiative by proud, entrepreneurial and dynamic local government executives.

CONCLUSIONS

One important implication of the historical perspective laid out here is the extremely recent nature of the decline in local government activism and vigour. It is a commonplace notion that the creation of a centralist welfare state by the post-war Labour government undermined localism in Britain, but this is clearly a misleading oversimplification. Rising local government activism and expenditure was a continuous trend in Britain for almost 110 years until it appeared to hit a roadblock in 1979. For the first time since reliable statistics begin in 1820 there emerged, after 1979, a peacetime reversal of the long-established trend in the statistics of secular real growth in local government expenditure, as a percentage of GNP. Two decades later, Table 2.1 shows that there had been a substantial 14 per cent reduction under the Thatcher and Major governments in the percentage of the nation's GDP spent by local government, falling from 10.7 per cent in 1979 (equivalent to 11.6 per cent GNP) to 9.2 per cent of GDP by 1998/9.

Although Conservative governments' rhetoric during the period 1979–97 talked of rolling back the state, central government spending in fact remained constant at about 40 per cent of GDP through the period 1979–97. The reality under the Conservative governments of the 1980s and 1990s was the rolling-back of elected local government for the first time in modern history. The last time there had been a period of stagnancy in British local government after the 1830s 'free market' reforms, it had had devastating consequences for the populaces of Britain's fast-growing cities. The attack on local government after 1979 has similarly been the prelude to two decades of relative decline in the health of those living in the poorest neighbourhoods in the country (Dorling et al., 2007). History indicates that no amount of Big Society volunteering over the next 5–10 years will reverse that trend, in the absence of a central government policy to support financially a reinvigorated democratic local government.

If there is a problem today with the effectiveness of local volunteering in communities, history indicates that the first way to stimulate this would be to re-empower elected local government by endowing it with financial resources to act vigorously to promote the efforts of those in the local community. The second historical lesson is that these financial resources need to be drawn in full proportion from local businesses and the nation's wealth elites to engage the attention and energy of those with most resources. On both previous occasions when local government and civic society has flourished in tandem, to the benefit of the social welfare of all in society, it has been achieved on the basis of a progressive local land tax, which the community's wealthiest citizens could not avoid. As a result, instead of free-riding, they actively participated in devising policies to spend the money most intelligently. In both cases, furthermore, the voice of the poor was facilitated and engaged, by appeal to magistrates in the era of the Old Poor Law and by dint of majority working-class votes in the era of municipal improvement.

This historical review would indicate, therefore, that if Mr Cameron and his advisors are serious about encouraging a Big Society as a contribution to social welfare policy, they need to start with the heart of local communities: local government. They should start by promoting the reinvigoration of accountable (primarily to its electorate, only secondarily to central government targets) local government in Britain.

History would suggest that each of the following four policies could help to bring this about; together they could confidently be predicted to have a powerful effect.

- Introduce a properly progressive land values and housing values tax, as in fact advocated by the Institute for Fiscal Studies in its recent review of the UK tax system, *Tax By Design*. Use the proceeds of this for a set of regional redistributive funds to ensure enhanced levels of local government finance for those local authorities with the greatest socio-economic burdens within each region. By making this fund redistributive within a region, not nationally, the intention would be to engage the self-interests and energies of the wealthiest enclaves in each region with how their tax money is being spent locally in their regions in the poorer districts. Parishes or even cities are probably too small today as units to encourage these important cross-class commitments.

- Arrange for business rates and for bond raising powers to be given to elected local authorities as two sources of relatively independent revenue to provide resources for local initiative and priorities. The 2012 Budget offers tax increment finance (TIF) to Regional Cities but this may be risky.[7]
- Ensure the continuation of fully funded Citizens Advice Bureaux and Legal Aid systems, to ensure that the voice of the poor is heard and that due respect is shown to their priorities and perspectives.
- Revive the political engagement of the voice of the local electorates though an experiment with compulsory voting. This could also be used directly as a pro-Big Society boost to local volunteering by enforcing it through a negative fine, with easy arrangements to transfer this, say £10 payment, to the local charity/voluntary sector cause of their choice for each voter, so that not voting would become uncool, needlessly denying local voluntary activity the financial support made so easily available to it by law. Another part of this strategy could be to bring down the voting age to 16 in local elections to engage school children and their parents – those who should be the prime focus for local politics.

Each of these policies to promote Big Society is imaginative and forward-looking, yet it draws its sanction as a plausible and effective policy from an understanding of how civic activism has worked in practice through vigorous local government over the long term in British history.

NOTES

1. Cameron speech, 14 Feb 2011, http://www.bbc.co.uk/news/uk-politics-12443396, (accessed 23 June 2011).
2. http://www.guardian.co.uk/politics/2011/may/23/david-cameron-big-society-project, (accessed 23 June 2011).
3. Danny Kruger, 'How a smaller state can serve the "big society"': http://www.ft.com/cms/s/0/aafdf77e-7d96-11df-a0f5-00144feabdc0.html#axzz1Q6dgF4L6 (accessed 23 June 2011).
4. Cameron speech, 14 February 2011, http://www.bbc.co.uk/news/uk-politics-12443396.
5. The original call was voiced by the report, *Setting Cities Free – Releasing the Potential of Cities to Drive Growth*, presented to the House of Commons on 23 May 2011. Business rates raise £2.61 billion annually, collected locally but held in a central account by the Department of Communities and Local Government and redistributed back to local authorities as part of the centrally determined local government finance settlement. The 2012 Budget has not fundamentally altered this.
6. Thus, the report goes on to state, 'The Government's approach in practice, however, has thus far been marked by inconsistency and incoherence, not helped by a definition of localism that is extremely elastic'. House of Commons Communities and Local Government Committee (2011).
7. http://www.telegraph.co.uk/finance/budget/9158975/Budget-2012-Regional-cities-given-go-ahead-to-raise-debt.html.

3. Big Society, legal structures, Poor Law and the myth of a voluntary society

Lorie Charlesworth

The Coalition government's 'Big Society' of mutuality and volunteering is being presented as a solution to tackling social problems. Its purposes are set out in a Cabinet Office document published in May 2010 within a week of the formation of the Coalition government (Cabinet Office, 2010). These aims are: decentralise power from central government via local government to communities, neighbourhoods and individuals. In the policy documents aimed at charities, social enterprises and voluntary organisations, the three core components of the Big Society policy agenda are empowering communities, opening up public services, and promoting social action (Office for Civil Society, 2010a,b). Proposals include: giving communities the right to bid to take over local facilities and services threatened with closure; training a new generation of community organisers; and supporting the creation of neighbourhood groups across the UK, especially in the most deprived areas. Schemes to train these 'community organisers' are already in place and yet definitions of 'society' or even 'community' remain imprecise. Essentially, Prime Minister David Cameron and his advisors seem to share an idealised view of English historical development based upon philanthropy and localism, both of which indeed played their part in the developments of our complex modern society. However, England's social developments, the virtues of our past, were not dependent primarily upon 'volunteers'. Rather they operated within a legal framework setting out rights, duties and obligations, which bound all classes and members of society together, much as they do today. What is increasingly evident in government pronouncements is that ministers have no knowledge of what went before.

In short, without a framework of both legal and fiscal obligations, any such voluntary system for social activism, local governance and even the relief of poverty is purely mythical, in the sense that it has no sanction in British history. What worked, and still works, is local government, regulated by law, financed by local and later additional national contributions, its duties enforced through the courts, by external agencies and government supervision and by citizens exercising their legal and democratic rights. Local government still responds to local needs and possesses some residual elements of its former legal local autonomy. Finally, philanthropy, charity in fact and in law, also operates in the context of a complex legal structure and a considerable legal history in the Courts of Equity, very different from the rules in common law (see Chapter 7, Charity and Big Society).

It is crucial to understand that the origins of English local government occurred as a by-product of Tudor legislation dealing with one of the social consequences of the reformation in England. Rushton has re-evaluated the poor relief expenditure of religious foundations, and concludes that the pre-Reformation ecclesiastical establishments were providing substantial, genuinely beneficial poor relief (Rushton, 2001), regulated by their canon law obligations and the individual rules of each order. Their closure by Henry VIII left a gap in relief and necessitated putting the relief of the poor in England and Wales upon a workable formal legal footing. The resulting Act for the Better Relief of the Poor 1601 confirmed, recognised and regularised this responsibility at a local level. The legislation instructed existing ecclesiastical parish vestries to function under the authority of legal duties and obligations that were set out within the terms of that Act and its many legal presumptions (for a full legal discussion of this, see Charlesworth 2010, Chapter 3). These activities were overseen and 'enforced', via the Justices of the Peace (magistrates) in local Sessions, under the authority of the overarching legal framework of the common law of England and Wales. This was certainly local and community based, but with joint and personal fiscal and legal liabilities; local civic society in England and Wales was not founded simply upon a cultural history of philanthropic volunteers, it was created by law.

THE POOR LAW AND THE ORIGINS OF ENGLISH LOCAL GOVERNMENT

In formal legal terms, the emergence of common law Poor Law is technically dated from the Act of 1601, which constituted the legal authority for all poor relief in England and Wales until 1948 and was so expressed in the case law. Although that Act may be read as innovative in part, it also embodied crucial legal presumptions underpinning and pre-dating it in a series of earlier, less complete and rather unsuccessful Poor Law statutes enacted during the previous seven post-Reformation decades. Most importantly, the obligation by each parish to relieve the poor was understood as in earlier statutes but was not articulated. Second, who was to be relieved was also understood or partially set out in the sixteenth-century precursor statutes: that is, a person born in the parish, or who had resided there for three years. This constituted the 'settlement' entitlement. Finally, in its terms this Act of 1601 cloned the ecclesiastical parish into a civil parish, whose residents were instructed to appoint annually unpaid parish officials (not exactly volunteers as this was a legal obligation for ratepayers) to administer the Poor Law, marking the birth of English local government and the first co-opted Big Society. Unpaid parish overseers of the poor collected the poor rate and paid poor relief, reporting and accounting monthly (if not more often) to the parish vestry.

The terms of the 1601 Act emphasised the civil administrative aspects of Poor Law. In brief, each parish was responsible for raising a poor rate from each resident householder, on the progressive taxation principle of being proportionate to the value of the property they occupied and according to local financial need. This rate was set annually, taking into account any money in hand, parish assets and parish debt outstanding from the previous year's expenses; it was demand-led and essentially uncapped. This figure and the parish accounts were presented to, and ratified annually by, Justices of the Peace at Sessions. As a result, each householder (occupier) in a parish or township, including the poor, had a legal obligation to contribute to the poor rate, and failure to do so would lead to the seizure of goods and imprisonment until full payment was made. The same legal rules continue today as an enforcement mechanism for non-payment of local council tax, successor to and descendant of the poor rate. Hence the system contained both financial and enforcement mechanisms supervised by all local Justices. Finally, this structure constituted a Poor Law system operating under the common law. Admittedly this system was not initially fully operational, nor in any way resembled modern, centrally supervised, welfare bureaucracies. Nevertheless, it constituted all the necessary legal and administrative elements that were to underpin and provide legal authority for poor relief for around the next 350 years in England and Wales.

Under England's Old Poor Law, welfare activities were highly organised between 1601 and 1834 on a local, community basis. However, this was not reliant upon the formula of mere voluntary association. On the contrary, local parish vestries operated under the authority of legal duties and obligations, set out within and enforced by the common law of England and Wales, its Justices of the Peace, Quarter and County Sessions and senior law courts. Local communities held joint and personal legal liabilities and were subject to sanctions for misconduct, including failure to perform their duties. These sanctions ranged from fines to terms of imprisonment, with possible criminal charges including manslaughter for failure to act if a poor person died of want. In short, although many of the key personnel involved, such as Poor Law overseers, were typically not paid for their services, these actions were far from merely voluntary, and this is why the system worked. Local church parish vestries, their clergy, churchwardens, beadles and parishioners, all who qualified to pay the poor rate, were seconded to the secular vestry and acquired legal duties. This was a world positively motivated, where the overarching framework of the common law allowed local flexibility but the assurance that the legal duties would be carried out. David Cameron's notion of a Big Society of mutuality and volunteering, without careful attention to a framework of legal as well as fiscal obligations, is untested in the English past.

It is important, however, to acknowledge that Poor Law was not the same as modern welfare law. The latter consists of public administrative law operating within a central bureaucratic framework, funded by a system of national taxation and directed by whichever government is currently in power. On the contrary, until 1865 and in some aspects beyond that date, Poor Law constituted an overarching common law legal system with local elements of autonomy, financial obligations, duties, responsibilities and *ad hoc* relief patterns based upon the parishes and townships of England and Wales. Quite lawfully, within this system, the localities manifested individual characteristics according to geographical, financial, social and property-owning circumstances. However, all relief decisions were made in the context of a legal framework, not simply the duty to set and raise a poor rate, but also the common law of settlement and removal, the right to relief, other legal rules and established legal processes.

In spite of the above, for many of those scholars writing about the history of welfare in England and Wales, even the basic legal truth that 'Poor Law was law' has slipped from collective consciousness. As a result, the legal underpinnings of that system of relieving poverty have been marginalised, misunderstood, forgotten and denied. Although most current welfare textbooks make reference to welfare's Poor Law past, few acknowledge that England and Wales (but not Scotland and Ireland, which each have a different welfare history) possess the oldest continuous legal system of welfare relief in Europe. This is a 400-year-old legal system of relieving poverty that more recently developed as a branch of public law.

Such is the degree of forgetting that the legal reality that the Poor Law encompassed a right to relief remains unrecognised or at best denied even among many historians. That right was founded upon the possession of a legal settlement, and to that end it may be stated as a legal opinion that the Law of Settlement and Removal was at the heart of the Poor Law. Its doctrines, encompassing rights, duties and obligations by all persons living in England and Wales, were such that the settled poor possessed a legal, enforceable right to relief from their place of settlement. This is the legal foundation for hundreds of years of poor relief payments in England and Wales. Record offices all over England and Wales bear testimony to the sustained efforts of thousands of local vestries (latterly county and borough councils) from the sixteenth to the twentieth century, in actively dealing with the problems of the poor. Whatever the personal motives and individual methods of those participants, poverty was relieved, local taxes on property were raised and local people occupied themselves with their responsibilities within a framework of legal obligations enforced by the common law courts.

From a lawyer's perspective it appears perverse that Poor Law's legal foundations are underestimated by legal historians and thus lost to others in the policy arena that follow their lead. One possible explanation for this law-blindness may be found in the influence of those reforms implemented via the terms of the Poor Law Amendment Act 1834. This initiated the New Poor Law with its national system of prison-like workhouses. Although the right to relief remained and settlement law was largely unreformed, the manner of that relief became both bureaucratised and brutalised according to the terms of the Act and was only supposed to be available under conditions of 'less eligibility', that is, less favourable than those of the very poorest wage workers living off a subsistence income. Consequently, the poor came to be seen as a problem to be contained and controlled. What is more, so influential and pervasive have been the negative aspects of those reforms that a cultural stigma surrounding poverty persists today despite the establishment of the welfare state in 1948.

In addition, other factors continue to influence current misunderstanding of welfare's legal past. The first is the persistence of a negative perception of the role of settlement in Poor Law, as concerned mainly with removal of persons, and not with the protection of rights. The second is that the abolition of Poor Law in 1948 left a message that nothing in welfare's past had value for society and the poor. The third is a result of that legal abolition: namely that Poor Law as a legal subject disappeared from legal education, practice and legal memory. As a result, a history of poverty has developed that does not take into account the power and formality of the Poor Law's legal aspects or, at best, seriously underestimates their significance for the poor, for local ratepayers and for those who administered the system.

Possessing a settlement (that is, the legal right to poor relief from one's settlement parish when destitute) was inherent if not clearly articulated within the 1601 Act, and it was a legal rule that everyone born in England and Wales possessed a settlement somewhere; the trick was to find the place. However, further administrative details of the settlement entitlement were clarified in an Act for the Better Relief of the Poor of this Kingdom, 1662, often erroneously titled the 'Settlement Act'. The terms of this Act confirmed that the 'settled poor' of any place were entitled to a share of the poor rate and added further details of how settlement was acquired. The residence qualification set out in the terms of early post-Reformation statutes was shortened to '40 days at the least'. In juristic terms, this Act formalised the legal status of possessing a settlement and was expressed as the legal authority for such in all subsequent case law. Settlement was from then on clarified as a legal right possessed by a settled individual who had an enforceable legal claim to a share of the parish poor rate when destitute. In addition, the Act was concerned with the removal of those poor seeking relief but not possessing a settlement in the place where they lived. Their removal was achieved through formal court hearings. However, the removal order could only be made to a specific named parish where the Justices were satisfied, from often complex legal proofs, that the pauper possessed a settlement.

There was a right of appeal by that named parish to Quarter Sessions, but only on the grounds that the poor person did not possess a settlement in their parish or for procedural errors (*certiorari*). These appeals could continue to the highest level, over time creating many thousands of settlement cases in the Law Reports. To summarise, in its earliest form, settlement as a common law right was acquired simply through birth or residence. However, gaining and proving a legal settlement became an increasingly technical matter. This law continued to evolve from those terms introduced and understood in the 1662 Act, via further amending statutes and developing case law, to become extremely complex and the major source of contemporary lawyers' incomes, equivalent to that earned from British criminal law practice today.

Settlement law thus protected and delineated legal civic status. It provided all individuals with legal recognition of their membership of a specific collectivity – a parish – and an undeniable right to the common wealth of that parish. An individual could only be settled in one specific geographical place. The acquisition of settled status elsewhere automatically destroyed the previous settlement, and responsibility for maintaining that person when destitute then lay with the new settlement parish. Any person could exchange their place of settlement for another via the qualifying rules for each head of settlement. A woman acquired her husband's settlement upon marriage, a family's settlement always followed the father's settlement and thus they were removed as a unit by one legal action. Individuals who had qualifying status acquired a settlement wherever they resided. Anyone, including the 'better sort', could be removed by legal process if they became destitute and had not acquired a settlement in the removing parish.

In order to access aid a poor person would approach a parish official to request relief and, once in receipt of relief, he/she was referred to as a 'pauper' – a legal term. The first legal requirement was to demonstrate that they were destitute, this initial decision lying within the subjective judgment of that official. It is this gateway decision that has caused much confusion and an emphasis upon conditionality, negotiation and local custom as explanations for poor relief payments. These factors may explain why officials sometimes refused relief but not why they were often overruled by the Justices. No matter how much any vestry or its officials wished to reduce or restrict relief, the legal position thwarted them. This legal right protected the poor from starvation.

Any poor person could approach a magistrate – in his court, in his home or even on the hunting field – state their destitution, explain that aid had been refused and ask for help. The magistrate could, and often did, make an Order and relief then had to be given. This was not an appeals procedure; on the contrary it represented a long-standing personal right that was eventually given a procedural formality in the terms of an Act of 1714. Parish officials were bound to assist the pauper and obey the magistrate's Order; failure to do so was contempt of court and officials incurred a personal liability. Most remarkably, this cost the applicant nothing at all.

Thus, settlement was not something imposed upon the poor; it was the source of their fundamental legal right to receive aid. It was also the explanation for the centuries of unexciting regular sums paid in relief and recorded by every vestry in England and Wales, all those uncontested payments which were annually ratified by Justices. Total expenditure on the Poor Law amounted by the early nineteenth century to fully 2 per cent of GNP, at that time by far the most well-funded welfare system in Europe.

FROM COMMON LAW RIGHTS TO PUBLIC LAW WELFARE

This was the position under the legal authority of the Acts of 1601 and 1662, and it remained so after the implementation of the terms of the Poor Law Amendment Act 1834. However, there were major direct changes in the lives of paupers, as the 1834 Act's draconian sections declared that the able-bodied poor could only be relieved in a workhouse in regimented prison-like conditions. Equally significant was the loss of a precious personal entitlement: a poor person's right to seek an Order from a Justice for relief payments was abolished. From then on Justices could only order relief in kind or medical aid and these solely in an emergency. Technically, this did not abolish the right to relief for the settled poor, as that constituted the legal foundations of, and explanation for, poor relief provision. However, this removal of a personal enforceable right to apply for relief payments from a Justice was truly a low point in English legal history. Even the modern welfare state has nothing as powerful in its armoury to offer the individual, if indeed it can be said to be rights-based at all.

With this legal development, the common law of Poor Law began its mutation into the public law of welfare. The personal common law rights of the poor were slowly submerged under bureaucratic decision-making processes. In this shift, poor relief as a legal obligation between fellow parishioners eventually mutated into the modern public law relationship between the individual and the state. Despite this change, local vestries especially in the North of England operated around the margins of the 1834 Act to exploit continuing elements of their legal autonomy. Each parish or vestry in England and Wales paid for its settled paupers whether in or out of the Union workhouses. In addition, each parish was still required to account to its own ratepayers for Poor Law expenditure and have those accounts annually verified by local Justices. Consequently, in the absence of actual fraud, parishes could spend as much as they liked and how they liked; their legal responsibility was to relieve their settled poor under the continuing authority of the 1601 Act. Nothing in the 1834 Act changed this fundamental legal rule.

However, the reforms of 1834 and after made a great difference to the poor and there is sufficient evidence of Poor Law protest and local resistance to show how bitterly this loss of legal rights was resented. Those reforms ensured that destitution increasingly became a route into the new Union workhouses for many. Almost unanimously, those historians who consider this matter have concluded that the poor were expressing cultural and social norms, not legal rights. Poor Law historians do not seem to have been prepared to listen to their witnesses, which is not only poignant and regrettable but also misleading. For the poor, the rights they claimed were indeed the legal rights they believed them to be. The Poor Law reforms of 1834 expressed a cultural shift in economic and thus social relations within English society, which permitted the creation of a punitive welfare system, whose basic norm was a mistrust of a large section of the poor, whom many believed – and still believe – were responsible for their own destitution.

There was no revival of the personal right to relief once possessed by the settled poor. This is unsurprising in that that right has been consistently undervalued, marginalised, denied and forgotten. This is not to minimise the subjective elements in the amounts and manner in which poor relief was given, nor to deny that proving destitution allowed discretion to parish officials – elements today understood as conditionality. However, the actions after 1834 of both the government in London and local responses in Ireland during the disastrous Great Famine of the 1840s illustrates how little relief might have been given to the poor in England and Wales over previous centuries without those legal rights protected by the settlement entitlement. Irish poor law in the 1840s was implemented under the terms of the post-1834 New Poor Law in the form of the Poor Relief (Ireland) Act 1838, which introduced a financially capped scheme and specifically excluded the right to relief, with truly tragic and deplorable consequences.

LEGAL DUTIES AND LOCAL GOVERNMENT

Local vestries concerned themselves with many other matters, duties set under a wide range of legislation, some pre-dating 1601. These included: road and bridge repairs; keeping waterways clear; ensuring nuisance removal; collecting county rates and appointing constables, overseers, surveyors of the highways; mole and sparrow catching; paying militia or their families; giving aid to travellers with passes; dealing with local disorder; pursuing disagreements over township boundaries; settlement enquiries concerning the poor; making visits to Sessions; and a myriad of other matters. Under the terms of the Act of 1601, local vestries apart from the duty to relieve their settled poor, were required to aid anyone in an emergency and set the children of the poor to apprenticeships.

However, each vestry had considerable autonomy in how they performed their duties. They could relieve poverty in any manner and amount they wished, be generous if they wanted, just so long as the poor were relieved. Ratepayers could choose any member of the vestry for the annual unpaid positions of overseer, constable, surveyor of the highways, and later they could pay extra officials to perform these roles. The vestry were accountable to their fellow ratepayers for expenditure, and generosity led to financial costs which could prove unpopular. Justices had to ratify accounts, payments and appointments, but did not choose officials. All Justices were ratepayers, too. Vestries were required to meet annually to appoint officials and monthly to deal with Poor Law and other matters; many had to meet more often. There were no expenses or payments, but the legal obligation and the local influence vestries carried ensured centuries of regular meetings across the parishes of England and Wales. This was Big Society localism in action.

Justices formed the coordinating mechanism and conduit between central government and the localities; centrally overseen, they had local concerns (Charlesworth, 2009). The administrative role of the Justices was considerable. They had extensive duties in connection with the Poor Law, ratifying the annual parish appointment of overseers of the poor, confirming the annual poor rate and the parish poor-law accounts and binding apprentices. Two Justices together had control of the sheriff, took oaths from undersheriffs and examined sheriffs' accounts. They were responsible for the licensing of alehouses. They also exercised a number of miscellaneous duties including making regulations in time of plague. Three or more Justices together had wider powers still, including examining the accounts of charitable foundations and exercising extensive authority concerning decayed bridges, gaols and sewers.

Overall, however, the statutes authorising these local Justices to act left them a very wide discretion in the exercise of governmental functions, which were performed within the traditional structure of presentment and indictment for non-performance. The effect of this approach was to give the rules and judicial processes of the common law primacy over statutory law in local county governance. This discretionary approach created the English model of local self-government and autonomy within a legal framework. At the end of the sixteenth century the main work of local government was being performed by the Justices and parochial officers, who regularly oversaw the activities of the parish vestry.

By the eighteenth century this pattern of criminal and administrative jurisdiction was an established feature of the role of Justices. Justices of the Peace were the most important and ubiquitous feature of local government in England and Wales. They were increasingly provided with professional legal and clerical staff, and were supported by the organisation and the local patriotism of the county. Yet, quite lawfully within this 'system', the localities manifested individual characteristics according to, amongst other factors, local geographical, financial, social and property-owning circumstances; but all decisions were made in the context of a legal framework. The Justices, in concert with the local vestries, both belonged to and represented the county. More importantly, they lived in specific parishes and their localism, and the great discretion they possessed in how they exercised their functions, bolstered communal feeling within individual parish and township. This combination of localism and historical continuity in local administration by Justices was enhanced and reinforced by general and local statutes. It is worth noting that central government increasingly disliked this element of localism and sought increasingly to exercise control over the localities. The first victory came in the passing of the Poor Law Amendment Act 1834, and the battle continues today.

Finally, charities as part of the third sector are clearly expected by the current government to bear a considerable responsibility for implementing a Big Society. Charities have a long history of helping people change the communities around them for the better; it was charities that established the first hospitals (Wilson, 1966) and many schools (Jones, 1938). Many successful charities embraced the principles of Big Society, before it acquired this label. Moreover, charity pre-dates the Reformation, which had a legal and operational impact upon charitable foundations and their functioning. As Richard Fries shows (Chapter 7, Charity and Big Society), charity also had its great foundational statute in 1601. It has been recently reformed but presents a number of legal issues. Crucially, a charity must be independent, so that it must exist solely for its charitable purposes, not for the purpose of carrying out the policies or directions of a public authority (Charity Commission, 2001). Quite unlike the history of welfare provision, there are no legal rights for recipients; trustees have a duty and obligation to perform the purposes of the charity, but if they choose not to act, no one has a right to make them do so. Charities have always provided an additional resource for the poor, needy and destitute, but however they are regulated, whatever social function they perform, no citizen can enforce a personal right against a charity.

CONCLUSION

The proposed, if amorphous, Big Society is not a creature of history, but something new; a retreat from the legal rights of citizens to a paternalist world of volunteers and amateur philanthropy. On the contrary, it must be emphasised that welfare in British history was not the creation of the brave new world of Beveridge in the 1940s, but represented a fundamental cultural and legal norm long embedded within our society; one that also initiated the legal structure and rights that are a basic constituent of local government in Britain. Localism has developed from, and within, a legal framework over a long period of time, and any social policy proposed by a government that dilutes or marginalises the rights of citizens should be regarded with grave suspicion. Poor Law also included one of our finest legal traditions, that of the right of the poor to be relieved. This earliest of human rights was once a fundamental aspect of our legal economy. Its legacy ensures that some form of welfare for all citizens, visitors and others, is deeply embedded within British society. A crucial point is that while its local participants were many and active (i.e. a Big Society), they performed legal obligations under the overarching framework of the common law with many fiscal and legal enforcement mechanisms to ensure and insure the substantial rights of the poor. Without a legal framework, 'rights' are meaningless and social policy becomes merely the gift of paternalist governments or dependent upon the good will of volunteers.

4. Mutual aid and the Big Society

Daniel Weinbren

When the Conservative leader's Director of Strategy, Steve Hilton, sought an image of the struggle to push back the frontiers of the state he settled upon the 1946 film, *My Darling Clementine*, as 'a fantastic description of our values and political approach' (Brooks, 2009; Hilton, 2010). David Cameron's inspiration appeared to be from a more conventional source in that his proposal to appoint a 'neighbourhood army' and to nourish '5000 community organisers', using the equivalent of a few loaves and fishes, may have had Biblical roots (Conservative Party, 2010). Neither these men nor (according to Stuart Hall) Nick Clegg have indicated interest in drawing on the experiences of previous Conservative-dominated governments' efforts to empower community leaders (Hall, 2011, p. 15). An important example of this had occurred between the wars when, following the 1911 National Insurance Act, the administration of UK health care was placed in the hands of mutual aid bodies. The resulting tangle of red tape nearly strangled the officially approved voluntary organisations and disillusionment with the voluntary sector was so extensive that the subsequent central state intervention of the 1940s was widely welcomed.

Employing a more homely image of the relationship between different forms of provision the architect of the NHS, William Beveridge, who was sympathetic towards the friendly societies, concluded that the 1911 'marriage between the state and the voluntary agencies has been followed by complete divorce' (Beveridge, 1948, p. 83). The reasons for the irretrievable breakdown of the relationship can be placed in four categories. First, the tasks set by the government were complicated. The mutuals had to create and support unplanned new branches of their businesses as well as maintain their old ones. Friendly societies and trade unions, designed for mutual aid, found it difficult to adapt to their new roles as officially 'approved societies' administering the National Insurance scheme. The marriage was not one between equals but unbalanced, as the actuarial conservatism of the system benefitted Treasury coffers at the expense of the mutual sector. Second, in addition to involvement in complex insurance management, the relationship between doctors and friendly societies, which had been strained prior to 1911, was not eased by the structures created to connect the administrative and professional, clinical bodies involved in the scheme. Third, in an era of retrenchment and cuts, economic and material considerations came to dominate ethical and educational ones, and democratic practices withered away. Fourth, the mutuals became associated with party politics and, when the government changed the perception of their party, bias was retained.

RED TAPE

The system of compulsory health insurance for lower-paid employed people, which was selected in 1911, involved only a modest state subsidy and was built upon the payment traditions and structures of the friendly societies and trade unions, some of which offered unemployment pay. All employed persons aged between 16 and 70, if they earned less than £160 per annum, or were manual labourers in the same age group regardless of earnings, had to join a society which had been approved by the government. The legislation provided between 11 and 12.4 million people with health insurance in 1912, and this figure rose in subsequent years as the population grew and the threshold for eligibility changed (in 1920 the amount earned for coverage was raised to £250, while in 1928 the upper age was reduced to 65 and, finally, in 1937 those younger than 16 were also covered if employed). By 1942 some 21 million workers were covered. If they lost their jobs they did not contribute to the scheme but were still allowed to claim. Employers paid 3d (three pence, an eighteenth of a pound), male workers 4d, women 3d and the government 2d a week. Women workers whose husbands were also insured qualified for double benefit.

Contributions were paid through a lengthy process. Employers purchased stamps at the post office, fixed them to the workers' contribution cards and deducted the workers' portion directly from wages. These cards were returned to the member's approved society, which returned them to the ministry as proof of contributory income. Although the day-to-day administrative decisions were supposedly left to the approved societies, in practice transactions between centre and each society were monitored through the process of audit. Collectively, the Controller, the official auditors and Government Actuary determined the ways in which the scheme developed. The process of audit was expensive and reduced the local autonomy of mutuals' branches. Every one of these had to keep track of nine different account books, 21 different categories of insured people and 22 different items of information about each member. The secretaries sent the books to the ministry as proof of income, which was then credited to the society twice yearly in arrears. This was after the ministry had checked on claims and certification and, if appropriate, withheld payment for 'improper' expenditure. The ministry then credited the mutuals with their share of contributions and the state's subvention, and audited the accounts. It decided every five years how much each approved society could offer in additional benefits.

This was calculated following consideration of the 'panel' doctors' per capita fee and data about the reserve values, contingency funds and investment. One of the largest mutuals, the Oddfellows, lamented that 'We never dreamed … we would be so governed by regulations. We had no idea that the Treasury grant would be bound up in so much red tape' (Whiteside, 1997, p. 477). The regulations were not only initially time consuming and confusing, but also there were numerous centrally imposed tweaks made to the scheme in almost every year between 1913 and 1945.

The workload of the mutuals' local secretaries increased something like three or fourfold and it became, for many, almost a full-time job, performed by part-time, often poorly trained, staff whose efforts were not always appreciated in Whitehall. In 1914 the Local Government Board concluded that 'the tragedy of voluntary effort is that it finds it difficult to maintain a high standard of efficiency' (Whiteside, 1997, p. 476). The mutual sector found it difficult to adapt to the new functions. There was no organised, centrally planned growth to take account of the needs, which arose when those friendly societies which were not numbered among the 2208 'approved' ones closed or merged. For example, in the Exeter area as a result of the Act, the Oddfellows opened four female lodges and recruited 2500 members, the voluntary and part-time Provincial Corresponding Secretary resigned and was replaced by a full-timer on a salary of £150 a year (*Oddfellows' Magazine*, February 1913).

In addition to being administratively complicated the scheme was also financially difficult to run as the influence on the approved societies of the Government Actuary and the auditors increased in the 1920s. The government reduced its contribution to the cost of the scheme and, as the number of unemployed rose, their contributions fell. The government had found a revenue-raising measure that fitted the political culture of the country and was popular because contributions to national insurance through friendly societies were not seen as a tax. Furthermore, it could evade criticism of the low level of benefit payments, the different levels of benefit payments and the fact that many people were not covered at all, by blaming the approved societies.

The mutuals were pushed into drawing on their own resources to make good deficits and implementing new regulations governing questions of access, levels of benefit and the policing of claimants and doctors. While the recession reduced contributions and raised the incidence of claims, the cost to taxpayers was very little because the Exchequer contribution was only paid on reimbursement of expenditure. Large sums were held within Whitehall as contingency funds and the interest used to offset the Exchequer contribution. Furthermore, any money that the mutuals made was held by the government. The conservatism of the actuarial science practised by the Exchequer was such that, by 1938, over £220 million of society investments were in centralised reserve funds. This was more than the assets of the Unemployment Fund (£130 million) and the Pensions Fund (£50 million) combined (Whiteside, 1997, p. 478). The interest accruing from this sum (c. £7 million p.a.) was used to offset the annual Exchequer contribution of £9 million to the scheme. Funds that might previously have swelled the coffers of the mutuals ended up as savings for the Treasury. Furthermore, it was easy for the government to tighten regulations unilaterally. In 1922, following the Geddes Report, and twice in 1925, following the introduction of contribution pensions and the Economy Act, society income from the Exchequer was reduced (Whiteside, 1999, p. 30). In 1932 women's benefit rights were cut and cover was removed from some unemployed. As the regulations became more complicated, so the autonomy of the mutuals was reduced. The Oddfellows, finding that it had high administrative costs compared to the cost of the benefits delivered, requested that it be allowed to pool the surpluses of lodges (an idea that the 1926 report of the Royal Commission on National Health Insurance recommended). This was not allowed (*Manchester Guardian*, 17 May 1932). Their societies received a flat-rate, per-capita subsidy and had to pay for their own running expenses and overheads. The Treasury paid only one-sixth of the total administrative costs.

SCRUTINY OF MEMBERS

The narrowing of their role left the mutuals less room to evolve. There were more claims made for illness and this was felt to be because the policing of who was allowed to join the mutuals had been relaxed, enabling people who were more likely to claim sickness benefits to join (Whiteside, 1987, p. 231). More generally, public attitudes towards poverty changed. Increasingly, state aid was seen as a right not as a gift. The adoption of new techniques and medications pushed up the cost of medical care. The main cost for a family of the sickness of the male breadwinner changed from the loss of his income to the payment of medical bills. This entailed a demand for larger and more varying sums, a pattern that fitted better the less personal and more businesslike methods of commercial insurers, which already sold more policies in 1912 than the friendly societies had members. It was also argued that people felt that malingering was acceptable and would go unpunished. In 1914 Dr Alfred Cox, Secretary of the British Medical Association, argued that the effect of the Act was that 'persons who formerly did not go to the doctor until they were really ill now go for more trifling ailments' (Digby and Bosanquet, 1988, p. 87). In addition, the decision to claim may have been guided by other factors than deciding that one felt ill. For example, by 1934–35 one-third of the chronic disability cases were said to be caused by nervous disorders, a trend partly explained by the recent respectability and prominence of psychiatric medicine and diagnoses (Whiteside, 1987, pp. 236–7). The criteria for payments under the National Insurance scheme were different to those made under the unemployment scheme. This may have encouraged people to claim the former, particularly as access to the latter was reduced and made more complicated.

Prior to the legislation, many doctors were employed by friendly societies and there was friction regarding clinical judgments, professional status and pay. Following the legislation, doctors were paid per approved society patient on their panel and this encouraged GPs to recruit the maximum number of panel patients and to spend the minimum time treating them. Payment was not for treatment so that doctors who made use of a laboratory for tests paid for it themselves. By contrast, private, middle-class patients received better treatment and sometimes had their own waiting room and better medical appliances and products (Digby and Bosanquet, 1988, p. 90). The mutuals tended to see doctors as part of the problem. The National Conference of Friendly Societies passed a resolution against an increase in panel doctors' pay in 1923 (*The Times*, 24 September 1923); and when the total amount of sickness benefits paid to claimants rose in 1927, partly due to an influenza epidemic, the Foresters claimed that this was also due to 'loose certification for sickness payments by panel doctors' (*The Times*, 10 August 1928). One delegate additionally pointed to the adverse effects of the right that patients had to transfer between doctors. The accusation of a 'laxity of certification among a proportion of doctors' was also made in 1931 (*The Times*, 4 August 1931).

The conditions for receiving sickness benefit were stringent, and sick visitors were appointed to ensure compliance. Albert Fox, an Oddfellows' Sick Visitor in Taddington, Derbyshire, recalled:

> You had to visit everybody on sick within a four mile radius once per week and report at the next Lodge meeting. There was one ... he was pruning his roses and the Sick Visitor of the day saw him doing it and reported him and he had his sick pay stopped for that. (Bathe, 1984, p. 30)

Frank Bagshaw, a member of the same lodge, also recalled the rules for receiving benefit:

> It was very keen, though. If you were off work they used to have a Sick Visitor, and he'd just drop in on you, any time. If he saw you cleaning your boots, you were in trouble. (Bathe, 1984, p. 30)

In nearby Disley Margaret Graham recalled that 'If you were on the club you couldn't go out after 7 o'clock at night otherwise you lost your club money' (Weinbren, 2010, p. 157). Monitoring the ill on behalf of the government, enforcing its labyrinthine regulations and blaming medical professionals when problems arose did little to improve the public image of the societies.

CONVIVIALITY

Whereas in the past collecting contributions, processing claims and policing against fraud had been balanced by the pleasures of voluntary thrift, proud parades and democratic self-government, the Act shifted the focus. The 'sympathetic visitor' who brought 'into the house of the afflicted brother ... not only the benefit which the sick member has contributed for, but also a word of cheer and comfort from his brothers in the Order', was replaced by 'cold officialism that will only perform so much service for so much monetary consideration' (*Oddfellows' Magazine*, 1913). Following the legislation the formerly 'warm-hearted, sympathetic sick visitor [now] "rushes round on Friday night or Saturday, hands the money in ... takes a receipt for the benefit and goes"' (*Oddfellows' Magazine*, June 1909, September 1911, March 1912; Alborn, 2001, p. 595). The effect of being 'approved' was, as one Oddfellow pointed out, that members became 'actuarial friendly society men rather than actual friendly society men [whose] souls were in pawn to the devil of arithmetic, who blew our ideals sky-high' (*Oddfellows' Magazine*, June 1915). Members of friendly societies relied on their lodges (branches) for fellowship. In 1913 the Oddfellows' Grand Master, Walter Wright, claimed that the legislation marginalised the need 'to build up character as well as to build up health' and to educate 'men and women in the virtues of self-denial and self-help'. He felt that the Oddfellows was veering towards being 'a mere commercial undertaking', that 'social and educational gatherings are becoming a rarity'; there was less ritual and there was a danger of 'creating a nation of spoon-fed puppets instead of a nation of free and independent men and women' (*Oddfellows' Magazine*, July 1914).

Although the Act specified that an approved society had to be subject to the 'absolute control of its members including provision for the election and removal of the committee of management', this requirement was satisfied when a dozen clerks who worked for the Prudential held a meeting in its London office. Such commercial organisations benefited from legislation that was supposedly intended to promote mutual aid. The number of policies issued by commercial collecting societies (which were also permitted to administer the scheme) rose by more than 350 per cent between 1915 and 1945. Between 1918 and 1932, despite an increase in the overall insured population, 2700 branches of the larger societies had ceased to operate and total membership fell to below 3 million. When the Act was passed there were over 15 000 separate approved society units (that is lodges, courts or branches). By 1938 only 5700 of these remained (Whiteside, 1983, p. 169). For many members the pleasures of lodge sociability were reduced because membership involved more travel and social activity in unfamiliar and enlarged lodges.

The new system also did little for mutuality across gender lines. When most of those who were insured had been men, their friendly societies had tended to meet in pubs from which women were excluded. The 1911 legislation reflected the idea that women depended on men for survival. The scheme was open to workers but not their spouses or children. Men were expected to be the bread-winners. However, women joined the scheme in large numbers, as domestic servants (the most common paid work for women between the wars) and war workers. The 1911 Act forbade meetings to be held in pubs but meetings in school rooms were not as popular as the commercial agencies' solution. This was to ignore traditions of fellowship, avoid the problem of members who forgot passwords or disputed as to whether women members should be allowed a vote or not (the franchise for General Elections was extended to women aged over 30 in 1918) or indeed any issues regarding participation. They favoured collecting door-to-door. Through their weekly visits to working-class house-holds, the commercial insurance sales teams offered a personal service to clients, combining public administration with private business. While this may have enhanced female control of the household economy, it was not mutuality.

PARTY POLITICS

The legislation had the effect of associating friendly societies with political parties because the future of health provision was the subject of considerable party political debate. When the idea of a national health service was raised, the High Chief Ranger of the Foresters felt obliged to point out that 'while state administration might be, and was, good in many things yet when it came to health insurance it was at best a machine without a soul' (*The Times*, 7 August 1928). Two years later, in the face of a cabinet committee's interest in this matter, the executive of the Foresters proposed 'strenuous opposition' to any move away from the 1911 Act (*The Times*, 31 July 1930). A year later, the organisa-tion's High Chief Ranger was reported as saying that the one quality that the organisation

> most desired in our national life today was a reawakened sense of national re-sponsibility ... multitudes had come to visualise the state as an organisation equipped with limitless funds the proper employment of which was to release all citizens from doing anything positive for themselves or their families. Their great Order, he was glad to think, stood for the antithesis of such doctrine. (*The Times*, 4 August 1931)

Similarly, J.H. Lear Caton of the Independent Order of Rechabites, Salford Unity and President of the National Conference of Friendly Societies 1923–24, argued that 'the approved society method was preferable to a State-adminis-tered scheme. Under the latter sick claims would tend to increase' (*The Times*,

19 September 1931). In 1929 a Past Grand Master of the Oddfellows and its Parliamentary Agent produced a pamphlet, which was sent to every lodge secretary. It was headed, 'National Health Insurance, created by Liberals, raided by Tories, threatened by Socialists' and it was published by the Liberal Publication Department (*The Times*, 23 May 1929).

Stanley Baldwin was Prime Minister for over seven years between 1923 and 1937 including during the 1926 General Strike. He was associated with appeasement and was perceived as the *de facto* Prime Minister in a coalition government headed by Ramsay MacDonald, the Labour Prime Minister who was expelled from the Labour Party. He was also a Forester and an Oddfellow. He told the Oddfellows conference that the actuarial tables on which the legislation of 1911 was based were derived from the Oddfellows and argued that the Society's lodges provided 'the perfect training to fit men throughout the country for all the responsibilities that have been laid upon them in the past half-century in local government and national government' (*The Times*, 24 May 1934). Neville Chamberlain, who succeeded Baldwin as PM, was a member of the Ancient Order of Foresters. Addressing their annual delegate meeting in 1926 he told delegates that

> the whole national system of health insurance was founded upon the work of friendly societies. The Act of 1911 was not a new departure it was an extension of the fabric already built by the friendly societies. (*The Times*, 3 August 1926)

This association with Conservatives and Liberals may not have bolstered the societies' claim to be politically neutral.

Quite apart from any antipathy towards ideas associated with the other main parties, many within Labour's ranks were hostile because they classified the friendly societies with the commercial providers. The Secretary of the Prudential between 1915 and 1931, Sir George May, headed the Committee on National Expenditure. According to the sometime Secretary of the Charity Organisation Society and honorary Oddfellow, Charles Loch Mowat, the May Committee's report, delivered in 1931, emphasised the government deficit (which was 'judged to be shatteringly large at the time') and it was given to the press without being offset by any government statement. It thus made the British financial position appear 'much more precarious than it really was' (Mowat, 1944, p. 356). The Labour Cabinet split over implementation of the report and the government fell from power. Labour did not win power again in the Commons until 1945. Scholars have noted Labour's antagonism (Finlayson, 1990, pp. 187–8). One concluded that 'for some Labour leaders in the 1920s and 1930s the approved societies came almost to be the embodiment of blood-sucking capitalism' (Sutherland, 1973, pp. 425–6). The 'party itself believed at the time' that the government was destroyed by its enemies (Phillips, 1992, p. 59).

By 1945 the Labour Party, which had run innovative health services at local level, had categorised all the approved societies as inappropriate bodies to run national insurances and had decided that it favoured a comprehensive health plan run at national, not municipal or local, level by state officials. The friendly societies could not compete with the popularity of Beveridge's ideas for insurance, outlined in 1942. When the National Insurance Act 1946 provided a far more comprehensive insurance provision than had previously been the case, the Oddfellows' Grand Master, G.H. Barrow, a stalwart who had joined the Order in 1916 and risen through the ranks, was one of many friendly society officials who became civil servants. The 1911 National Insurance scheme had helped to position mutuals as part of a sector that Labour disparaged, a situation which left the party uninterested in further engagement with them on taking power in 1945.

CONCLUSION

In 1945, 8.7 million people were members of friendly societies. There were over a million members of the Oddfellows, which also had over a million National Health Insurance 'state members'. Even if widows, members of female societies, honorary members (of whom there were 1913) and other members are included in that year, there was still a decrease in Oddfellow membership of 6800 members. The Secretary of the Order presented a positive face arguing that the nation had become more insurance-minded and that there remained a role for friendly societies, while the Grand Master, M.V. Sweeney, stressed that although welfare was of importance, 'we are part of the great traditional social life of the country' (*Oddfellows' Magazine*, December 1945). Nevertheless, a further 9500 left in 1946 and almost twice as many as that in 1947 (18 600). The decrease doubled again to 35 500 in 1948. This was largely due to lapses rather than deaths. Men returned from the services and did not resume payment. It was difficult to trace many of them and, as the level of contributions also rose, some other members left. In 1948, two years after the National Insurance Act, 205 of its lodges had closed and, including 2400 juveniles there were only 6170 new joiners. This was the lowest figure for the Oddfellows in over 50 years. While this rapid decline was not entirely due to the legislation, it appears that so unpopular had the approved societies become that as soon as the opportunity to leave arose then reliance on the state became widespread. Mutuals had become associated with a system in which seven different government departments were involved, with three different and mutually exclusive benefits for unemployment, three different types of pension and different schemes for the blind, the disabled, those with industrial injuries and the sick who earned less than £250 a year (Gilbert, 1970, p. 53). Mutuality had rested upon local, democratic, supportive lodges in which the government was not interested. It imposed a system on the mutuals that was efficient only in its own terms. Having shifted their perspectives, the mutuals were then relieved of their administrative role and had to struggle to find a new one.

For over 30 years governments enabled mutual associations to deliver a public social welfare function in a manner deemed economic and cost-saving. This formalised a long tradition of symbiotic, two-way traffic in ideas, personnel and funding between official and voluntary welfare provision. However, the terms of this engagement meant that, although those commercial organisations that carried out the administrative tasks of governments benefited, the scheme became an important contributory factor to the loss of direction and the decline in popularity experienced by many friendly societies. An understanding of this context might be of value to those voluntary organisations contemplating servicing the current government's requirements under its Big Society agenda. While Steve Hilton might see his recommended film as a celebration of civic order, it can also be read as a warning as to what can happen when a member of a fraternal group (in this case Wyatt Earp) takes responsibility for a state task. By the conclusion of the film half the brothers have been killed and Wyatt is left in the wilderness.

5. Big Society and the National Citizen Service: young people, volunteering and engagement with charities c. 1900–1960

Kate Bradley

Whilst Big Society has yet to be firmly defined as a concept, certain elements that formed part of the picture had crystallised before the General Election in 2010. One was the need to involve more young people in volunteering projects, to encourage them to mix with other young people from different backgrounds to build up their social capital, and to then take up positions of leadership in their local communities. This element came together under the banner of the National Citizen Service (NCS) scheme. NCS was piloted in summer 2011, with 12 schemes of vigorous outdoor activities followed by action in the community for over 10 000 16-year-olds in England (DirectGov, 2010). A nationwide scheme will roll out in summer 2012. Government figures suggest that the first year of the scheme cost about £13 million, due to rise to £37 million in 2012 (Phillips, 2011).

The NCS is not a compulsory scheme, unlike its namesake, the National Service that was operational between 1939 and the early 1960s. The choice of the scheme's title very clearly aims to tap into the popular idea of National Service as a period of positive transformation in the lives of young people, without conveying its more problematic aspects or the real differences between what is suggested by this evocation and what is actually proposed. National Service was conscription into the armed forces in order to fight the Second World War and, later, to aid Britain's commitments to its Empire and peacekeeping activities during the Cold War. As the actor Michael Caine's enthusiastic endorsement of the NCS launch suggests (BBC, 2010), National Service has come to be seen as a positive, character-building force in the lives of young men in the mid-twentieth century. In this way, the NCS is an attempt to hark back to a golden age of disciplined young people who gave their time to their country and their community.

However, to see the period from 1945 to 1960 as a golden age of socially engaged young people is inaccurate. Throughout this period, contemporaries were anxious about rising crime figures for all age groups, but especially amongst the young. Corporal punishment as a recourse of the courts had been abolished in 1948 but, as a result of the upward trend in the crime figures, there were frequent calls for its restitution in the 1950s. Furthermore, there is much evidence to suggest that many young men dreaded receiving their call-up papers, on account of the disruption it would cause to their education, as well as their working and private lives (Prest, 2011). For some, National Service was a rewarding period in their lives and, in some cases, it got young men away from bad influences, such as Teddy boy gangs (see Hickman, 2004), but it would be incorrect to view it as a panacea for the problem of wayward youth. Rather, it should be seen as what it was: a military expediency, not a form of deliberate and purposive youth work. The NCS is intentionally positioned to evoke a highly selective account of the past, and thus it is essential that it is given thorough interrogation by historians.

The NCS is an investment in young people, and this is to be welcomed, at least in principle. However, the expenditure on the NCS needs to be set next to cuts in local government spending following the Spending Review of October 2010 which, in some areas, have led to the cutting of youth services – notably in Prime Minister David Cameron's constituency in Oxfordshire. Shiv Malik in the *Guardian* (2011) reported the case of a young man who organised a picket of Cameron's constituency office to protest the closure of local youth clubs and was pulled out of class by anti-terrorism police to be given a stern warning about his activities. At the time of writing, Oxfordshire youth clubs are being shut down, but not without a vigorous campaign by the young people of the county to prevent this. These are young people who have clearly benefited from youth clubs in stimulating their abilities to take the lead on issues of concern to them, to organise themselves and to work in a team, yet their participation in the Big Society is not recognised as being a positive force. Unlike National Service, youth clubs do not come with the same connotations of inclusive, universal, transformative, disciplined and structured activity. They do not call up this golden age of National Service, and they predate it by some hundred years. In effect, one form of youth work is being instituted at the cost of another that was apparently already delivering its social goods.

Whilst the NCS evokes compulsory military service through its name, in its execution it draws upon long traditions of organised youth work in Britain. The aim of this chapter is to take a longer view of youth work, using the settlement movement as a case study, to explore which factors determine the relative successes or failures of youth clubs in engaging young people over time, and as a counterpoint to the historicism of the NCS project. The settlement movement is useful as a case study because these were charities that deliberately brought young graduates to the deprived areas of British towns and cities in order that they might live, learn something of what it meant to be poor and become leaders in these communities. In this way, the settlements resonate with many elements of the aims of the NCS and the Big Society more broadly: ideas around building social cohesion through bringing people of different backgrounds together. However, as this chapter will demonstrate, much settlement youth work succeeded not because it necessarily brought people together, but because it appealed to a sense of locality and community, and created space for young people, along with encouraging the development of certain forms of social capital. Social capital can be bonding or bridging and linking: the former tightening links within a community, the latter creating links across communities and networks of power (Putnam, 2000, pp. 22–4; and see box in Introduction).

Samuel Barnett, an Anglican priest working in the East End of London, was inspired to establish a 'settlement of university men' in the early 1880s in order to engage young Oxbridge men with social questions and philanthropic solutions (Briggs and Macartney, 1984, pp. 3–6). Barnett was dissatisfied with the affluent, female volunteers who came to his parish during the day and went home, as he saw it, without engaging with the needs of East London (Barnett, 1918, p. 307). The settlement was a means for volunteers to become fully involved in the community, to 'defeminise' social action by drawing in young men, to provide an outlet for religious service, and also to create positive role models for boys and men in the East End. Barnett believed that the working classes of East London were too tired or incapable of leading themselves, and also that exposure to middle- and upper-class standards of behaviour would have an uplifting effect on the ways in which the poor organised their home lives (Meacham, 1987, p. x). Barnett's idea was an extremely popular one, leading to the formation of the first settlement, Toynbee Hall, in Whitechapel in 1884. It was named for Arnold Toynbee, the Balliol economist who, before his death in 1883, had spent his vacations volunteering with Barnett (Barnett, 1918, pp. 308–13). Settlements rapidly sprang up across London and other major British towns and cities, across North America, Europe and Asia. Some had an overtly religious agenda and affiliation, whilst others, like Toynbee Hall, took a non-sectarian approach. Although Barnett was interested in creating a space for men's volunteering (Toynbee Hall was exclusively for male volunteers), women also actively embraced settlements and they provided opportunities for single women to live away from the family home and to do voluntary or paid work with the needy (Bradley, 2009, pp. 34–46). Settlements were principally a means to engage the young middle and upper classes with voluntary work, but they were secondarily concerned with getting these young volunteers to work with the children and young people who thronged the city and town streets of the later nineteenth century, as a form of developing their own bridging and linking social capital.

One of the most popular settlement solutions to the question of children and young people on the streets with (supposedly) nothing to do was the boys' or girls' club. Such youth clubs appealed because they were relatively cheap and cost effective: the basic need of a club was a room. Some settlements were purpose-built and thus had suitable rooms that could be given over to clubs, or those who had converted houses often hired or borrowed space elsewhere, at the local church or neighbourhood school. Club membership was dependent upon the payment of a small weekly fee or 'sub', which provided an income that could be given over to meeting running costs and buying equipment. In time, some clubs – like the Fairbairn Club at Mansfield House in the East End – had purpose-built facilities that included libraries, gyms, woodwork rooms and theatres, along with grounds outside London that were used for sporting events or annual camps. Boys' and girls' clubs were also highly photogenic and newsworthy. Visits by dignitaries to clubs made for excellent photo opportunities (and later, newsreel); club football teams and boxing players featured in the local newspaper sports pages. For the young settlement residents, they were also exciting places to work. As many settlement residents' memoirs suggest, working in a club was exciting and frightening in equal measure, taking the affluent resident into a very different world for young people.

However tempting the fare on offer, settlement club leaders recognised the need to treat new members well and to encourage existing members to bring new people in. The manager of the Fairbairn House boys' club wrote in the settlement's magazine that:

> They [the former club members] have made an atmosphere, and in Fairbairn House the beginnings of gambling are soon checked, bullying is discouraged, a foul word is seldom heard, clear eyes look into clear eyes, and boys can grow up to be strong, healthy, clean-minded, helpful men. One can watch the progress. The newcomer is brought in by a pal; he is welcomed to the Club, and put in the friendly care of an older member; he is shown the glories of the place, the gym, the boxing room, the tennis court, the library. ('The Need for Boys' Clubs', *Mansfield House Magazine*, 1918, p. 160)

The club managers were interested in improving the behaviour of the young men, and thus their relationships both within and beyond the club. Here, the check on gambling sat well with the Nonconformist ethos of Mansfield House, if religion was otherwise worn lightly at such clubs. For example, at both the Mansfield House clubs and those at the Jewish Bernhard Baron Settlement, prayers often formed part of the opening and closing rituals of club evenings, but otherwise religious practice was kept to a discreet minimum in order to avoid deterring the less observant. It is also clear that joining a club offered affordable access to a range of tempting leisure pursuits that were not easily come by in the home or on the streets. Formally and informally, the club worked to make the experience of joining as friendly as possible.

At the most basic level, clubs were an affordable and congenial place to go to meet one's friends and acquaintances away from home or work. However, clubs were more than just a space to go to. Clubs provided opportunities for young people to demonstrate their prowess in sports and cultural activities, with the possibility of making one's way out of a working-class district into other worlds: one consequence of building an individual's bridging social capital. The actor Terence Stamp recalled how he had initially relished life at the Mansfield House clubs, waiting eagerly for the clubhouse doors to open so that he could get on with discovering the joys of the theatre (Stamp, 1987, pp. 81–5). Sports of all varieties were important at boys' clubs, providing opportunities to compete with other clubs in the region as well as nationally. The Fairbairn House clubs produced major sporting stars, for instance Jimmy Barrett, the West Ham and England football player. Clubs were a place of discovery, but this discovery need not be limited within the club walls. For both boys and girls, the year was topped off by the annual summer holiday to a camp on the English coast, a chance to enjoy the fresh air and to try out different kinds of physical activities.

Aspirational and creative fare was not just available to boys. The girls who attended the Canning Town Women's Settlement clubs were active in regional club competitions in the interwar period, often coming first. Some of the most common girls' club activities were based around homemaking and beauty. Such classes tapped into concerns at the start of the twentieth century that the working classes were physically degenerating through poor diets, household management and child-rearing practices. For the settlement volunteers this was one way of tackling a national problem; for the young women, this was useful preparation for their adult lives as wives and mothers. Yet the club also brought on women who became successful in public life. In 1937, Daisy Parsons, a former club member, became the first female Mayor of West Ham. Parsons had been a domestic servant after leaving school, before embracing the suffragette movement and becoming a Labour councillor in the early 1920s, and returned in her mayoral year to address the settlement girls about her work. Other speakers included, in 1924, Margaret Bondfield, then the first female Cabinet member. The club's activities can be seen as being grounded in the realities of the girls' lives in the not-so-distant future, but also as opening up much wider horizons at the same time.

A club is, by definition, an exclusive entity and, in the case of the settlement clubs, exclusion and inclusion were defined by territory. As the Fairbairn House membership books reveal, groups of boys from the same or neighbouring streets joined up at the same time; shared surnames indicate that family also had an important role to play in joining clubs. The use of neighbourhood and community operated in other ways. At Bernhard Baron Settlement in Stepney, membership of the adults' clubs was conditional on having been a member of the youth clubs and further agreeing to help manage these clubs. The researchers of the *New Survey of London Life and Labour* commented on how well this worked in terms of bonding the community together (Llewellyn Smith, 1935, pp. 135–6). Parents could also get involved in helping to run the clubs. Whilst appealing to a sense of neighbourhood was an effective means of including everyone within that community, it was also an exclusive measure, generating bonding rather than bridging social capital. For example, the East End was ethnically and religiously diverse, and the various communities were concentrated around particular streets, went to different places of worship, and sometimes different shops, schools and clubs. As Jerry White has shown, children played on 'their' own streets in order to avoid fights with children from other groups or abuse from adults (White, 2003, pp. 133–5). Apart from intra-club sporting matches and competitions – which certainly introduced young people from different backgrounds to each other, if in a sometimes combative fashion – clubs did not necessarily encourage, say, Jewish children from Stepney to mix with Irish Catholic children from Wapping. If the local neighbourhood did not shape the club's intake, the club managers sometimes actively encouraged the club to become the province of one group. Bernhard Baron grew out of the Oxford and St George's Club founded by Basil Henriques in 1913 in order to provide a club specifically for Jewish children and young people, as all the others in the district were run by Gentiles, some of whom were proselytising (Henriques, 1937, p. 29). Where there was an element of extending links across different social groups in settlement youth work, it occurred at the level of the young middle- and upper-class volunteers and project workers attached to the clubs, who came from very different backgrounds to their young charges. This was the point at which any bridging took place.

The other way in which clubs brought people together – or kept them apart – was through gender. Clubs were run separately for boys and girls, certainly before the 1960s when it became more fashionable for mixed clubs to be offered and there was less consternation about the sexes mixing (Collins, 2003, p. 88). By the same token, the settlements were also segregated by sex, and it followed that men's settlement residents would become involved in running boys' clubs whilst women's settlement residents would run girls' and younger boys' clubs. This model of organisation reflected wider sensibilities, but also ideas about suitable adult [middle class] role models. However, the young people did not blindly accept their leadership by the settlement residents. Miss M. Child of the Lady Margaret Hall Settlement in Lambeth took to her challenge with aplomb, as she recalled in 1957:

I do not know whether a man would have thrown some of them out early on or put up with their pretty ways long enough for taming to set in as we did. They mostly turned out good enough boys after a bit. I reckoned on a real Rough House about once a year when the lights would suddenly go out & chairs fly through the air & tables be hurled over. (Lady Margaret Hall Papers, 1957)

In Miss Child's account, her success with the boys of Lambeth arose from her tenacity – not an uncommon theme in club workers' accounts of building trust with their young charges. On the other hand, Canning Town had a period in the 1920s in which they found it difficult to keep leaders for their boys' clubs, as the women volunteers found the boys' behaviour too challenging. It was not the case that men found it any easier. Basil Henriques, later Warden of the Bernhard Baron Settlement, recalled in his memoirs how he had to prove himself to the boys of a club in Bermondsey through showing prowess and leadership in sports (Henriques, 1937, p. 25). Of course, some children and young people were impervious to attempts to mould them into club members, and thus were thrown out or prevented from joining. Innovative attempts to engage these young people were made from the 1950s onwards by detached youth workers, who provided 'clubs' that were not 'clubs' – informal café facilities and 'detached' youth work – in order to engage these hard-to-reach young people, though such work remained outside the mainstream of settlement youth club work before the 1980s (Bradley, 2009, pp. 115–18). Later, by the 1970s, a combination of new immigrant communities in the East End and the movement of older groups out of the area disrupted these older territorialities, bringing new community groups into the youth work market and thus forcing a repositioning of the existing settlement projects.

What comes out most clearly in these accounts of instilling discipline in boys' clubs is the way in which the settlement residents felt that *they* succeeded in imposing *their* will upon the boys. What is more implicit is the way in which this experience changed the residents as young people *themselves*. For example, Henriques admitted that before attending the club his only experience with the working classes had been through having domestic servants; he was surprised that the boys would speak to him as though he was their social equal (Henriques, 1937, p. 25). The settlement residents were young people used to a privileged world: encountering this working-class environment required reflection, flexibility and adaptation; a different, bridging iteration of their own social capital. These settlement workers may have been young, but they still had considerable power to shut clubs down or to exclude members, not to mention the power exerted in their other roles as home visitors and the like. Yet it would be wrong to say that the working-class users of the settlements were without power of their own. For instance, if the club leader wanted an easier time, they had to alter their behaviour in order to be listened to. Whilst hard-up working-class parents may have had greater difficulties in negotiating with welfare workers in times of trouble, their children certainly had the power to make the lives of inexperienced club leaders miserable.

An important precept was the creation of democratic principles of management. Fairbairn House had a standing committee drawn from its membership, whose role was to oversee the daily management of the clubs, supported by a member of settlement staff. The boys were keen to ensure that their fellow members participated as fully as possible, demanding to see members who were not felt to be as energetic as they could be in joining in with the full range of club activities. Membership of the standing committee was something taken on only by those who were sufficiently dedicated to the club and willing to police their friends and neighbours. Whilst settlement residents would often overlook certain behaviours as an expediency in maintaining overall standards, the boys at Fairbairn had no such qualms but unlike their leaders, they were part of the community and evidently felt more comfortable in being stricter. Taking up the leadership of one's club was a first step in becoming socially active. Some of the young women at Canning Town offered to take on the running of the senior club themselves, and another volunteered to take the Sunday afternoon Bible class. In 1930, some of the older girls took it upon themselves to run their own club for younger children. These cases were not radically innovative by any measure, but they were nonetheless examples of young people being empowered to take responsibility for the well-being of others, an opportunity that would likely not have been there without the settlement as a framework.

Despite the perils of overly punitive club members, the boys' club sometimes came to occupy a special place in the affections of its members. This was most clearly seen during the Second World War, when young men in the forces regularly wrote home to their club leaders to give them news about what was happening in their lives and to catch up with events at home. A common feature of many of the letters was the feeling that the experience of being in a boys' club in their youth had helped to prepare them for the trials of war:

> The spirit of the Club has made each of us, I am sure, give that little extra bit over the next man. All those little extra bits add up to something, and the final amount is but part of the Club's total effort. (Henriques, 1951, p. 107)

Crisis gave the members the opportunity to reflect upon what the clubs had offered them as boys and young men:

> Over the impressionable ages of boyhood and youth, the Club convoyed me safely through the temptations that breed on the street corners of slums, where youth is like a high-speed ship without a rudder. (Henriques, 1951, p. 117)

The former youth club members believed that the experience of the clubs had changed their lives. Some saw the experience as putting them on the right path, or of providing opportunities they may not otherwise have experienced. But, for many, clubs provided opportunities to make new friends and to further develop their sense of identity and self. Writing back to the club also gave the young men a sense of stability in a world that was both boring and dangerous.

CONCLUSION

Where settlement youth clubs were successful in creating vibrant cultures, it followed that they had, whether by accident or design, provided a club environment that provided a range of opportunities to suit a variety of tastes, whilst also fitting into the rhythms and networks of the neighbourhood. The club members felt an ownership over their clubs, and settlement residents, managers, club members and alumni worked hard to sustain the clubs over longer periods of time, literally bringing in different generations of club members. Yet it did not necessarily encourage anything other than the tightening of bonds within the community. Whilst this integrated the club in the immediate community, the club did not necessarily open up the community to anyone other than the settlement workers it brought in. If a desire to serve others for religious ends brought young people to settlements as residents, religion was also a powerful divisive force between communities. Clubs were not specifically about getting young people to volunteer. What they were concerned with was getting children and young people to act in collegiate ways with each other, and in several cases social action followed from that, on however small a scale. If club leaders were very clear that their agenda was to create good, all-round citizens, their methods on the ground were often more subtle: and they were far from immune from the process themselves. What is less tangible to the historian is the way in which this general sense of fellowship, religious or otherwise, impacted on the community more generally, in the ways in which people behaved with each other beyond the club, whether individuals might otherwise have taken different directions through life had they not had the opportunities the club provided.

In comparing the work of the settlement clubs with the present day some important caveats apply. First, clubs thrived in a world before individual bedrooms for children in a family, central heating, television and computer games; second, they also grew in an environment shaped by the public school ethos of team sports, houses and (religious) service. Yet youth clubs and organisations remain important for young people, as evidenced by the enduring popularity of the Scouts and Guides. Youth clubs are still going strong: London Youth alone has over 400 youth clubs working with 75 000 young people (London Youth, 2010, p. 4), or around 5 per cent of the London population aged 10–24 (Office of National Statistics, 2003, p. 17). There are far more leisure opportunities for young people, but clubs remain popular, for the fellowship they offer and the broader field of opportunities. The NCS, with its short burst of volunteering, may well appeal to young people who otherwise remain outside current programmes, but given the range of youth work that already achieves the NCS's aims – and the importance of building up relationships with the community over time in order to get young people and their families to engage with it – the NCS runs the risk of duplicating existing work and being something that has only a transitory impact on the young people who participate in it. It is not clear how the NCS will differ from older forms of youth work in bringing young people from different backgrounds together: bonding social capital appears to go with the territory. The money would perhaps be better directed to those groups who are quietly working towards such objectives already.

6. Charities, voluntary organisations and non-governmental organisations in Britain since 1945

Matthew Hilton

1 INTRODUCTION

The Big Society is a deeply historical concept. According to one of its chief proponents, Phillip Blond, the author of *Red Tory*, 'civil society' has 'disappeared'. While the state and the marketplace have continued to thrive, 'All other sources of independent autonomous power have been crushed. We no longer have, in any effective independent way, local government, churches, trade unions, co-operative societies, publicly funded educational institutions, civic organisations or locally organised groups that operate on the basis of more than single issues' (Blond 2010a, p. 3). For Blond, this is part of a much deeper malaise in our social fabric such that 'something is seriously wrong in Britain'. To put it crudely, and Blond certainly does, 'things were better in the past' (2010a, p. 2).

Blond and Conservative politicians have built upon a narrative of decline prevalent among proponents of the social capital thesis. Most commonly associated with Robert Putnam, the thesis holds that citizens no longer 'join in'. They no longer attach themselves to the forms of associational life that sustain social bonds, build trust and ultimately strengthen democratic participation (Prochaska, 1988; Putnam, 2000; Prochaska, 2006).

Certainly, there is much evidence to support such an account. Membership of the two main political parties has slipped from over 3 million to just under half a million over the past 50 years (Marshall, 2009). Over the same period, membership of the churches fell by around one-third (Matheson and Summerfield, 2001). While trade union membership peaked at over 13 million at the end of the 1970s, it has subsequently fallen dramatically, reaching about half this level just 30 years later (Achur, 2010). And to take just one example of a type of voluntary organisation, women's groups have suffered the severest losses. The Mothers' Union had 538 000 members in the 1930s, but only 98 000 by 2009. Membership of the National Federation of Women's Institutes fell from 500 000 to 205 000 from the 1950s to the present (Beaumont, 2001, 2009). The types of organisation federated to the National Council of Women – the Women's Co-operative Guild, Married Women's Association, Townswomen's Guilds, Women's International League for Peace and Freedom – either no longer exist or have been long forgotten. If we follow the social capital thesis it ought not to surprise us, then, that a collapse in the institutions that generate social trust have a consequent impact on levels of political trust. It is well known that turnout at general elections has fallen steadily from over 80 per cent in 1950 to under 60 per cent in 2001.

Yet these figures capture only one trend. Indeed, it might be argued that the Big Society is flourishing. In 2008, the most recent year for which consistent figures are available, the National Council for Voluntary Organisations (NCVO) calculated there to be 171 000 voluntary organisations in the UK. If the widest definitions of the sector are employed, such that all forms of associational life are included, the NCVO estimates there to be approximately 900 000 organisations all over Britain, ranging from the tiny, local and informal to the huge, global and highly organised leaders (NCVO, 2010).

The purpose here is not simply to play a numbers game. It is, rather, to draw out one prominent trend in British associational life since the Second World War. This is the rise of the large-scale charities, non-governmental organisations (NGOs) and professionally run 'voluntary' organisations. While these are often dismissed, ignored or discounted by the proponents of the Big Society – Lord Wei, for instance, controversially criticised the big charities for being 'bureaucratic and unresponsive' to citizens (Asthana and Helm, 2010) – what their existence does is point to a very different set of relationships between politics and society, between the state and its citizens and between the public and associational life. These often single-issue pressure or 'cause' groups have seemingly relied on a more passive type of membership, required to do little more than not cancel their direct debit statements. Yet their existence points to the ways in which citizens have continued to engage in various forms of civic participation. If the Big Society, with its focus largely on local, community-based organising, cannot take into account the reasons people have chosen to support large-scale, professional organisations, it risks making the same misinterpretations about the past as Blond. It becomes based on a nostalgic attitude to voluntarism as naive as John Major's unfortunate reworking of George Orwell's paean to warm beer, village cricket and 'maids bicycling to Holy Communion through the morning mist' (Major, 1993).

The Big Society, if we are to use the term, is a dynamic, not a static, phenomenon. Associational life has been transformed over the last half-century, and largely for reasons that demonstrate a rationality on the part of a supposedly more passive citizenry. Understanding this transformation ought to lie behind any attempt to make civil society organisations serve the ends of the political fashion of the day.

2 EXPANSION AND GROWTH

What is immediately obvious in any survey of the history of voluntary organisations, charities and NGOs is that, while there has been decline and stagnation in certain sectors, there has been growth and expansion elsewhere. The number of registered charities, for instance, has grown steadily over the last few decades (see Figure 6.1), rising to over 180 000 by the 1990s. So, while the number of people joining traditional women's groups might have fallen, the number of people choosing to support environmental organisations has expanded significantly. For instance, the total cumulative membership of the ten leading environmental and conservation groups in 2008 (and accepting much double counting) was nearly 7 million (for more detailed data, see Hilton et al., 2012). Likewise, reflecting a society that spends more on leisure and personal consumption, membership of many outdoor and recreational groups has continued to expand.

Part of the reason the Big Society protagonists and social capital theorists are able to make sweeping judgements about the past is because of the problematic nature of much of the evidence. Data collected on rates of volunteering, for instance, is dependent on different methodologies and types of question asked in social surveys. Consistency is the one thing that is missing from measures of voluntarism. However, if we survey as much of the available evidence as is possible, collating many types of evidence collected over the last few decades, then it appears that rates of volunteering have not actually declined and may well have increased (see Figure 6.2). Not only are we supporting more organisations through our donations but we are helping them out with our time too.

It has to be acknowledged that the form of volunteering may well have changed and that the types of organisation supported are varied, too. New social movements, such as the Campaign for Nuclear Disarmament, account for much of the growth. Yet it is not all due to radical political causes. The 1960s also gave rise to the socially conservative National Viewers' and Listeners' Association and a period of mass affluence provided the backdrop to the proliferation of medical charities, both large and small. Some groups, such as Amnesty, are very much the single-issue campaigning organisation, but many of the humanitarian aid agencies, in contrast, such as Oxfam, Christian Aid, War on Want and Save the Children, can trace their origins much further back and their developmental work involves them in a complex web of global economic and political subjects.

The point is that there is an incredible diversity to the Big Society. It cannot be reduced to just one form of participation. In the arena of homelessness, action is not solely the preserve of Shelter or the Advisory Service for Squatters (that is, those more radical groups associated with the campaigning initiatives of the 1960s and 1970s), but also established charities such as Centrepoint,

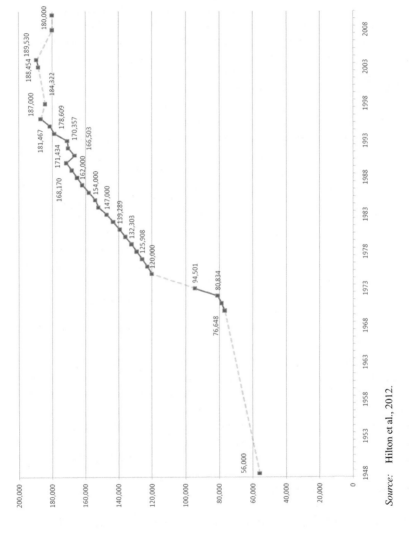

Source: Hilton et al., 2012.

Figure 6.1 Number of registered charities

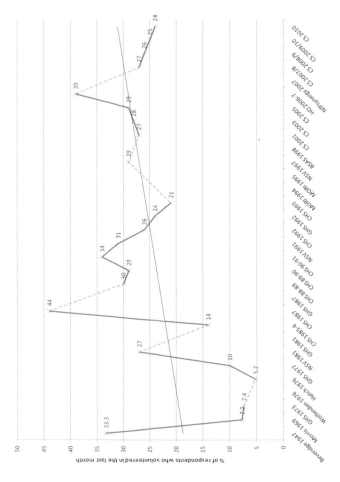

Key: GHS = General Household Survey; NSV = National Survey of Volunteering; CHS = Charity
Household Survey; BSAS = British Social Attitudes Survey; HO = Helping Out; CS = Citizenship Survey

Source: Hilton et al., 2012.

Figure 6.2   Volunteering in past month, according to various surveys, 1947–2010

faith-based initiatives such as the Church Army, Emmaus, the Salvation Army and Quaker Homeless Action, and more recent self-help ventures such as the Big Issue Foundation (Humphreys 1999; Hutson and Clapham, 1999; Swithinbank, 2001). Likewise, environmentalism and conservation incorporates local activism organised through Friends of the Earth initiatives, elite, policy-oriented bodies such as the Green Alliance, global campaigns led by Greenpeace and truly mass memberships as in the National Trust (Lowe and Goyder, 1983; Rootes, 2007, 2009).

The growth of these varied organisations has been impressive. The total income of all charities has risen from around £12 billion in 1970 to over £50 billion today. Within this, it is obvious that many of the larger charities predominate, with much of this income being enjoyed by what are just a handful of NGOs. The sector has become a formidable presence in British society and politics, and an economic powerhouse in its own right. For instance, the total assets held by 'general charities' has tripled over the last 30 years, from a figure of just over £30 billion in 1980 to one of around £100 billion today (NCVO, 2010).

It is undoubtedly true that small-scale, local community organisations have continued to emerge. But it is the creation of highly professional, prominent, expert-driven, 'voluntary' (as many still incongruously calls themselves) bodies that is a key feature of contemporary civic participation. NGOs, as charities and voluntary associations have increasingly come to be called, have proved adept at creating sustainable and viable organisations able to marshal the research conducted and evidence compiled by their highly trained staff. University-educated engineers, scientists, lawyers, planners and economists have founded, developed and run these organisations. They are a far cry from local community activists or political radicals. They have been, as one historian has put it, 'experts with their mouths close to telephones and their heads full of reasoned papers' rather than 'crowds with their feet close to main squares and their heads full of movement material' (Yeo, 1976).

So much has the sector become professionalised that it is now not uncommon for an individual's career to move from one organisation to the next, the skills being brought to the charity or NGO being so technical that it matters little that the organisations concerned are tackling very different subjects. Des Wilson, for instance, began his career as a journalist. After fronting Shelter in the late 1960s his media skills saw him highly valued by other organisations and he subsequently went on to found or work for the Campaign for Lead-Free Air, Friends of the Earth, the Campaign for Freedom of Information, Citizen Action, Parents Against Tobacco, the National Council for Civil Liberties (now Liberty), the National Trust and even a number of private corporations (*Who's Who*, 2011).

3 CIVIC PARTICIPATION

It is precisely because these organisations have been so professional, technocratic and expert-driven, that they have been overlooked in the Big Society discussions. They do not mobilise citizens to participate in the organisation at every level. They do, however, mobilise citizens to support them and to trust them. We need to understand why it is that the public chooses to exercise its civic participation more through the likes of Oxfam than through the Women's Institute.

First, it needs to be understood that civic participation in the post-Second World War period cannot be imagined as some sort of ideal Tocquevillian democracy. The world has become a far more complex place and political solutions have accordingly become more technocratic. Issues about climate change, global justice, human rights and the limitations of welfare have become too technical to be either understood in their entirety by ordinary citizens or easily absorbed into the traditional ideologies associated with the mainstream political parties. NGOs have stepped in to focus in on these issues. Within governments, such issues have been increasingly 'de-politicised'. That is, they have been pushed away from parliament to be dealt with by planners and technocrats. Citizens cannot hope to influence such processes and this is why political scientists have long claimed that professionalisation and specialisation have led to increased levels of political apathy (Stoker, 2006; Hay, 2007). However, another response has been possible: that is, of bringing expertise to expertise. The seemingly passive support of solely making a financial contribution to a professional campaigning organisation may not look like evidence of an active citizenry, but faced with such complexity, in both the subject matter and the way in which it is debated 'behind closed doors', it has made sense for the public to support experts who can speak more effectively on their behalf.

Second, media-savvy groups have transformed the ways in which political communication has taken place. They have bypassed the formal channels of party politics and spoken directly to the public through the media, through publicity stunts, through educational work and through the mobilisation of support at key moments. They have also sought to lobby and have influence at Westminster and in the corridors of Whitehall, and they have attempted to bring the public in at key moments. To give just one example, the ways in which they have operated in a space between the traditional lobby group and the mass social movement becomes apparent. When the second report of the Brandt Commission, *Common Crisis*, was published in 1983, the World Development Movement organised a letter-writing campaign. It sold 100 000 copies of its letter-writing guide creating such pressure that 400 MPs wrote to either the Prime Minister or the Foreign Secretary for clarification on the government's position (Mitchell, 1991). This was a strategic mobilisation of a perhaps usually dormant support which had, nevertheless, signed an unwritten contract, whereby the NGO would be trusted to act as the expert body while the public donors would not be called upon to do very much except at key moments

Third, large-scale charities, voluntary organisations and NGOs have been supported because they have been seen to work. The examples are legion and range from the permissive legislation of the 1960s to any one of a number of minor amendments to government policy in, say, consumer protection legislation, brought about by *Which?* (Hilton, 2003). Within the environmental and conservation sectors, for instance, influence has not just come from recent initiatives such as the Big Ask coalition that paved the way for the Climate Change Act in 2008. It has also come from the work of the Coal Smoke Abatement Society and the Smoke Abatement League in the lobbying for the 1956 Clean Air Act that followed the devastating London smog of 1952, and from single-issue campaigns such as Des Wilson's CLEAR group, which advocated the use of lead-free petrol in the 1980s. Each instance of 'success', which a campaigning group will then trumpet to its members, is used to spur further donations and subscriptions to the cause.

4 A QUESTION OF TRUST

At the heart of the relationship between the public and the state there has lain a host of intermediary institutions that have served a function from the public's perspective. If they seem too professional, too powerful and too divorced from their ordinary members to be regarded as classic forms of associational life, they are nevertheless crucial to understanding how citizens have elected to engage with the world around them over the last few decades. Key to this is the notion of trust. The social capital thesis holds that trust is a product of participation in associational life. Social bonds lead to greater social trust which, in turn, encourages higher rates of political trust in democratic institutions. Yet trust has not simply been the consequence of membership. It has also been the cause of membership. That is, trust is an active category: it is something we decide to do. While recorded declining levels of social trust might be due to more general trends emanating from the transition to a society of mass affluence, declining levels of political trust might be due to the active decisions taken by members of the public. Arguably, they have chosen to trust politicians less while at the same time placing greater trust in charities, NGOs and voluntary associations.

Indeed, evidence suggests that 'people in Britain have a remarkable understanding of different kinds of political trust' (Li and Marsh, 2008). Certainly, they have not lost their interest in political issues. Survey data from the 1970s onwards conducted by the Audit of Political Engagement and others has measured attitudes to politics and the figures show remarkable consistency, if a slight tendency for the obstinately uninterested to increase (Hansard Society, 2010). The public has demonstrated persistently low levels of trust in journalists and politicians, for instance, yet much higher trust in the professions and the charitable sector. Taking just one example, conducted at the end of the 1990s by the National Council for Voluntary Organisations (NCVO), it was found that nearly everybody (91 per cent) respects what charities are doing (Tonkiss and Passey, 1999). A study commissioned by Action Aid in 1988 found that 70 per cent of respondents believed that politicians were not doing all that they could on international aid and development issues. Trust in charities, by contrast, was much higher (National Council for Voluntary Organisations, 1998).

The public has chosen to trust the expertise of large-scale, professionally run non-profits more than that of other institutions. The Ipsos MORI 'Trust in the Professions: Veracity Index', commissioned by the Royal College of Physicians, shows persistently higher rates of trust in the professions than for business, governments or journalists (IPSOS MORI/Royal College of Physicians 2008). When we break down these figures still further, it becomes even more apparent. A poll conducted in August 1993 found that 38 per cent of the public trusted government scientists. The figure for trust in industry scientists was around the same at 41 per cent. Yet for scientists working for environmental organisations that figure was 73 per cent (Porritt, 1994). This suggests that among supporters of NGOs there is an emotional attachment as they trust the organisation to act on their behalf when dealing with other experts. The public itself lacks the expertise about a particular issue, but has made a calculated decision on who to trust to act as an expert.

All of this is not to argue that organisations such as the National Trust, Shelter and Oxfam represent the vanguard of a new great age of civic participation. There are too many problems and limitations with them for that. For instance, there are constraints on the levels of inclusion. For all that these types of organisation can mobilise citizens otherwise disillusioned with party politics, they fail to reach a stubborn core of the uninterested. Even at the height of voter turnout rates in this country there remained a good fifth of the adult population that chose not to vote. It seems likely that this cohort remains unmoved by any of the organisations one might imagine to constitute the Big Society and, indeed, the levels of disenfranchisement might be even higher. NGOs, voluntary associations and charities remain the organisations of the affluent and the educated, no matter how much this section of the population has expanded.

The effectiveness of this form of civic participation can also be called into question. For all that moments of success and influence can be found, there are also stories of failure. More problematically, there is nothing about civic participation in any form that can guarantee access to the political centre or ensure that social issues are tackled. In this sense, political parties will ultimately prove resilient because of the assured pathways they provide to the political centre. Finally, the nature of the relationship NGOs, charities and voluntary associations have with their supporters is problematic. Trust might be given, but it might be done so in ways that demonstrate an ignorance of what it is the charity wants to do. This is a classic problem for the humanitarian agencies that rely on public donations in times of emergency, but not all of that public knows the full range of subjects the NGO devotes itself. The organisation can then become constrained by the limited expectations placed upon its more innocuous charitable role, forcing it to the political mainstream when more fundamental solutions might in fact be necessary.

5 REDEFINING THE BIG SOCIETY

Nevertheless, the relationships the public has developed with politics, with the state and with these professional organisations they have chosen to support are very different from the assumptions made in the Big Society proposals. Here, in the words of David Cameron, the aim has been to provide 'a new focus on empowering and enabling individuals, families and communities to take control of their lives so we create the avenues through which responsibility and opportunity can develop' (Cameron, 2009). The Conservative MP, Jesse Norman, imagines these avenues to include not only civil society organisations, but the churches, the market, the family and the rule of law (Norman, 2010). In similarly Burkean fashion, Blond looks forward to 'a revival of groups and genuinely intermediary associations' that make 'liberty both real and specific' (Blond, 2010a, p. 172).

The key issue comes down to the types of institutions being imagined as the bulwarks of the Big Society. Mutuals, cooperatives and social enterprises are all mentioned, paving the way for the entry of commercial organisations to develop non-profit subsidiaries that can compete for government contracts. But the types of social organisation considered are essentially local and community based. Given the nature of the investigations undertaken by the Conservatives into what they consider to be good practice, organisations are based upon a community bounded by geography rather than values or belief (Norman and Ganesh, 2006; Duncan Smith, 2007; Davis and Strevens, 2010; Wind-Cowie, 2010). It is in this sense that their vision becomes deeply nostalgic and chooses to ignore the myriad organisations that have come to replace the Mothers Union in our institutional life.

The first lesson that the proponents of the Big Society must learn from this historical overview is, therefore, that the Big Society cannot be regarded as an entity that is static in character. Constant evolution and adaptation is the principal feature of the sector. As long ago as 1948, William Beveridge noted that:

... philanthropy has shown its strength of being able perpetually to take new forms. The Charity Organisation Society has passed over to Family Welfare. Within this century entirely new organisations have arisen, such as the Boy Scouts and Girl Guides, Women's Institutes, the Workers' Educational Association, the National Council of Social Service, Training Colleges for the Disabled, Women's Voluntary Services, and Citizens' Advice Bureaux. The capacity of Voluntary Action inspired by philanthropy to do new things is beyond question. (Beveridge, 1948)

The rise of the modern NGO is the latest stage in this history of constant evolution. Any consideration of the potential of the Big Society has to acknowledge the important role these bodies have had in altering the forms of civic participation.

A second lesson follows from this. Politicians have constantly debated the Big Society and its predecessor labels not because there is an interest in voluntarism in and of itself, but because it is regarded as a potential saviour to the perceived failings elsewhere. But precisely because the sector is so dynamic and constantly evolving, it means that it can never be controlled according to the politician's interests. The interventions of the charity commissioners, the consultations encouraged with government departments, the conditions attached to funding and the types of contract signed, all constitute forms of control of the NGOs and the voluntary sector. To create an army of local community activists engaged in the sorts of services that others might feel are better dealt with by central or local government represents another form of control, too. But the lesson is clear. These represent only partial controls: of the organisation and of the sector. The constant adaptability of the sector, and the ease with which its supporters can switch their loyalties and affinities, means that NGOs as a whole will continue to be an incredibly dynamic force. If they are not seen to be responding to their supporters' interests, then such support will rapidly wither and new organisations will be found to channel these energies elsewhere.

Finally, the Big Society, however understood, is not an alternative to the Big State. Yet Conservative rhetoric would have it so. As Cameron himself put it in his important speech of November 2009, 'the size, scope and role of government in Britain has reached a point where it is now inhibiting, not advancing the progressive aims of reducing poverty, fighting inequality, and increasing general well-being. Indeed there is a worrying paradox that because of its effect on personal and social responsibility, the recent growth of the state has promoted not social solidarity, but selfishness and individualism' (Cameron, 2009). However, what is clear is that the public has supported expert bodies because of their interconnections with the state. They have operated on the frontier of welfare reform. They have acted not as radical opponents of governments, but as moderate cooperators. Indeed, they have worked so closely with the institutions of government as to make their own label, non-governmental, almost disingenuous. Collaboration, cooperation and complementarity better describe the relationship than the competition of alternatives. From one extreme, it would be crude to suggest that NGOs as pressure groups have adopted a Keynesian frame of mind (as the Big Society proponents would put it) to the effect that they call solely for further government intervention on behalf of citizen's rights. They have done so at times, but they have served other functions too. From the other extreme, it would likewise be crude to see NGOs, charities and voluntary associations as the providers of services that step in once the state retreats.

The Big Society has therefore always been with us. It might be very different now from what it was in the 1950s. And it might even be the case that how it existed at any one point in the past was better than it is today. But such normative definitions miss the crucial point that civic participation has constantly evolved. Subscriptions and support for large-scale professional organisations ought not to be ignored as somehow representing a lesser form of civic participation. Instead, it ought to be recognised for what it is: a deliberate and rational decision by citizens to alter social and political engagement in response to the social and political world around them. It is a vital part of the dynamism of the Big Society that must be appreciated before nostalgia for the past and policies for the future become confused.

7. Charity and Big Society

Richard Fries

INTRODUCTION

The concept of the Big Society clearly includes charity. One of the questions this raises is, if the Big Society is new where does so old an idea as charity fit into it? Some may say this just confirms that the Big Society is more a repackaging of long-existing social forces than a substantive innovation. But if the Big Society concept really is innovative, albeit incorporating long-established elements of British society, how does charity fit into it?

These questions are timely. Though – or perhaps because – charity is long-established in the texture of British society and economy, it has been undergoing a long period of reform. The Charities Act passed in 2006 was presented as the most fundamental reform of charity for 400 years. And the Act itself provides for a review of its provisions after five years – now under way. So it is timely to ask how charity and Big Society fit the needs of Britain in the twenty-first century.

It is striking that David Cameron hardly mentions charity as such in presenting his vision for the Big Society. To quote his relaunch speech of May 2011 (Cameron, 2011b), the Big Society is 'all aspects of life that fall outside our dealings with the state, or with the market'. That space is more commonly called the third sector or civil society, terms used by the previous and present governments successively to label the Cabinet Office Unit responsible for state/sector relations. Charity is certainly in there.

Of course charity 'has dealings with the state' – some charities might be mistaken for being part of the public sector (British Council, Arts Council); and many charities operate 'in the market', as social enterprises, to use the fashionable buzzword. But clearly charity is neither state nor market. Public benefit defines charity and always has, long before it was controversially highlighted in the 2006 Act. The ethos of charity could indeed be described as 'to make our country a better place to live', to quote David Cameron's rhetoric on the Big Society.

One might say that, with a couple of hundred thousand charities, Britain already has a Big Society. The Chief Executive of the Royal National Lifeboat Institution (RNLI), to name but one representative of the sector, has said just that (RNLI, 2011). At one end of the spectrum of size and character, the largest charities might not be regarded as part of David Cameron's local community vision. But the National Trust, for instance, with nearly 4 million members and over 60 000 volunteers, led by a council independent of government, is a prime example of citizens taking on responsibilities in the public interest, for an issue – heritage – which the state cannot, and indeed should not, meet single-handed. That great Victorian philanthropist, Octavia Hill, might certainly have seen it this way in founding the Trust.

So, even the largest charities can be part of Big Society. And it is true that the great majority of charities are small bodies, often coming into existence through the commitment of ordinary citizens with the determination to tackle issues which they passionately believe need to be addressed. Many of these bodies are indeed purely voluntary. But much of the charitable sector consists of small to medium-sized organisations with professional staff equipped to tackle professional issues. It is important to be clear that the voluntary sector does not consist purely of engaged amateur citizens. Paid staff with the relevant professional skills and properly resourced are an integral part of it.

The test of charity in the modern world is whether it provides a legal and institutional framework which enables people's vision to flourish and public confidence to be maintained. The test of the Big Society idea is whether it encourages this diversity and commitment to flourish.

CONCEPT OF CHARITY

The everyday meaning of charity is doing good, helping others. That is certainly captured by the law; but there is much more in the legal concept of charity. In law, as in colloquial discourse, the essence of charity is public benefit. How that is determined is a vexed question, but for immediate purposes it is sufficient to note that a body which does not serve the well-being of the community cannot in law be a charity.

Equally important in the legal definition of charity is the concept of not-for-profit. It is important to note that this not-for-profit element in charity does not mean that charities cannot make a profit. Many charities are trading bodies that generate a surplus – what they may not do is pass on this surplus to shareholders. Thus charities should more accurately be described as non-profit-distributing bodies. Charities often are, and have for centuries been, social enterprises, long before that label became fashionable. It must be admitted that charities themselves have often not thought of themselves in entrepreneurial terms, so the present emphasis on enterprise is salutary, provided equal emphasis is given to the 'social' part of the label – for the community not personal benefit.

The third element that determines charity, equally important to the other two, is independence – again a vexed issue, easily stated, much more difficult to determine. The law is clear: a charity is the responsibility of its trustees, its board, whatever title they have (management committee, directors, etc.). The absolute duty of trustees is to do what is best for their charity, overriding personal interests and, equally important, overriding the interests of other bodies including those that may have appointed them. A trustee cannot 'represent', for example, a local authority or central government. This captures the sense of citizen involvement, which the Big Society notion emphasises. It also highlights the essential point that charities have their own point of view, their own policies. They must not be agents of the state. Part of the richness of charity is their voice and the innovation they bring.

This leads to another element, which might be taken as a fourth determinant of charity, namely the political dimension – an even more vexed issue. That charities should not be party political is undisputed; but to say, as the law appears to, that charities must not be political in a much wider sense would seem to contradict this emphasis on the independent voice. At this point it is sufficient to say that, first, the law is quite firm (if not clear) on the fact that charities may not have a political purpose; and, second, that so long as they have a charitable purpose the trustees may take part in the political process, including campaigning, if they reasonably believe that doing so is a good way of achieving their charity's objectives.

ORIGINS AND GROWTH OF CHARITY

Charity has a long history in Britain. Charities have been part of the texture of society for centuries. One of the strengths of the concept of charity is the way it has retained public support. The fact that the law has developed, enabling the institutional basis for charity to keep pace (more or less) with changing society and new needs, is one of its strengths. If the Big Society concept takes root it will be but the latest challenge to charity to show its relevance.

In England, the modern concept of charity goes back to 1601, to the Elizabethan Statute – the Charitable Uses Act of that year – significantly the year of the Poor Law reform (see Chapter 3). The 1601 Act has, naturally, long been repealed, but its famous Preamble cast a long shadow over the development of the concept of charity. The Preamble (quoted in Luxton, 2001) sets out, in gloriously Elizabethan language, a list of purposes that were then recognised as proper objects of charity. (A sample will have to suffice: 'for releife of aged impotent and poore people, for maintenance of sicke and maimed souldiers and mariners, schools of learning … for marriages of poore maides, for supportacion ayde and help of younge tradesmen handicraftesmen and persons decayed …') The underlying purpose of the 1601 Act was to secure the better administration of charitable trusts. Given the social and economic upheavals of the Tudor period it was vital that private money given to public purposes should be used for those public purposes ('accordinge to the charitable intente of the givers and founders'), such as relief of poverty and advancement of education. Queen Elizabeth herself apparently took a close interest in the legislation. (Clearly this partnership of private philanthropy with government in pursuit of the well-being of society mirrors the concept of the Big Society – 'people doing the right thing is an essential quality of the good society – of a strong society' as David Cameron put it.)

The Preamble would only be of interest to historians if it had done no more than codify charity for the first Elizabethan era – the Charities Act 2006 of its time. But the place of the Preamble in the determination of charity has meant that it remained a living document for centuries afterwards. The mechanism for deciding whether something is charitable is clearly vital to the continuing relevance of charity. Laws get out of date. Charity is a prime example of common law evolved by the courts. Both the 1601 Preamble and the modern list of charitable purposes in the 2006 Act set a framework. What is critical is how the courts apply and interpret that framework. Does it constrain? Or is it a flexible instrument enabling charity to keep pace with changing needs? The latter is the boast of charity law, most eloquently set out in a judgment given by Lord Wilberforce:

> It is not the wording of the Preamble itself, but the effect of decisions given by the courts as to its scope, decisions which have endeavoured to keep the law as to charities moving according as to new social need arising or old ones become obsolete or satisfied. (Scottish Burial Reform and Cremation Society case, 1968)

For years the Preamble was treated as the touchstone of charity. New purposes had to be within 'the spirit and intendment' of the Preamble. In 1891 Lord MacNaghten's judgment in the Pemsel case (Income Tax Special Purpose Commissioners, 1891) classified (not defined) charity into four 'heads' (or purposes): poverty; religion; education; and other purposes beneficial to the community. The 2006 Act, replacing the four Pemsel purposes with its list of 13 purposes, incorporates the notion of 'analogy' to existing purposes, which has proved quite a flexible modernising mechanism in recent years. The framework of charitable purposes codified in the Charities Act 2006 shows how far charity has developed. The fact that the promotion of human rights is now accepted as charitable is but the most obvious example of this. It has to be said, however,

that the progress has been hard won. It was not until the 1980s that race relations was accepted as charitable. If ever there was an issue calling for a Big
Society response, it was communities responding to the challenge of immigration. And indeed the community relations movement had its roots back in the
1950s. The process of building on court judgments inherent in the common law
system was slow and uncertain. In fact it was the Charity Commission that took
the initiative in respect of race relations and was subsequently able to acceler-
ate the modernisation process.

The development of the Commission and its role has been a crucial element
in the development of charity. Until the Commission was established in 1853,
as an administrative alternative to the time-consuming expense of the Chancery
Court, charity law was a rigid and uncertain basis for philanthropy. A century
earlier, the Mortmain Act of 1736 had introduced the paradoxical situation that
charitable bequests of property were void – on the basis that they disinherited
the rightful heirs. Thus many court judgments determining something to be
charitable were made precisely to void them – a curious basis for developing
the scope of charity. Unsurprisingly, would-be philanthropists in the eighteenth
and nineteenth centuries sought to avoid these constraints by setting up as philanthropic societies or companies.

It was only with the reforms initiated by the Nathan Report in 1952 (Lord
Nathan, 1952), which led to the Charities Act 1960, that the Charity Commission established a comprehensive register, covering all types of charities for the
first time. The reforms were gradual – half-hearted one might say with hind-
sight. The status of the Commission was ambiguous – was it an extension of
the courts or an administrative government department? The expectation that
the Commission would hold charities accountable, which the establishment of
the register created, remained unrealised. Indeed, in the pre-IT era, the register
was an inadequate, inaccurate vehicle and the Commission, despite extensive,
even draconian, powers of inquiry, lacked supervisory resources. The IT age,
in which details about the activities and resourcing of registered charities are
accessible on the Charity Commission's website, has since transformed their
openness and accountability.

THE REFORM OF CHARITY

The Charities Act 2006 was presented with the hyperbole that it was the most
substantial reform of charity for over 400 years – a clear reference to the 1601
Act. It was nothing of the kind; but it was the culmination of a long process going, with stops and starts, since at least as far back as the 1970s. This reflected
concern that the law of charity not only did not correspond to the expectations
of ordinary citizens who were the ordinary donors – bad enough for public

confidence – but worse, that it was not fit for the needs of voluntary action in the modern world.

First, a brief sketch of the reform process that has led to the 2006 Act. The National Council for Voluntary Organisations (NCVO) was the leading voice in the sector advocating reform. Even in its earlier incarnation as the National Council of Social Service (NCSS), it set up a review chaired by the ubiquitous Lord Goodman, which reported in 1976 (NCSS, 1976). Setting the course subsequently followed by later reviews, the Goodman Committee considered whether the concept of charity should be substantially changed, for example to embrace the whole of the not-for-profit sector; but, in common with subsequent reviews, Goodman took the view that charity was too well-established and valuable a feature of the social and economic life of the country, and that therefore reform rather than replacement was what was required. The end result was a recommendation to replace the 1601 Preamble with an up-to-date framework of 'guidelines' (as the report put it) setting out in modern language the scope of charity as it had evolved.

The recommendations of the Goodman Report were not taken up by the government and, indeed, when reform finally did reach the political agenda, it focused on the need to modernise the Charity Commission. The reforms of the Charities Act 1993, which consolidated the provisions of the 1960 Act, strengthened the powers of the Commission, given effect with a substantial increase in funding enabling proper IT systems to be introduced; meanwhile, the concept of charity was left untouched. This moved NCVO into action through the Commission chaired by Nicholas Deakin on the future of the voluntary sector, which reported in 1996 (NCVO, 1996). While endorsing the value of the concept of charity, the Deakin Report recommended that it be redefined in statute in terms of benefit to the community. Reform of charity law was not, however, on the agenda (or 'message') of the New Labour government, which took office the next year.

It took yet a further NCVO review to get the issue back on the political agenda. The NCVO report 'For the public benefit?' (NCVO, 2001) yet again considered and rejected the case for replacing charity, and built on the Deakin Report by proposing a universal public benefit requirement. The government now felt confident enough to grasp the nettle, at least to the extent of setting up yet another review, this time within government. The Cabinet Office-led review, drawing in a wide range of people from the charitable and legal worlds, made its recommendations in a 2002 report 'Private action, public benefit', essentially focusing on the public benefit test (Cabinet Office, 2002).

The process from the Cabinet Office report to the 2006 Act was long drawn-out and fraught. A draft bill was published in 2004. A scrutiny committee of both Houses of Parliament, drawing in a number of peers with close knowledge of and involvement in the charity sector, examined the bill closely and critically, flushing out the key issue of just what difference a public benefit test would make, the point being that the legal concept of charity includes the criterion that any charitable purpose is for the public benefit. The reform came down to the fact that, for the Pemsel heads of poverty, religion and education, but not for the fourth head of 'other purposes', public benefit was under previous law assumed unless rebutted, but would now have to be demonstrated.

CHARITIES AND THE POLITICAL PROCESS

The concept of the Big Society centrally involves charities sharing in the provision of public services. Government recognition of that must be welcome. Of course it is hardly new. In the Victorian era philanthropy flourished, attempting to fill something of a vacuum in tackling the problems of industrialisation and the growth of cities, which the state was slow to deal with. The professionalisation and nationalisation of social welfare provision, which reached its high point with the creation of the welfare state, did not supplant charity. Barnados, the National Society for the Prevention of Cruelty to Children (NSPCC) and the Red Cross, for example, did not lose their role because the government recognised the need for coordinated state provision. What the creation of the welfare state did do was change the terms, the relationship between charity and state – and then only in varying degrees. The debate about the role of charity in the new order was perhaps slow to start, but it has certainly been going strong since the 1970s. Indeed, the Big Society initiative can perhaps best be seen as a contribution to that debate: the latest focus for the vital, ongoing discussion of what the responsibilities of the state are, and how citizens, individually and collectively, can contribute to the public well-being.

One distinctive feature of the post-welfare-state voluntary sector has been the growth of campaigning charities. Take Shelter as an example. This is by no means new: the great Victorian philanthropic bodies combined provision with campaigning. Raising public awareness about the evils of the new urban society that desperately needed tackling was the driving force of much Victorian philanthropy – citizens taking responsibility, as David Cameron might put it. And taking responsibility includes, often starts with, challenging the way things are done – public policy – as well as the way things are. A strand in the debate over the role of charities in the welfare state has been just that. The recognition that state provision is not the end of voluntary involvement has been a key impetus to the growth of the sector in recent decades – and to the debate about the proper role of charities and their relationship to government. It remains a key issue in the Big Society debate.

The voice of charities is acknowledged in the Big Society concept. David Cameron may not emphasise campaigning in his exposition of the Big Society concept, but he does acknowledge that people should play a role in 'helping to design policy, scrutinise legislation' and, in short, 'to hold government and the public sector to account'. So how does charity law deal with this aspect of the role of charities? On the face of it, the principle that charities cannot have a political purpose seems to limit their engagement in the political process of developing policy and legislation. That is not, of course, a role reserved for political parties. There is nothing new in the recognition that public policy depends on the contribution of interest groups and lobbying. But the law does not only exclude charities participating in party politics. Charity law, as laid down in a 1917 judgment (Bowman, 1917), defines 'political' as extending to the law and public policy. The rationale for this is that charities are subject to the law and the courts, and that changing (or indeed upholding) the law and policy is the business of Parliament. As reaffirmed in court judgments since then, the courts, in overseeing charities and determining whether they are acting within the confines of charity law, hold that the courts are not able to judge the public benefit of the law or government policy, that being the preserve of Parliament and the political process.

Applied rigorously, as was done until quite recently, this meant that charities could not campaign. Given the vigour of philanthropic campaigning in the nineteenth century, it is difficult to square the 1917 judgment with the realities of charitable engagement. Fortunately, the law, or its interpretation, is not that restrictive. Resting on the distinction between a charity's objects and its activities, it has been possible to confine the rigour of the law to precluding charities from having a *purpose* that is political (in the wide sense described above) – for example to repeal a specific law – whilst allowing charities to engage in political activity (in this wide sense) in pursuance of their objects – for example by lobbying for a change in the law on the basis that this helps achieve the charity's objects.

CONCLUSION

The headline conclusions are that charity is at the heart of the Big Society; that the Big Society agenda is not new, but may all the same be a worthwhile repackaging of the process of growth and change through which citizen engagement and the state have been going in recent decades; but that there are elements in the law and discourse of charity that should with advantage be highlighted in the Big Society debate.

One virtue of the 2006 Act is that it sets out clearly in modern language what charity covers. The issues David Cameron cites as examples of the vital areas of public policy and provision that will benefit from the Big Society approach – issues like education, health and care, crime reduction, drug rehabilitation – are all covered by the list of charitable purposes in the 2006 Act. And they are, of course, issues that charities have been seeking to tackle for years. 'More freedom for professionals to innovate' is music to the ears of charity. The capacity for innovation has been one of the planks out of which the case for charity has been made in the world of the welfare state. As noted above, it is *professionals* who make the contribution, not just amateur volunteers (and see Chapter 6). This needs proper resourcing.

One of the strengths of the 2006 Act list is that it explicitly includes such issues as human rights and citizenship as legitimate objects of charity, in the past regarded as political. Two points arise. The call for anyone who has 'ideas and the people and the commitment to tackle our most deep rooted social problems [to] come forward and play a role in our public services' is welcome, even if an endorsement of what charities have always been doing. But this is not just a matter of implementing government policies and priorities. Government must accept the central contribution of charities to policy formation – and to its criticism. The independent participation of charities in the political process must be upheld.

This highlights the importance of the place of 'voice' in the legal basis for charities. The compromise between the restrictive – I would say anachronistic – law prohibiting 'political' purposes for charities on the one hand, and the permissive law on 'political' activities on the other, is frankly an unsatisfactory fudge. It constantly gives trouble over registration by the Charity Commission.

The Big Society idea goes wider than charity in its encouragement to citizens to act together in pursuit of their interests. Often these will be advantageous to the community; but often they will be sectional, even divisive, for example setting one group of citizens against another. The criterion of public benefit makes charity narrower. But it is an attractive element. Given its central place in charity, and the focus on it in the reform process, the reliance on the inherited body of common law and its capacity to determine what constitutes the public benefit in the modern world, and to develop it, is a key issue. In common sense public benefit is a perfect shorthand for what distinguishes charities from voluntary bodies serving more private purposes and sectional self-interests. But it does not encourage confidence that the 2006 Act leaves its determination open. The Charity Commission has worked wonders developing guidelines on the difficulties of how to draw the line between public and private benefit; but it is worrying that, for example, the criteria for schools or hospitals that charge high fees to be charitable should immediately fall into controversy, based on hotly contested interpretations of a limited number of court judgments. The fact that the Commission is having to revise its guidance as a result of challenge in the tribunal highlights the uncertainties.

The Big Society agenda includes promoting giving and volunteering. These are both important, and their perennial appearance on governments' agendas for the voluntary sector, from the Thatcher era of the 'active citizen' and before, testifies to the fact that they are neither new nor easily realised.

Two points here about them: promoting giving means that there must be worthy recipients. That charities effectively deliver public benefit rightly enjoy public confidence is the necessary corollary of promoting giving. That has been the object of the charity reform process. Charities must be accountable for the use they make of the resources, and tax benefits, they receive. The transparency of this reporting and accounting, which the Charity Commission has promoted in recent years, is a necessary advance. The fact that the Commission's resources have been drastically cut threatens its ability to secure the compliance necessary to maintain public confidence. And volunteering is about ordinary citizens joining in. Some of this can be done individually, for example helping in hospitals and schools; but again having organisations in which people can volunteer is an essential corollary of the volunteering agenda.

Charities depend on resources. Private and corporate giving is essential, as is discussed by Cathy Pharoah (Chapter 9) and Diana Leat (Chapter 10); but it is unrealistic to think that public sector funding can be dispensed with. David Cameron has emphasised that the Big Society initiative is not a cuts agenda. He must hold to that. There are real worries as to whether this is being translated into action. The government must hold to both parts of the promise to 'put power – and money – in people's hands', and not just in the hands of citizens as 'consumers' but as 'Big Society' deliverers.

The great value of charity, which the Big Society discourse reflects, is its independence. This is at the heart of the legal concept and requirement for charities. But legal independence, not always easy to maintain in any case, is not sufficient. At a time when the proportion of charity income deriving from public funding has been growing and amounts to at least a third of the total, the need to make independence a reality has never been greater. The fact that a committee chaired by Dame Anne Owers has been established is both a sign of this and a reassurance. Government must heed their views. To ensure that the state piper does not call the tune requires understanding on the part of the public sector paymasters and commitment on the part of charities engaging in partnership with public authorities. It must be the ethos of the trustees to make partnership a reality, not to become agents of the state.

That highlights perhaps the most important element in charity, the trustees. If the ancient form is to remain relevant in the modern world, effective trusteeship is vital. It would be welcome if David Cameron emphasised trusteeship as one of the forms of citizen volunteering most important to realising his vision of a healthy society.

PART II

Policy

8. 'Big Society' as a rhetorical intervention

Martin Albrow

Who gets excited by 'Big Society'? Certainly not the general public who, by all accounts, find it uninformative and boring. Conservative MPs have allegedly experienced frustration on the doorstep as they have had to work harder to win any interest. Tory MP Jo Johnson was reported as saying it was 'intangible and incomprehensible ... and unpersuasive'. According to the same report Phillip Blond, author of *Red Tory* (2010), said government departments had yet to grasp it (Beattie, 2011).

In an age of mediatised politics it is no accident that on the very day – 11 July 2011 – when Parliament was debating the Murdoch media empire and phone hacking, the scandal of scandals, the Prime Minister was promoting his Big Society programme elsewhere. For these are two sides of the same coin. One side sabotages the media machine, as the other endeavours to keep the wheels moving. While once class conflict revolved around the factory floor, today a more widely diffused conflict centres on the means and methods of communication.

Jonathan Powell, who served as Tony Blair's chief of staff, describes the process of searching for 'big bold policies or big ideas to define their approach for voters' (Powell, 2010, p. 174). On his account Blair spent most of his ten years looking for a way to present a conceptual framework that included modernisation and fairness. But, so often, contemporary processes of political communication brought it down to a catchphrase or sound bite. For the 'big idea' doesn't even have to be an idea.

A slogan is intended to evoke a response rather than signify a meaning, and the use of 'society' as a slogan suggests that the strategy professionals behind it see it as an empty signifier. Margaret Thatcher's famous throwaway remark that society did not exist led the way, but it only picked up on a mood among intellectuals of both right and left who had already discarded 'society' as a term with a serious content. Cameron is able to distance himself from her without giving hostages to fortune by way of clearly defined policies flowing from the concept.

'Big Society' as rhetorical intervention crafted by media professionals invites us to revisit the theme Antonio Gramsci made famous in his account of the hegemonic role of intellectuals (Gramsci, 1957, p. 120). Picking up on the older Marxist model of class society he pointed to the production process being 'mediated' by a vast superstructure staffed by intellectual workers. Their involvement in civil society was as vital to engineering tacit consent to the established order as was their role in state coercive institutions.

Gramsci was pointing to the development of specialised intellectual roles in modern society to the detriment and neglect of the intellectual capacities that all people possessed. For him, civil society and bureaucrats mediated between the two great classes of industrial workers and owners of capital. Things have moved on since his time, with a specialised communications industry now working to manufacture consent among a mosaic of class fractions.

Yet we have to ask, is society quite so anodyne and content free? The government's PR machine and the owners and controllers of the mass media are in a symbiotic concentration of power far removed from the everyday life and concerns of the general public. Both Big Society and the phone hacking scandal are two aspects of the same phenomenon – the mediatisation of politics distancing politicians from the place where trust is generated, in the everyday complexity of social relations or, as some would still call it, 'society'.

In that scandal the media professionals and politicians alike bow down before something intangible but seemingly all pervasive, the norms and values of wider society. It suggests that the mediatised politician is too far away to see that there is, after all, a real big society beyond 'Big Society'.

AN ENDURING DIVIDE: ELITE AND EVERYDAY DISCOURSE

It was always thus, or at least it was 400 years ago. In an essay 'Of vanity', a retired magistrate from Bordeaux, Michel de Montaigne, wrote from the comfort of his rural chateau:

> These great and tedious debates about the best form of society, and the most commodious rules to bind us, are debates only proper for the exercise of our wits: and, as in the arts, there are several subjects that have their being in agitation and controversy, and have no life but there. (Montaigne, 1842, p. 442)

So there we have it: across the ages one member of the country gentry speaks to another. While this may leave Montaigne's legion of admirers, among whom I count myself, spluttering with indignation, David Cameron's Big Society has something in common with the outlook of the great essayist.

There ought to be a rural equivalent to 'urbane' to describe how Montaigne can hold intellectuals in disdain at the same time as captivating and disarming them with an effortless display of elite culture. He may have scorned scholastic concern for the concept of society but he was entirely confident in writing of society in all its manifestations, a legacy that has delighted generations of scholars and general readers ever since.

Big Society is likewise David Cameron's gift to the chattering classes, all-embracing and Delphic at one and the same time, open to as many interpretations as there are ideological positions. They can and do construe its meaning at such length as there are columns to fill. But crucially its very amorphous, even everyday, quality allows him to make it a signature idea that he can take in any direction the politics of the day demands. The insouciance with which he tosses 'society' around aggravates academics who have consigned the term to the history of ideas.

On the contrary, 'society' sits within everyday discourse as easily as ideas like nation, country, class or immigration. And again it was always thus. It will strengthen this point to take as an example a writer from the next century, as celebrated as Montaigne, but offering a rather greater challenge for the Conservative Party of today.

John Milton, urbane, university-educated city dweller, for many second only to Shakespeare in the pantheon of English literature, is renowned also for the defence he wrote in 1644 of liberty and press freedom in his *Areopagitica* against an order in Parliament of the previous year that required that no book should be printed except under licence. He argued in 'Of Education' for a 'complete and generous education, that which fits a man to perform justly, skilfully and magnanimously all the offices, both public and private, of peace and war' (Milton 1644 [1927], p. 46). Consistent too with his fervent belief in freedom, he challenged religious authority and advocated the possibility of divorce. In that context society was an ever-present consideration.

In 'The Doctrine and Discipline of Divorce' (1643 [1927]) Milton spoke variously of civil and godly society, household and conjugal society, blissful and peaceful society, mutual and human society, moving easily between them, with no more complex reflection on the concept than his concern for the right to divorce required. Society was for him what anthropologists today would call a thick concept, embedded in everyday language and experience, not the thin, precise product of theoretical definition.

For all practical purposes we, as ordinary people, know what society means, and we know how to handle its blurred boundaries, vagueness and ambiguity. In that respect the way we use it differs not at all from the way Montaigne and Milton did. We refer to it as unselfconsciously as we might to people, relationships, life, nature, or the world. Cameron relies on that taken-for-granted quality and uses it effortlessly as a political resource.

PERSUADING THE PUBLIC

Cameron does what all politicians do in communicating with their public, whether it's Harold Wilson explaining the sterling devaluation crisis of the 1960s in terms of 'the pound in your pocket' or Margaret Thatcher likening national finances to household budgets. Big Society then has to be understood in the first instance as a rhetorical intervention, seeking to send a message to the general public, before we begin to construe any technical policy directions that shelter under its umbrella.

Rhetoric, 'mere rhetoric'? Nothing could be less 'mere' than the formulae that contemporary politicians employ as the pegs on which to hang whole series of speeches, often framing political party campaigns over many years. Slogans in politics are as important as brand names for business, debated, crafted and subject to endless team discussions before being launched. They are not arbitrary either. They deserve all the serious attention that academics can give them.

In a world split between intellectuals and the general public, slogans have to be robust too, for they have to mediate between the two. Just as Montaigne assumed the mantle of the common man, even if he is steeped in Burke and Hayek, Cameron has to beware of those intellectuals who will assault him in some dark back alley with 'those great and tedious debates'. Mediation means finding a common space between two or more points of view, enabling them to meet and communicate with each other. It is no accident that the terms 'mediate' for resolving conflict and 'media' for the means of communication have a shared root and that, in politics, the mastery of both is a necessity.

If that observation appears to emphasise the importance of Cameron's experience in public relations, we should recall that all politicians are professionals in rhetoric. At least since Periclean Athens, this has been a main tool of their trade, whether they have made it a subject for study or not. Powell noted in his *The New Machiavelli* (2010, p.189) the enduring truth of his sixteenth-century predecessor's emphasis on presentation.

The Conservatives make as full use of the opportunities for shaping public opinion that the media revolution provides, as did their New Labour predecessors. Cameron's own background in public relations is well known and his former chief strategist, Steve Hilton, used to work for Saatchi. The Big Society Network, established in March 2010 as an autonomous cheerleader for Cameron's idea, has, on the evidence of its website, a managing team dominated by media and marketing professionals, strong on experience in television, film-making, and event organising.

There is ample anecdotal evidence of the importance that contemporary political leaders give to the spoken word, to the speeches they make and, in particular, to the word or phrase on which the speech will pivot or resonate through the media and public discourse generally. The memoirs of Michael Waldman, *Potus Speaks: Finding the Words that Defined the Clinton Presidency*, tell in great detail how ringing phrases like 'the end of big government' or 'building a bridge to the future' would emerge from a process where a text would shuttle back and forth between writers, advisers, interns and the President himself. In the case of 'a bridge to the twenty-first century' Clinton wrote, crossed out and rewrote until he arrived at the phrase (Waldman, 2000, p. 138).

Clinton's phrases tended to stick around for longer than Blair's. Powell notes how short-lived a lot of his were, gaining the next day's headline and not much more, and how it was a mistake not to think through a phrase. He observes, somewhat gratuitously, that speaking of 'forces of conservatism' pejoratively was a mistake, since it alienated Conservatives (Powell, 2010, p. 174). He credits himself with 'Education, education, education', claiming inspiration from estate agents' 'location, location, location'.

Finding a durable phrase, a peg for a programme, an everyday slogan would appear to be then a key aspect of political communication and it is in that light that 'Big Society' deserves serious consideration as a rhetorical device. It has after all so far survived the many months since Cameron showcased it in his Hugo Young Memorial Lecture on November 10 2009.

On the face of it 'Big Society' has not much going for it, certainly less than 'education, education, education' which, on the authority of speech-making expert and communications researcher Max Atkinson (1984), has at least the attraction of being a triple list, a rhetorical device with a strong record of success. It lacks the popular imagery that Clinton displayed so effectively in his speeches and the adjective 'big' has all the appeal of the bun in a burger.

SOCIOLOGY AND ITS DISCONTENTS

But then the question arises, why does Cameron persist with it despite his own party's discomfort, regardless of the scorn of the commentators and ignoring the disdain of academics who regard it as an intrusion into their own domain? I recall one meeting of senior sociology professors where I ventured to say that the Big Society theme opened up possibilities for their and my own profession, if the Conservative Party were elected in May 2010. The facial expressions told everything about their response. Perhaps they were concerned not to appear to take crumbs from a Conservative table, but there could also have been discomfort with engaging publicly on 'society'.

In point of fact the term 'society' has been a matter of private grief for sociology for many years. For the academic discipline with 'the study of society' as its most common founding definition, it is embarrassing that within the profession there is no longer any consensus that society is its overarching topic, no agreement on how to define society, whether it is real or, indeed, even exists. John Urry (2000) has documented many of the reasons for his unease, associated with the appropriation of society by the nation-state and the fluidity of contemporary social life; he proposes to move on with mobility rather than society as the core concern for sociologists today. For some sociologists it is the accelerating processes of individualisation that make it difficult to speak of society.

But an emphasis on individuals as the primary bearers of social life was no obstacle to early sociology. Herbert Spencer, who did most to popularise the subject in the latter half of the nineteenth century, promoted a fervent ideological individualism as well as an insistence on the reality of society. It was another, subsequently much more influential, founder of the modern discipline who set up a resistance to the use of collective concepts in sociology, namely Max Weber. For him, compared with the reality of thinking, acting and feeling individuals, society was an imaginary entity and rigorous science required that all social analysis of collective entities had in principle to focus on interpreting the course of individual actions (Albrow, 1990). Talk of the state, nation or capitalism could only be shorthand for accounts of the different ways countless individual citizens, voters, workers or owners of capital related to each other.

This doctrine, which by mid-twentieth century became known as methodological individualism, reinforced an insistence on the rigorous distinction between social science and ideology. Weber detested the intrusion into academe of appeals to the nation and class masquerading as objective science. It was an outlook that gained post-Second World War support from Karl Popper (1957) who saw, in collective concepts, the roots of totalitarianism of the left and the right. What both Weber and Popper understood very well were the political uses to which such concepts could be put. In neither case did this preclude their fervent ideological commitments outside the lecture theatre, in Weber's case to an exalted notion of the destiny of Germany as a world power.

In the 1970s and 1980s the rise of neo-liberal political theory of the right and postmodernist cultural theory of the left provided additional intellectual support for a reductionist individualism, and sociologists put up no effective resistance to what eventually became the trademark phrase for Thatcherism, 'there is no such thing as society'. While happy to inveigh against neo-liberalism they have put up no full-scale defence of the idea of society.

Compared to the evident relish with which economists mix in public debate over the economy, sociologists prefer to back off from full engagement with party politics, retreating behind the curious doctrine that while no research is apolitical, it is a virtue when it is not party political research (as in Brewer, 2011). Why an ill-defined disposition (usually leftist) should be preferable to an explicit commitment to one party or another is not entirely clear to me. Anthony Giddens (1998) has been a notable exception to this rule but even his foregrounding of civil society in his *The Third Way* was not accompanied by a vigorous defence of the idea of society.

The equation of scientific rigour with the rejection of collective concepts has lent additional strength to the barriers between the public sphere of debate and the academic world, to the detriment of both. For there is no more reason for sociologists to be reluctant to pronounce on society, class or community than there is for meteorologists to refrain from talking of weather, clouds or storms. They are all fuzzy at the edges, hard to define and far reaching in their effects. The real world is like that. It is full of neighbourhoods, communities, societies and corporations, collective concepts and real entities all. Montaigne and Milton lived there. Cameron clearly gets it, too. On one occasion I'm told, when the meaning of 'Big Society' arose in a discussion among senior officials they received the authoritative response, 'Don't try to define it. It's meant to be mushy'.

THE DEEP STRUCTURE OF 'BIG SOCIETY'

A notion that underpins communication and recurs in sciences like sociology, anthropology and politics is that human thought and action are fundamentally organised around polar opposites, binary concepts that structure the ways we form a view of the world and our place in it. Hence good and evil, mind and body, material and spiritual, us and them, are paired ideas that regulate a vast variety of everyday expressions and decisions (yin and yang in Chinese – this is culturally universal).

Cameron assiduously employs 'Big Society' as the positive one in a pair:

Big society advances as big government retreats. (10 November 2009)

There is such a thing as society, it's just not the same thing as the state. (31 March 2010)

The Big Society agenda ... get rid of the centralised bureaucracy. (19 July 2010)

We need a Big Society approach rather than a big state approach. (15 February 2011)[1]

Government, state and bureaucracy seem to serve equally well as the counterpart negative pole to the Big Society and in this respect secure a line back to Thatcherism's declared hostility to the state. It also marks off this particular evocation of a society theme in political rhetoric from its previous use in

Lyndon Johnson's Great Society programme, which depended on an overarching philosophy of social reform and renewal led by government.

The seeds of that construction of the Great Society had already been sown early in the twentieth century in the friendship between the greatest of American journalists, Walter Lippman, and Graham Wallas, first Professor of Government at the London School of Economics whose book *The Great Society* (1914) promoted a concept that partnered 'Great Industry', and argued that only new machinery of state could carry the appropriate organisation of a collective will that would be adequate for the new complexity of society that was not just national but international. Wallas himself was active in establishing the New School of Social Research in New York (Dahrendorf, 1995).

The problem for Lyndon Johnson's version of managerial liberalism was that it came up against the resistance of local communities. In the words of one historian of the period, there was 'no natural constituency beyond the experts, politicians and bureaucrats who were central to its creation. It led to an image of the Great Society as an alien or imperious bureaucratic monster' (Andrew, 1998, p. 17). Community in the American tradition is a more powerful encompassing concept than society. The writer of the main Johnson speech on the Great Society, which he delivered in May 1964, subsequently declared that the problem with government was precisely the necessity for bureaucracy and the loss of participation in an organic community (Goodwin, 1974, p. 75). It was to this anti-government localist tradition that Clinton sought to reach out with his declaration of the end of 'Big Government'.

In so far as the same tradition has a hold in Britain, Cameron, too, declares an end to Big Government and has sought to neutralise statism with a localism agenda, by applauding local social enterprises and by embracing community activists as key agents in the Big Society.

'Big' therefore has its own soundbite history and resonates against the background of earlier political campaigns.

For those working in advertising and marketing there is nothing surprising in the repeated use of the same cultural symbols over successive political campaigns. They operate in a mature market where it is the total set of campaigns over time that frames the creation of a winning message (Leymore, 1982). All of which highlights the irony of Cameron, the public relations professional, declaring that the failure at the core of New Labour was that 'It was always a communications strategy rather than a proper governing one' (31 March 2010).

'*Big* Society' operates in the same product field as '*Big* government' and Cameron seeks to occupy the same field as Thatcher, even if his 'society' explicitly affirms what she denied. He is therefore connecting with a mature market, arguably more directly than Blair (1998) managed to do with 'The Third Way', for which there was no significant antecedent phrase with popular resonance and only relatively obscure intellectual origins. 'Society' by contrast is massively commonplace, and it is both as durable and productive of debate as Montaigne long ago declared it to be.

Tagging 'society' with 'big' makes a catchphrase that prompts recall of recent ideological debate. This is the 'mere' rhetoric. It is the froth that, perhaps deliberately, conceals the vast and intricate embeddedness of 'society' both in everyday language and in academic discourse. For this is where the Cameron rhetoric commands much more than the space of a political marketing campaign. The power of the idea of society derives from extensive usage and from its employment in a whole series of fundamental paired concepts, not just society and the state, but society and individual, economy, nature or culture. Each of these can be invoked as and when required.

'Society' can switch in an out of different pairs as context requires. So, beginning with the opposition of state and individual, society can be introduced as the energies of individuals released by the withdrawal of the state. 'A new role for the state: actively helping to create the big society' but also 'the big society requires mass engagement'; 'we must use the state to remake society' but also 'bigger society not bigger government' (10 November 09). Here we see society as an operator, switching activity from government to people, an explicit move that figures in Cameron's early leadership campaign declaration that 'there is such a thing as society, it's just not the same thing as the state' (31 March 2010).

Just as important as this switching function is mediation. This occurs whenever an attempt is made to bridge a deep polarity, most obviously expressed in oppositions like in- and out-group, citizen and foreigner, us and the other. Here society mediates between both, pointing to shared qualities and bonds. It can also be employed as Cameron does to mediate between the state and the market: 'In the past, the left focused on the state and the right focused on the market, we're harnessing that space in between – society – the hidden wealth of our nation'.

Here there are, to be sure, traces of the older tripartite frame, state, third sector and business, which New Labour adopted from American usage, and where the Conservatives have replaced third sector with civil society. That is what 'the space in between' suggests. But in talking of society as 'the hidden wealth of our nation' Cameron is tapping a profounder sense of society, a Durkheimian collective consciousness underlying, and a precondition for economic activity, that 'will create the conditions for a more aspirational, entrepreneurial culture' (Cameron speech 23 May 2011, 'Building a Bigger, Stronger Society').

This is a sense of society that corresponds with the everyday notion of open-ended human interaction, which is the medium though which all relationships are built, private or public, cooperative or conflictual. It corresponds to William Outhwaite's (2006, p. 124) preference for a flexible concept of society, one that fits with what what Jürgen Habermas calls a postnational world.

BEYOND THE 'BIG SOCIETY' RHETORIC

Let me be clear in asking the reader to treat Cameron's speeches as more than 'mere' rhetoric: I am not endorsing them as examples of fine rhetoric. Indeed, in the peroration to a speech of 23 May 2011, the structural components of his thinking are all too visible and devoid of the metaphor and imagery that would connect to a wider audience. A list of authorities from Burke to Oakeshott and references to the philosophy of individualism, market, state, entrepreneurial culture deprive it of any charm or appeal beyond the chattering classes and, given the anti-intellectualism of British life, probably leaves most of them cold, too.

I am not suggesting, either, that Big Society represents a worked-out coherent political ideology. The makings of that are more to be found in Phillip Blond's *Red Tory* (2010) than in Cameron's Big Society – but 'Red Tory' will never be a sound bite.

What 'Big Society' achieves is a connection for Cameron between the language of the street, or at least of the popular press, and the language of the professional political analysts in which he is steeped. It makes it easy for him to bridge the communication gap between community centre and social capital, between parent's group and stakeholders, between charities and civil society. At the same time it may be a step too far in exposing his government to the test of what is credible in daily experience.

This account says nothing about the viability of any of the policies that the rhetoric may announce, although it does suggest the pitfalls to which policy measures under the Big Society banner may be prone. The very comprehensiveness and resilience of a rhetorical structure that has society as the key component may encourage too casual an adoption of measures that together amount to a ragbag or, at worst, are inconsistent in practical terms. The tensions between localism, community or third sector initiatives, state welfare and social justice were apparent in the Blair period and nothing suggests that the Conservatives have yet found an answer to alleviating them.

A media campaign invoking 'society' highlights the gap between the arduous negotiation of trust in everyday social relations – in other words, society as lived in daily life, and processes of media manipulation. As Neil Washbourne (2010, p. 45) points out in his recent textbook, 'the work of political consultants seen as "spin doctors" working to promote leaders, may actually produce the conditions for greater levels of distrust'. Referring back to Gramsci we can understand this as a communications industry failure to replace hegemony with an equivalent kind of taken-for-granted acceptance of social order in the new fragmented class structure of contemporary society.

Giddens (2007, p. 189) has pointed to a generalised change in contemporary conditions whereby trust is no longer something passive, hidden and taken for granted, but has to be worked for and gained actively through partnership. New Labour's reliance on spin was symptomatic of a failure to generate active trust. Cameron's public relations campaign, invoking 'Big Society' as it does, runs an even greater risk by drawing direct attention to the cleavage between society and the class that lives from politics. It may divert attention away from the economy, banking and budget deficit reduction, but it does so at the risk of exposing the gap between a media power elite and the rest. Society as a theme can easily open political discourse to debate on fundamentals and thus raise issues of fairness, distribution of wealth and control of corporate power. 'Big Society' may well turn out to be the sound bite that bites back.

NOTE

1. The Cameron speeches to which reference is made here are:

    – 10 November 2009, 'The Big Society', The Guardian Hugo Young Memorial Lecture, Kings Place, London, available at: www.conservatives.com/News/Speeches (accessed 11 November 2009).
    – 31 March 2010, 'Our Big Society plan', at a Conservative party symposium in London to launch a pamphlet 'Big Society not Big Government: Building a Big Society', Conservative Party Office, Millbank, London, available at: www.conservatives.com/News/Speeches (accessed 5 July 2011).
    – 19 July 2010, 'Our Big Society Agenda', delivered at Liverpool Hope University, available at: www.conservatives.com/News/Speeches (accessed 20 July 2010).
    – 14 February 2011, 'On Big Society' delivered to launch the Big Society Network at Somerset House, London, available at: www.number10.gov.uk/news/speeches-and-transcripts (accessed 13 June 2011).
    – 23 May 2011, 'Building a bigger, stronger society' delivered at Milton Keynes, available at: www.number10.gov.uk/news/speeches-and-transcripts (accessed 13 June 2011).

9. Funding and the Big Society

Cathy Pharoah

Within new conservative ideology, the responsibility for welfare will increasingly shift from the state towards the Big Society concept in which the roles of the public, voluntary and private sectors in both financing and delivering welfare are rebalanced. The Coalition's vision for financing the role of 'social ventures' in welfare provision, that is of community organisations, charities, social enterprises and social firms, is set out in its social investment strategy (HM Government, 2011). This refers to the three 'pillars' of finance for social ventures – social investment, philanthropy and state funding. Uncertainties around the proposed reshaping of the funding base, however, have seen the role of the Big Society in relation to finance increasingly contested. Widely divided perceptions have arisen around issues such as whether the Big Society is on the supply or demand side of the finance market, or both. Issues of the sufficiency and timeliness of financial resources in a period of change have also surfaced as both crucial and contested. This chapter outlines the emerging debates, describes and analyses the models for financing social ventures in the Big Society context, and identifies some of the issues and implications that arise for funding social welfare through the Big Society approach.

THE EMERGING DEBATES ON FUNDING

Timing has been critical to the shape of the debate about financial issues in relation to the Big Society. With a four-year programme of government spending reduction of around 30 per cent under way, and many voluntary organisations experiencing grants cuts and service closures (London Voluntary Services Council, 2011), policy discussion has largely been subsumed within pragmatic questions that treat the Big Society as synonymous with the voluntary sector, and ask how it is to be funded and delivered. The vacuum surrounding the precise meaning of the Big Society allowed critics to interpret problems in their own way. In a major speech aimed at relaunching the Big Society concept early in 2011 Prime Minister David Cameron acknowledged that 'Some people say it is too vague', (Cameron, 2011) but still left the definition wide, saying that 'building a bigger and stronger society was a good thing' in itself, particularly at a time of public spending cuts. The parliamentary Public Administration Select Committee (PASC) launched an inquiry into Big Society policy in February 2011, focusing on 'the consequences of reductions in public expenditure for the delivery of Big Society, and the appropriateness of using charitable income or volunteer labour to subsidise costs of public service delivery' (PASC, 16 February 2011a). Third sector organisations have also voiced concern. For instance, in an open letter to David Cameron, the Association of Chief Executives of Voluntary Organisations (ACEVO) wrote 'Big Society has for too long been promoted as a Utopian ideal with calls for more giving and more volunteering. But the reality is the hard grind of charities trying to provide services for more, against cuts in their funding' (ACEVO, 2011).

The government's concept, however, is that a successful Big Society is one where communities generate their own local solutions to meeting service needs, through alternatives merely to asking for more external funding. Cameron, for example, asked 'If there are facilities that the state can't afford to keep open, shouldn't we be trying to encourage communities who want to come forward and help them?' (Cameron, 2011). Negative responses to the Big Society approach were interpreted as mainly due to timing issues by Phillip Blond, a recognised architect of new conservative thinking, who wrote that 'the drive for immediate cuts and deficit reduction is running too fast to give people the chance to take over the state and create the conditions for a civic economy' (Blond, 2011). The Coalition's vision is that alternative models of financing will emerge as part of a cultural shift to stronger local empowerment and engagement in service delivery. Blond argues that the strength of the Big Society is 'its unprecedented scope for ... shifting the private and public sector models of production, provision and consumption. Conceived properly, the Big Society could be the answer to the consternation that the public-sector cuts are causing' (Blond, 2011). The current policy gap in the government's approach is that, while spending cuts are estimated at a potential third sector loss of £3–5 billion (Joy, New Philanthropy Capital, 2010), the speed and feasibility of acquiring alternative funding are unknown. The PASC concluded that the success of the Big Society project would depend on 'substantial change in Whitehall and to the nature of government' (PASC, 2011b). The next sections of this chapter look in more detail at the Big Society funding models, beginning with its social investment strategy.

THE SOCIAL INVESTMENT MODEL

What is the meaning of social investment as a 'pillar' of finance in the context of Big Society policy? Its use has been diffuse, referring variously to a special type of philanthropy, finance or investment, or the uses, purpose or distribution of finance. Related terms include 'philanthrocapitalism' and 'venture philanthropy' (Nicholls and Pharoah, 2008; Westall, 2010). An all-encompassing definition was used in an Open University seminar series in 2008, for example, 'the provision and use of finance to generate social, or social as well as economic, returns'. In marked contrast, the definition of social investment in the Coalition's strategy is more specific: 'money that blends financial return with social return' (HM Government, 2011). The emphasis on money sets the direction for a social investment strategy directed primarily at the supply of capital and the Big Society bank proposition was renamed 'Big Society Capital' in July 2011, when the Financial Services Authority stated that it was not a bank.

The 'normalisation' of social investment as part of mainstream investment gives it a new and more specific steer but, in many ways, the Coalition's social investment strategy draws heavily on previous centre-left, or 'Third Way', developments (Giddens, 1998); and in this it is similar to other strands in Big Society thinking (Alcock, 2010). Progressive conservative thinking has easily assimilated centre-left approaches to the economics of the third sector, as they were strongly influenced by Thatcherite neo-liberalism. The Third Way aimed for state and third sectors to drive local social and economic regeneration through capturing the principles of successful private sector enterprise and growth. As Giddens wrote, 'The new mixed economy looks … for a synergy between public and private sectors, utilising the dynamism of markets but with the public interest in mind' (Giddens, 1998). The influential ideology of 'social entrepreneurialism', which emerged in the 1990s (Leadbeater, 1997) and evolved throughout the next decade, combined the notions of locally based regeneration, entrepreneurialism and community access to finance in ways adopted within the Big Society concept. This chapter cannot cover in detail the history of social enterprise thinking and practice, but it describes the main features of a 'financial landscape', which developed around ideas of innovation, entrepreneurialism and sustainability in social welfare (Nicholls and Pharoah, 2008) and which is incorporated into the Coalition's social investment strategy.

On the supply side, new top-driven funds and funders have been established by government. Some charitable funders are shifting from traditional grant support to a more sophisticated use of finance along mainstream market models, including loans, loan guarantees, underwriting and other financial mechanisms, long-term 'patient capital' or quasi-equity investment. The intention is that the new approach will be attractive to both philanthropic and commercial funders. Approaches to risk and flexibility are key distinguishing factors in the new kinds of financing facilities. Intermediary and Community Development Finance Institutions (CDFI), including credit unions, operate largely as low-risk community and micro-credit finance providers. The Charity Bank, partly capitalised through donations, provides a low-risk loan facility, with larger social businesses served by mainstream social banks like Triodos. Innovative social investors include Venturesome, a philanthropically-based fund for early stage social enterprise, and the government's Futurebuilders, Adventure Capital and Social Enterprise Investment Funds (all now managed by The Social Investment Business), which also offer flexible financial packages of loans, grants and business support. For more developed social enterprises, the Big Issue Invest and Breakthrough offers patient capital investment and Bridges Ventures provides growth capital on commercial terms to business in deprived areas. Social Finance, meanwhile, is managing the new Social Impact Bond to the 'Community Interest Tax Relief' (CITR). This was introduced in 2003, to incentivise investment into deprived and potentially higher-risk areas and is available for investments made through a CDFI. Venture capital tax reliefs such as the Enterprise Investment Scheme can only be accessed by certain kinds of social ventures excluding, for example, charities.

Social investors have targeted charitable endowments and charitable grants as potentially important sources of finance because of the scale of charitable assets, which are at least £97 billion (NCVO, 2011), their inherent role in third sector resourcing, and their independence in using funds. An important step was the Charity Commission's recent clarification of the regulatory context for charitable investment, confirming that charities can take social gains into account when setting investment policy but that responsibility rests with the foundation (Charity Commission, 2011).

Although there is much growth in the supply side, demand for social investment has been slow to emerge. This has been interpreted mainly as a problem resulting from lack of access to appropriate finance and there are measures to stimulate the demand side. Supply-side issues remain central to policy for the growth of what are now termed 'social ventures', namely, community organisations, charities, social enterprises and social firms (HM Government, 2011). Enterprise potential was extended through the introduction of the non-profit Community Interest Company (CIC) in 2005, a structure allowing capital to be raised through, for example, shares while assets are kept permanently locked for public benefit. The CIC has proved attractive and there are now over 5000 (Office of the Regulator, 2011), though most are still small and below the formal reporting threshold (Department for Business Innovation and Skills, 2010). Alongside new entrepreneurial models, the Coalition's approach also embraces older mutualist and communitarian traditions, which have led to a revival of interest in cooperatives and credit unions (Kellner, 1998). The 'John Lewis model' is seen as an important example of how the cooperative structure can lead to major commercial success. The government's Pathfinders initiative involves running 20 public sector projects as mutuals in which public sector staff work with voluntary organisations, and is a trailblazer for the policy, but early reports suggest these public sector 'spin-outs' are experiencing mixed fortunes (Ainsworth, June 2011). Alongside supply- and demand-side initiatives, a number of new players have emerged to provide intermediary support including information, training and advice support.

CHALLENGES IN DEMARCATING A NEW FUNDING SPACE

The Coalition's social investment strategy recognises that the social investment space is still in an embryonic stage of development. There has been limited demand for the CITR and recent research indicates that community mutual ownership models need time and the right environment to grow (Woodin et al., 2010). Foundations have been generally cautious about switching from grant to social investment support (Chapman, 2011). The total scale of funds, which could be described as within the social investment territory, is around just £1 billion (NPC/NESTA, 2011, Table 9, p. 41). This is equal to one to two per cent of the income of the registered charity sector and has taken ten years to reach, although many charities access mainstream borrowing. Experience has shown the particular challenges of demarcating a new space for finance combining economic with social gain, which will need to be addressed if social investment is to play a significant part in future funding for social ventures.

The social investment model implies a deficit approach to third sector providers, which are perceived to have a weak asset base and to lack financial literacy and business development skills or 'investment-readiness'. While problems of growth tend to be located in organisations, little empirical research has tested theoretical growth models. Yet the one important exception to this, the evaluation of Futurebuilders, showed that external factors such as access to local markets are also crucial (Wells et al., 2010). This issue is acknowledged within the Coalition's Open Public Services policy, which sees the opening up of local welfare markets as a key factor, with community budgets, Local Integrated Service and participatory budgeting creating the context for social ventures to bid to run local services.

This deficit approach means that risk avoidance from both sides has continued to dominate financial decision making, inhibiting the growth of social investment. A specific intention of the CITR, for example, was to incentivise investment in higher-risk deprived areas, but eligibility criteria aimed at directing investment to these areas have come to be seen as the major barrier to its success. Subsequently, uptake of the CITR has been considerably lower than anticipated, with just £63 million of £672 million of CDFI investment raised in this way (HM Government, 2011). And it has recently been argued that the CITR should be replaced with a tax relief related to investment in the ever-growing CICs (Heaney, 2011).

NEW INVESTMENT MODELS AND THE SOCIAL IMPACT BONDS

Funding models that focus on the third sector's particular strengths and assets rather than its weaknesses in relation to the commercial sector are the least developed aspect of the field. The recent pilot development of the Social Impact Bond, a government-backed investment bond that is largely supported by institutional charitable investors and whose returns are related to improved social outcomes resulting in efficiency savings, aims to make a breakthrough in several ways. One is that investment risk is transferred away from the investee to the investor. Another is that it is being piloted in prisoner rehabilitation services, where certain kinds of intervention have been shown to reduce re-offending rates and hence costs to the state. There is considerable government interest in identifying other areas of social care where such a model might work. Early intervention programmes for young people at risk are under consideration (Allen, 2011) and the development of a potential social impact bond in this area has been funded, though it will be difficult to assess its social effects. For investors such as Sir Ronald Cohen, a key figure in the development of venture capital in the UK, the critical success factor is under-capitalisation. He has continuously promoted the proposition for the type of social investment capital facility which is central to the Coalition's social investment strategy, and which forms the Coalition's main source of new funding for the third sector, writing recently 'there needs to be a wholesaler to channel capital into the social sector, which has, to date, been disconnected almost completely from capital markets' (Cohen, 2011).

BIG SOCIETY CAPITAL (BSC)

The idea of creating a bank-type facility, taken up in the Conservative election manifesto 2010, resulted from feasibility work spearheaded by Cohen, now Chair of Big Society Capital (Commission on Unclaimed Assets, 2007). While rooted in earlier development (Cabinet Office OTS, 2009), however, the BSC has undoubtedly developed as a distinct proposition, in terms of both ideology and substance. Unlike earlier hybrid notions of a provider straddling public, charitable and private finance, and combining wholesale and retail finance roles, BSC is solely a wholesale finance operation. It will supply capital to front-line finance providers who tailor products to the social venture market. The decision about whether to invest in such products will rest with BSC, which will be a private sector body and will have to maintain long-term sustainability, though with a 'locked-in' social mission. BSC will be independent of government when making decisions about priorities, risk, financial return and social gain. While earlier conceptions of a bank-type proposition were explicitly aimed at strengthening the third sector (Commission on Unclaimed Assets, 2007), BSC will support all types of public, voluntary, mutual or private social ventures, whether large or small and from 'a variety of market sectors, business models and legal structures'.

The reframing of the banking proposition and the locating of social investment more clearly within mainstream finance brings a clarity that some will welcome. However, BSC's role as a wholesale capital provider and its requirement for financial sustainability raises questions of its own. BSC might continue to fall between social and financial funding. On the one hand, the BSC concept has moved away from original visions of a facility tailored to social ventures dependent on grants, and whose business is so embryonic that investment would carry risks on both supply and demand sides (Westall, 2010). It may not be able to support or subsidise investment where market potential is limited, as seen with the CITR. The main beneficiaries of the BSC are likely to be small-to-medium established social ventures that need capital to grow and expand. On the other hand, BSC's relationship with mainstream finance raises the risk of unfair competition and, at the time of writing, the BSC has been referred for approval under EU state aid requirements. This may involve arrangements such as setting up of a new 'neutral' body to actually own the money transferred in, with strict limits in scope (Gregory, 2011). This could risk its attractiveness to private finance. Because of the delay, the Big Lottery Fund is now distributing dormant account funds, with its first award allocated to the Private Equity Foundation to develop a social impact bond in early years intervention.

With an estimated capitalisation of between £300 and £400 million from dormant accounts, and a further £200 million from the four largest high street banks (Barclays, HSBC, Lloyds and RBS), the role of BSC in welfare investment will still be small in comparison to the potential market. For example, local authority expenditure on social protection and health is around £38 billion, of which just 11 per cent is in the voluntary sector. This means that a key role for BSC may be to provide social ventures with a bridge of mainstream private finance. The social investment strategy claims that over the years social investment could become a £10 billion market. For welfare activities which cannot enter this market, the Coalition's strategy is to increase philanthropic giving as a source of support.

PHILANTHROPY AND GIVING IN BIG SOCIETY

Private giving by individuals (including legacies), companies and charitable trusts represents a large proportion of the funding of voluntary activities and social ventures. It can be estimated to be worth over £18 billion per year

(Pharoah, 2011), around one-third of the income of registered charities, a similar proportion to statutory funds. Increasing discussion refers to philanthropy instrumentally as a source of income for charities and Big Society, as for example the statement from the Secretary of State for Culture, Media and Sport that 'what government is looking for is ... an opportunity ... to turn philanthropy into a tap that could support the arts as effectively as the National Lottery' (Hunt, 2010). Giving has been actively promoted by successive Conservative and Labour governments since the 1980s, when extensive private wealth resulted from the expansion of global capitalism, and the Conservative administration expressed its belief that the frontiers of the state should be rolled back, allowing a greater role for private initiative, including philanthropy. The Coalition's promotion of philanthropy as part of Big Society lies directly within this tradition (also see Leat's chapter). Debate on philanthropy, however, was pre-empted by general anxiety about funding the Big Society, as discussed at the beginning of this chapter, and many responded to the reduction of the government's subsidy to the Arts Council by asking whether philanthropy would fill the funding gap for arts and culture organisations (Glynn, 2010; Youngs, BBC, 2011). Prolonged public debate led the DCMS specifically to refute any link between promoting philanthropy and spending cuts, saying that 'Nothing could be further from the truth' (Hunt, 2010). The DCMS set out an action plan to boost philanthropy in December 2010, which included a new matched funding scheme to prompt major donations and support for building new endowments for arts and culture organisations. The National Council for Voluntary Organisations (NCVO), however, also expressed a belief that the importance of philanthropy 'will proportionately increase as state funding declines' (NCVO, 2011). The extent to which philanthropic funding is likely to increase in line with rising needs and hopes, however, has not been assessed. The next section of this chapter looks at the evidence around the likely role philanthropic funding might play within the needs of Big Society.

POLICY AND THE *GIVING WHITE PAPER*

While aimed at public benefit, philanthropy is a form of private action. It presents huge opportunities to promote public benefit without government intervention but, as seen in the discussion above, may be at risk if perceived as an instrument of government policy. The Coalition's approach to philanthropy is set out principally in the *Giving White Paper* (GWP) launched in May 2011 (Cabinet Office, 2011). Its goal is ambitious, aiming to 'stimulate a step change in giving'. To achieve this, its programme of action is embedded in the behavioural economics approach, intended to 'nudge' people towards desired behaviours (Thaler and Sunstein, 2009) (see also Chapter 11). The GWP takes a different approach from other White Papers and avoids setting out an overarching government policy towards philanthropy. Its approach is largely practical, with an eclectic mix of policy amendments, new ideas and examples of innovative current practice aimed mainly at market innovation in fundraising techniques and transactions. A need for cultural change in social attitudes towards giving is also highlighted in the GWP, which introduces measures to increase public celebration and awareness of private and corporate giving. While this approach is influenced by the US model of philanthropy in which there is wide formal public acknowledgement of the role of private wealthy donors in building civic institutions, many major public buildings such as museums, art galleries, libraries, housing and baths in the UK's inner cities still bear witness to the philanthropy of the successful and wealthy entrepreneurs of the Victorian era who founded them, through their name wall plaques, statues or paintings of the donors. As with social investment, however, policy interdependence is an important feature of the Coalition's approach to philanthropy and it anticipates that increased giving will result naturally from policies to increase local community engagement, such as localism and the encouragement of local volunteering.

In particular, the GWP focuses on case studies demonstrating the principles of behavioural economics and use of new media, both of which government believes are important for generating behaviour change in relation to philanthropy. These focus largely on ways in which giving might become more integrated into daily life, in particular through the computerised electronic transactions through which most of us now handle our daily financial management such as ATMs, payrolls and card payments. Specific projects include 'round pound' schemes, which enable small gifts when paying bills in restaurants, etc., and developing an infrastructure for giving at cash machines. A further strand of policy is to remove bureaucratic and transactional barriers. In line with Cameron's claim that the major culture shift needed to build Big Society 'will not happen overnight', the GWP aims more at giving behaviours in the long term than on short-term funding gaps or targets.

Fiscal incentives remain important as a way of incentivising behaviour, though with little additional government money available, policy has been limited to small-scale changes to existing tax reliefs at top and bottom ends of the gift range. Other ideas building on previous initiatives include further financial support for a major donor advice and information infrastructure, and a commitment to a new promotional campaign for the payroll giving scheme. Its attraction is that it embodies behavioural economics in being linked into daily working life and that it has scope to extend corporate involvement in philanthropy. But the revived interest in the payroll giving scheme flies in the face of consistent evidence of low penetration and slow growth since its inception in 1988.

PHILANTHROPY AS WELFARE FUNDING

While there are clear expectations of philanthropy in Big Society, there has been little fleshing out of what this might mean in material terms. There is, for example, almost no discussion of where, when, how and how much government feasibly expects philanthropy to contribute to welfare provision. Currently, giving is approximately equal to just 2.7 per cent of government spending. In contrast, the Philanthropy Review (2011), an initiative led by donors and charities concerned with short-term fundraising targets in the current environment, sets out highly specific targets against initiatives.

The question of what philanthropy will fund is also problematic. Motivation to give results from a multiplicity of personal determinants and social influences (Walker and Sargeant quoted in Walker and Pharoah, 2002) and there is considerable evidence that private giving choices vary considerably from statutory spending priorities. Giving to the major fundraising charities, for example, is concentrated in areas such as international development, cancer, animal welfare and religious causes; while, in contrast, statutory funding prioritises arts and culture, social welfare and special needs causes alongside international development (Pharoah, 2011). About one-quarter of all corporate giving is dedicated to arts and culture, and heavily skewed to the major national institutions, while small local arts organisations are more dependent on statutory grants (Arts & Business, 2010). Local arts organisations struggle to get the corporate support that flows to the major charities.

There are few published studies of the distribution of charitable giving and philanthropy in relation to social justice, but studies in north-east England have shown that registered charities were least likely to be located in the most deprived areas, while the opposite was true for small non-registered local 'below the radar' organisations (Northern Rock Foundation, 2011). US studies have found limited evidence of redistributive effects from the non-profit sector more generally (Clotfelter, 1992; Reich, 2005). It seems that an increase in philanthropic funding along current trends would be unlikely to replace statutory funding in any like-for-like way.

Although the building of Big Society may need greater diversity in giving, there is strong evidence from research on long-term trends in donating that the donor population has increasingly narrowed towards older and wealthier donors over the last three decades (CGAP/CMPO, 2011). Participation in giving has declined steadily in all age groups except the over-60s, whose share of total giving by value grew from 24 to 35 per cent over the 30-year period. While the real value of donations amongst donors increased, lower participation rates meant that the population percentage of spending on charity did not change over that time.

Research evidence also raises questions about how far levels of philanthropy can be raised through transactional approaches. Results of a study of three decades of giving from 1978 to 2008 shows that, in spite of a number of factors such as significant change in fiscal incentives, the use of new technology and communications, and new approaches to major donors such as social investment opportunity, yet giving as a proportion of gross domestic product only increased in line with general expenditure (CGAP/CMPO, 2011). Research suggests that giving habits are generally fairly resistant to change, even in recession.

CONCLUSION: GOVERNMENT AND THE NEW FUNDING MODELS

The evidence presented above suggests that, while increased wealth appears to be linked to increased giving, philanthropic support is partisan, part of a pluralist society but not inherently pluralist. While philanthropy is a vital part of Big Society, it does not necessarily have sufficient resources and a diverse enough donor base to extend easily into meeting new needs arising from an expanding Big Society, which might include entering areas such as libraries, an early victim of statutory cuts. Local giving and philanthropy is strong in the field of health, but the extent to which locality in itself could become a stronger focus for fundraising is unknown.

The analysis of Big Society funding policy outlines the specific ways in which it is envisaged that social investment and philanthropy will increasingly rebalance support for welfare activities away from the state. Considerable policy and practice challenges remain and the timing gap between old and new models is likely to mean that the question of finance and the Big Society remains contentious.

Within funding models, the finance available for welfare activities in Big Society will increasingly be driven by private preferences and investment choices. Even if the philanthropy and social investments markets grow, there are strong indications that finance in the Big Society will play a different role from that played by state funding in the third sector. This change will be driven partly by the increasing alignment of social investment with other mainstream private rather than public sources of finance. Big Society is often treated as synonymous with the voluntary sector, but the changing funding base is likely to mean that it will develop quite differently. The research has shown where funding gaps in terms of social welfare activities will be likely to appear.

There is some evidence from the previous financial crisis of 2008 of both US and UK donors, particularly institutional donors such as charitable trusts, responding to emerging needs. Some drew on capital to maintain spending, or reviewed their spending priorities. This response was, however, focused on the immediate crisis, and on issues such as the poverty and homelessness resulting from rising unemployment and home repossessions at that time. Some trusts provided stop-gap funding for others who were unable to meet commitments because 'parent' financial services institutions had collapsed. Institutional donors, however, are generally wary of meeting gaps in government funding. In terms of the general donating public, however, there was little evidence of change in the causes supported, although subjectively fears were expressed that giving might, for example, switch from environmental or arts causes to social welfare, or from international to domestic giving. There is currently little evidence to suggest that, on current trends, philanthropy might grow in a prolonged period of economic recession because of changing perceptions of need. The research quoted above (CGAP/CMPO, 2011) suggested that giving falls in periods of recession, though at a lower rate than other types of expenditure. It picks up as we move out of recession when incomes, the main determinant of levels of giving, begin to rise again. It is difficult to predict the possible effects of a more prolonged period of global recession on people's spending priorities, and how far philanthropy might be a casualty, or might prompt more people to give, raise their giving or shift its focus.

10. Government, foundations and Big Society: will you be my friend?

Diana Leat

INTRODUCTION: PHILANTHROPY, BIG SOCIETY AND THE 'NEW GOVERNANCE'

The philanthropic world is changing. The headline news is that philanthropy is fashionable among the mega-rich, with followers including Bill Gates, Warren Buffet, Ted Turner, Oprah Winfrey and Madonna. In the context of philanthropy, there are those who want to be giving friends and then there are those who want to be taking friends. Having long been of little interest to governments in many countries, philanthropy is now reluctantly auditioning for the role of knight in shining armour riding to the rescue of cash-strapped governments. In England, for example, government has great hopes for philanthropy as evidenced in Big Society rhetoric and the *Giving White Paper*. In the US, state governments are currently going even further to access support from philanthropic foundations by creating 'philanthropy liaison' offices. In parts of Australia, meanwhile, creation of new lookalike philanthropic foundations is one of the new tools being used to raise money and channel it into public priorities.

In England, the current 'discovery', or perhaps rediscovery, of philanthropy is part of the wider Big Society project which, in turn, is arguably part of a more fundamental new governance discourse. This new discourse includes the notion that it is necessary to rethink governing, policy and administration in the light of changing social processes. Problems and solutions, so the argument goes, no longer conform to the established boundaries of policy and administration, thus requiring a change in both. The 'new governance' for the 'network society' is often linked to development of information technologies, globalisation, individualisation, and so on (Hajer and Wagenaar, 2003). In fact, however, the fluidity of responsibilities and relationships across and between sectors is nothing very new. Certainly, as the discussion below illustrates, philanthropic foundations and governments have a long and tricky relationship in various parts of the world (Anheier and Toepler, 1999). This chapter begins by examining the definition and scope of the foundation sector in the UK and then briefly looks at the policy context as it relates to foundations. The following two sections consider the theory and the practice of relationships between government and foundations; in both these sections thinking and research from the US provides some interesting and timely challenges to the somewhat woolly and cosy approaches to the role of foundations in the UK. The conclusion is that in refining the Big Society agenda of a closer relationship between government and foundations, both parties need to be reminded of the inherent differences and tensions between them.

FOUNDATIONS IN THE UK AND THE CURRENT POLICY CONTEXT

Foundations are probably one of the least understood players in the UK charity sector. Although legally there is no distinction between foundations and other charities, in practice there are important differences. First, foundations, also sometimes described as 'trusts' in the UK, differ from the majority of other registered charities in that they do not typically raise funds but rather live off the income generated by the investment of their endowment or corpus (i.e. the gift with which the foundation was created). There are some exceptions to this general rule; for example, community foundations do seek to raise new funds but their aim is to build the sort of endowment that other foundations already have. Similarly, some corporate giving programmes are referred to, or style themselves as, 'foundations' even though they lack an endowment. The estimated total number of foundations in the UK is 8800 (ACF, 2007). In 2004/5 the top 500 foundations (about which most is known) had total assets of around £33.3 billion, a total income of around £4.5 billion and made total grants of around £2.7 billion (ACF, 2007).

In the UK foundations have traditionally kept a low profile, emphasised their independence from government, and seen their roles in terms of 'risk-taking', 'innovation', and 'pump-priming' (Leat, 1999).

A second difference between foundations and the majority of registered charities is that the majority of foundations in the UK do not operate their own programmes but rather seek to achieve their goals by giving grants to other implementing organisations. Like all registered charities, foundations are required to submit annual accounts of their work to the Charity Commission (see Chapter 7 for more on the Charity Commission) but, unlike fundraising charities, foundations do not have to account to the general public and, if they choose, they can maintain a profile that borders on the invisible. In other words, they do not need 'the oxygen of publicity' in order to survive. In England and Wales, the Charity Commission has played an important role in mediating the relationship between foundations and government, and simultaneously providing government with some reassurance that foundations are properly scrutinised. Thus, unlike foundations in the US, UK foundations have led a very quiet life untroubled by the sort of scrutiny the US Congress and Senate have periodically visited on US foundations. This is because, until now, philanthropy in the UK has not been big enough to be threatening to government. But, with the advent of the Big Society agenda and public spending cuts, this is likely to change.

THE POLICY CONTEXT IN THE UK: ENCOURAGING GIVING

Whatever 'Big Society' may or may not mean, the government's desire to encourage private giving for public benefit is clear. The *Giving White Paper*, issued in May 2011, tells us that levels of giving have flatlined for years so 'government is taking action', 'introducing policies to make giving give back, cut red tape and spark innovation' (Cabinet Office, 2011). The specific recommendations contained in the White Paper, however, raise questions about how much the Coalition government really understands those they are trying to woo.

The proposed policies include: improved access to local philanthropy advice and networks; enabling donations through government websites; cashpoint giving via LINK's member banks; various tax incentives; improvements in payroll giving; and cultural change to create new norms and incentives such as linking giving to the honours system. The White Paper sends a mixed message. On the one hand, it is about giving, philanthropy and altruism; on the other hand, there is a set of messages about getting a return for money spent, which is less about giving and more about something akin to shopping.

Focusing on the narrow question of Coalition government's encouragement of giving, what are the considerations? Leaving aside the question of whether the proposed measures will work, it is important to examine the inherent tensions in the government's encouragement of giving. The government's most powerful weapon in this sphere is assumed to be the tax incentive. But tax incentives are in some ways a rather blunt instrument because, first, they cost government money in foregone revenue. Second, they are very broad in direction and may result in giving to areas of little policy relevance, such as dogs' homes, rather than drug rehabilitation schemes (also see Chapter 9). The third tension is that, where public money is directly or indirectly given, there will be demands for accountability but foundations do not generally like such rules. Indeed, foundations often seem to be more concerned with distancing themselves from government and protecting their independence than working with government. Political neutrality has traditionally been an important part of the ideology of foundations – although, in some cases, neutrality is highly selective.

For these reasons, foundations are reluctant to accept directions as to what they fund. High-end philanthropists prefer to dictate their own timetables and types of giving. They do not take kindly to direction on needs, methods, quotas or overheads. So perhaps the first message for government when cosying up to philanthropists is that they may look cuddly but they may be challenging companions who know what they want and are used to getting it. The expectation that foundations and government might engage in fairly frequent interaction is not that far-fetched. Foundations and governments share a common interest in the pursuit of public benefit. Thus, while in theory we might expect them to work closely together, in practice this tends not to be the case – at least on the surface. For this reason, in the next section, I examine the US experience.

THE US CONTEXT

While philanthropy has a long history in the US, there remain several points of tension. First, there is lingering, mutual suspicion as the US government periodically fears the power of big philanthropy and philanthropy fears government's interference (Dobkin Hall, 2006; Anheier and Toepler, 1999). As one group of Senators in the US complained:

> The tax base is being dangerously eroded by many forces, among them tax-exempt trusts and foundations ... (and) even more harmful social and political consequences may result from concentrating and holding in a few hands and in perpetuity, control over large fortunes ... (quoted in Dobkin Hall, 2006, p. 54)

But the counter-argument is that governments gain as much as they give. For example, in the US it has long been argued that:

> tax exemption is a means of preserving the strength of the private sector and insuring that our cultural and educational life is not wholly subject to the monolithic dictates of government ... The policy is based on the wise conviction that we will be better off if these activities so crucial to the core of our national life are participated in by individuals and groups with a wide range of points of view. We don't believe that Big Government has all the answers; we want a lot of people in on the act. (Gardner, 1970, pp. 215–16)

This statement, which criticises 'Big Government', might well have been written by David Cameron in the last year.

A second important tension is that endowed foundations are, as Nielsen (1972) has pointed out, strange creatures in the jungle of American democracy – like giraffes, they should not exist but they do. Endowed foundations are, in theory, independent organisations with no constituencies and no customers. They have a more or less guaranteed income and, if they choose, can exist in perpetuity almost whatever they do or fail to do, whoever they please or fail to please. In effect, as Ylvisaker (1990) has pointed out, foundations give the rich a vehicle through which they can buy influence in public affairs if they so choose. By this Ylvisaker does not simply mean that foundation founders buy kudos but rather that foundations, in effect, 'buy' influence in the public sphere through funding this topic rather than that, or starting a service and then lobbying for continued support by government. Choosing which issues to champion and which advocacy groups to fund – and not fund – is another element of foundation power. Awareness of their anomalous position in a democracy may be part of the reason that foundations tend to be fearful of government restraints on their freedom. Within the constraints of tax and charity law, and despite some further restrictions post 9/11, the US foundations have considerable freedom to fund what, when and how they choose.

In the US, the Council on Foundations has recently made it clear that, in order to be most effective, foundations have no choice but to become involved with government policy. The Council has developed a very active public policy strand and encourages its members to contribute to policy debates (www.cof. org). Similarly, Gara LaMarche at Atlantic Philanthropies (a foundation based in New York, giving grants all over the world) has argued that, given philanthropy's limited resources, the 'public option' is not an option but a necessity. LaMarche argues that foundations' arms-length relationship with government in recent years must change if foundations are to address the changes they wish to see (LaMarche, 2010).

FOUNDATIONS AND GOVERNMENT – THE THEORY

The fact that endowed foundations have no shareholders, constituents, members or customers means that they are, unlike most other organisations in society, resource independent. Interestingly, however, foundations' relationships with (applicant) non-profit organisations are more often discussed in terms of foundations' independence of the wider non-profit sector *and* their dependence on the sector. For example, Prewitt argues:

... foundations are linked to the nonprofit sector in a pattern of reciprocal dependency. It follows, from consideration of self-interest as well as more lofty motives, that foundations actively work to expand the scope of the nonprofit sector and to strengthen its functioning. Without a nonprofit sector, foundations would have too few places to spend their funds. (Prewitt, 2006, p. 357)

In other words, Prewitt suggests, just as non-profit organisations need foundations or funding, so foundations need non-profits to be their 'operators' – without grantees, foundations have no means through which to fulfil their missions.

Leave aside the accuracy of Prewitt's generalisation; there is a parallel question about how foundations see their relationship with government. Is that, too, a relationship of reciprocal dependency, or do foundations have a fundamentally different relationship with governments – which do not need them in the way that grantees do? Judging by the tendency of foundations to stress their independence of government as one of their defining characteristics, it seems unlikely that many foundations would admit to a relationship of reciprocal dependency. Is the rhetoric of 'independence' a cover for fear of entering into a relationship in which foundations would typically be the junior partner? That may indeed be part of the issue but foundations' stress on their independence has other roots. Stressing their independence gives foundations a framework to define their roles, and a means of maintaining the autonomy to do what government does not, cannot or should not do; it enables the legitimate refusal to act as a substitute for government; and it enables them to stand against government injustice (as, for example, the Rockefeller Foundation did in Nazi Germany when it helped dismissed scholars to escape).

From government's standpoint, relationships with resource-independent foundations may appear a world away from their relationships with fundraising, operating, non-profit organisations. For many fundraising, operating organisations, governments hold the keys to their financial futures. Endowed foundations not only do not need governments in the same way but they have something government itself does not have and very much wants: resources free from political constraints. Or, as Peter Goldmark, former Rockefeller Foundation President, once put it:

Foundations lack the three chastising disciplines of American life: the market test, which punishes or rewards financial performance; the ballot box through which the numbskulls can be voted out of office; and the ministrations of an irreverent press biting at your heels every day. (quoted in Arnove and Pinede 2007, p. 422)

This does not mean that foundations are free of any accountability require-ments. As discussed earlier, they are subject to the constraints of charity (and tax) law and in England and Wales the requirements of the Charity Commission to submit accounts of their work. Moreover, foundations may also be criticised by the press. Goldmark's underlying point is that none of these constraints touches a foundation's continued existence (unless the Charity Commission finds that it has behaved illegally). A tabloid newspaper, for example, can criticise a founda-tion as much as it pleases –that may be uncomfortable for the foundation but it is not career threatening. The foundation does not need public approval.

A further theoretical consideration concerns the ways in which foundations may serve certain meta functions for governments. For example, Prewitt (2006) argues not only that democracies require an enlightened public to which foun-dations contribute, but also that foundations serve liberal values in other ways. Prewitt goes on to argue that governments welcome foundations not because of what they do but because of what they represent:

> The liberal society wants public goods at the least cost to economic and political
> freedoms, and it turns to private foundations as non-coercive funders of public
> goods ... The foundation is not necessarily measured by how well it does its job
> or by whether it is redistributive or capable of bringing about important changes.
> It is welcomed because of what it represents – directing private wealth to the pro-
> vision of public goods without encroaching on political and economic freedoms.
> (Prewitt, 2006, p. 359)

In other words, the existence of foundations reassures us that minority/niche needs can be met without requiring me to contribute (via taxation) to something I do not support. But this contains within it its own tensions: government, through regulation and taxation, influences private expenditure patterns; foundations re-verse the flow of influence by spending tax-free funds on advocacy grants to *alter* government spending priorities. For example, government indirectly encourages private giving to, say, education – but a foundation may then spend some of that money attempting to change government policy or practice in education. So, if we focus on the theoretical tensions inherent in government–philanthropy inter-action there is some reason to be cautious in seeking closer relationships.

FOUNDATIONS AND GOVERNMENT: THE PRACTICE

The issue of how foundations and governments relate to each other in practice may hold the key to resolution of a fundamental tension in governance be-tween foundation autonomy and democratic accountability. What is the proper balance of autonomy and substantive accountability for the foundation sector?

Society grants unique privileges to foundations and in return requires that philanthropic wealth promote the public good. But there is a circularity in this formulation. What emerges as the 'public good' is itself the result of private deliberation. There is no effective mechanism by which various interests in society can voice their preferences for what public goods are appropriate as foundation agendas (Prewitt, 2006, p. 375). Where foundations and governments have relationships of mutual understanding and perceived benefit, does this effectively diffuse this tension?

What little we know about relationships between foundations and governments in practice suggests that relationships vary between countries and over time (Anheier and Daly, 2006; Schluter et al., 2001, pp. 268–81; Karl and Karl, 1999). Why we know so little about these relationships is an interesting question to which the answer is probably a mix of academic lack of interest in the study of foundations and foundations' reluctance to spend precious funds on 'navel-gazing'. In the US, Karl and Karl suggest that the relationship between foundations and government is a:

> functional one with a few episodes of genuine respect, periodic moments of very close cooperation both sides are quick to conceal, and a certain amount of bitter hostility, but held together by a utility that may be too profound to be acknowledged by either side. (Karl and Karl, 1999, p. 58)

However, governments' pleas for closer relationships with foundations may itself change the relationship. Writing of the Reagan years in the US, Karl and Karl note that: 'the call for philanthropy in general and the foundation world in particular to "take up the slack" has played around the relation between foundations and government like Casper the Friendly Ghost, obviously eager to be loving and sociable, but surprised at the alarm he seems to raise' (Karl and Karl, 1999, p. 66).

The reality, however, is that we know very little about day-to-day relationships between foundations and governments in this country. This may be because they rarely exist. While this may be true to a degree: (i) we know that some relationships do exist; and (ii) in this respect the past may be a poor guide to the present and future.

Much recent exploration touching on foundation–government interaction has focused on foundations and public policy, but the question of how foundations relate to government is both narrower and wider than this (see, for example, Anheier and Daly, 2006; Arnove and Pinede, 2007). It is wider in that foundations and governments may relate to each other for purposes other than policy influence. It is narrower in that government is only one of a number of potential audiences for policy influence. For example, a foundation might try to influence policy via the media, funding for research or service provision, and so on; it might also try to influence corporate or non-profit sector policies. To judge foundations' interactions with government by the time or money spent on advocacy is undoubtedly misleading.

Grantcraft recently published a piece entitled 'Working with Government' (Grantcraft, 2010). This highlights the growing interest – from both sides – in this subject, as well as some of the rationales and reservations. It identifies a range of different types of relationship, as well as some of the challenges stemming from different cultures and constraints. But the Grantcraft study is necessarily a snapshot and is limited to the US. Whether or not the findings would apply elsewhere is debatable. Anheier and Daly (2006) led a pan-European research team looking at foundations' roles in relation to government in various member states. But this study was necessarily at a high level of generality. The many questions on which further research is needed include: when, why and how do foundations relate to government, and vice versa? At what level and with whom do they relate? Do relationships vary with geography and 'industry'? What triggers or prompts relationships? What sustains relationships? What forms do relationships take? And so on. The answers very probably vary between countries as LaMarche's reflections suggest.

Reflecting on working in several countries, LaMarche illustrates some of the potential variety. In Ireland, he notes, there is little tradition of investigative journalism and few think tanks to influence policy. Civil servants are of high quality and government very centralised: 'so we form relationships with them. This has paid off in co-investments by Atlantic Philanthropies with the Irish government in youth development programs and in the appointment of key ministers to advance the concerns of older adults in both the Republic of Ireland and Northern Ireland.' In South Africa, Atlantic programs negotiate with government departments to support costs, supply services, and so on. In Vietnam the government's role is 'quite pervasive' and Atlantic has to interact quite closely with it at many levels. In the US, relationships with government, LaMarche notes, take two forms: adversarial and partnership. For example, Atlantic works with the US Labor Department to provide more 'encore' (retraining) career opportunities for older adults in New Mexico and with the city governments of Oakland (in California) and Chicago to match Atlantic's investments in integrated services for middle school students (LaMarche, 2010).

LaMarche's choice of countries to compare obviously reflects where the foundation works. But his comments are of interest here in so far as they suggest a pragmatic, context-specific, purpose-specific approach towards a degree of engagement with government. They are also interesting in suggesting that foundations may relate more closely with governments when working overseas and/or in situations where government is seen as the only/most powerful agency to get things done.

Within the UK, foundations illustrate a common, somewhat wary, arms-length relationship; but some foundations (e.g. Nuffield Foundation and the Diana Princess of Wales Memorial Fund, among others) play important convening roles, and others adopt a more adversarial quasi-lobbying role. In England, too, some community foundations play a 'government agent' role, distributing funds from government programmes. In wider Europe, relationships also take a variety of forms including convening and policy influence. In Queensland, Australia there is a further interesting development in the use of the foundation 'form' by the state government to deal with funding and creation of infrastructure projects in the mining town of Gladstone (this is part of what is arguably a growing trend for governments in various parts of the world to use foundations or foundation-like structures to deliver public benefit).

CONCLUSION

So, what might we conclude from this brief look at the theory and practice of relationships between government and philanthropy? What are the implications of the discussion for the Big Society agenda? As noted elsewhere in this volume, the Big Society agenda is difficult to nail down; but shared responsibility and closer relations between government, non-profits, philanthropy and private action are central elements. In some aspects there appears to be an assumption that foundations/philanthropy might become the core of provision in a return to a 'golden age' before the state 'stole' our sense of civic responsibility (but see Chapters 2 and 3). In considering this approach we may do well to remember two points emerging from the discussion above.

First, we should remember that the post-war welfare state was created because, valuable though philanthropy may be, it is insufficient and particularist. Philanthropy does what it wants to do, in uneven and limited quantities. In other words, philanthropy does not do equity. Second, we should not forget that philanthropy is not democratic. Thus, while foundations works in tandem and in tension with the public democratic, legislative and administrative process, it is not bound by the same structures of accountability as public donors. As Mavity and Ylvisaker suggest, philanthropic foundations carry out privately a function that is the counterpart of what is done by government:

> They listen to public opinions, identify social problems, analyze the issues, choose ways of dealing with those issues, resolve at least to their own satisfaction the competing claims of supplicants and advisers, assemble financial resources, appropriate money, and then evaluate performance. (Mavity and Ylvisaker, 1977, p. 794)

Foundations and government differ in the fact that they (foundations) intervene without having to levy taxes or get elected, they work by persuasion and not force of law, and particularly through the persuasive power of deploying their financial resources, which have the character of a gift to the beneficiaries, but they are ultimately subordinate, or at least accountable, to the public legislative process in the sense that government could (and, in some countries at some times, does) deny foundations the right to exist. Foundations are also, of course, subordinate in that they operate in a policy and legislative context dominated by government. When this comparison is made, Mavity and Ylvisaker suggest, one can immediately understand the kinship and rivalry, and the 'love–hate' relationship likely to exist between philanthropy/foundations and government. They are practitioners of the same art and each a competitor 'to keep and expand its own share of the market for social influence' (ibid., p. 800).

For all of these reasons philanthropy and government have good reason to work together for public benefit *and* equally good reason to approach friendship with caution. At times of public expenditure pressures, foundations may be additionally wary of functioning as government's: 'pain child: absorbing the anguish and blame that goes with what has to be done, trying something new when political reality rules out trying what's been tried before' (ibid., p. 831).

Finally, whether the Coalition government is really trying to become friends with foundations, or simply courting them for their money, is debatable. If friendship is the goal then it may require change and compromise on both sides. Philanthropy needs to be aware of its own strengths and weaknesses, but change is also required from government. Government needs to recognise that foundations have functions that are different from government and that they can do things that government cannot or should not. But foundations are not a substitute, supplement or back pocket. Foundations are potentially most valuable when they are free to experiment, make mistakes and stimulate debate. In order to do what they do best, foundations need to be free of performance measures, free to think the unthinkable, free to fail. At the same time, foundations need to be encouraged to learn and share that learning, and actively to communicate their learning. Governments need to listen and show serious commitment to considering ideas and practices that foundations can demonstrate are feasible and affordable routes to greater public benefit. It remains to be seen how the relationship between foundations and government will develop in the UK. With ongoing cuts in public spending, there might be an expectation that foundations will step into the gap. But, as has been argued in this chapter, given the tendency of foundations to maintain their independence and autonomy in choosing how and what to fund, even if foundations step into the gap, they are hardly a substitute for the 'public option'.

11. Can we 'nudge' citizens towards more civic action?

Liz Richardson

INTRODUCTION

At its heart, Big Society is an idea about a more civically active society. Potential roles for citizens are varied and range from individual acts of socially responsible or collectively orientated behaviour, such as recycling more and acts of compassion to neighbours, through to voluntary organisations running public services. The term civic activity encompasses many things including exchange and reciprocity between citizens, e.g. time credit and time bank schemes; charitable donations of time and money and philanthropy; mutual aid; community self-help; lobbying and campaigning; involvement in decision making; voting and standing for election; community self-management; informal and formal volunteering; and civic governance. Leaving party politics to one side, there are some social scientists who have agreed with these broad normative aims and some who are less comfortable. Many policy-focused political scientists have a commitment to the creation of a well-functioning democracy and vibrant civic life, regardless of their views on the policies of the government of the day (Crick, 1964; Stoker, 2006). If these are good goals for public policy, then the critical question is whether it is possible for sufficient civic activity to be generated and sustained, in order to meet the demands of policy-makers or, indeed, the desires of political scientists.

Taken as a whole, there are stable, long-run trends in overall volumes and levels of different sorts of civic activities in the UK and elsewhere (Richardson, 2005). Policies to increase or deepen civic activity often require governments to make policy interventions. Some interventions have not been effective; for example, from 1997 to 2008, UK central government investment in adult volunteering increased fivefold (Das-Gupta, 2008) without a corresponding five-fold increase in the number of volunteers. However, there remains a firm interest in getting citizens to participate in volunteering as well as different forms of civic action (see Chapter 12). For example, the Coalition government's ambitions for the scale of what they termed 'social action' were made clear in the launch of the *Giving White Paper*, with policymakers talking about their desire to create: 'a US-style culture of philanthropy' (Greening, 2011). Yet, it is difficult to assess whether existing levels of donating are healthy or not. For example, figures for UK giving vary from 73 per cent of the population donating within the last month in 2010 (CAF 2010a, p. 12), with the country being ranked amongst the highest in the world, to a 'more accurate' figure of 56 per cent of adults donating in 2009/10 (CAF 2010b, p. 26).

'Nudge' has emerged as a newly coined term in the ongoing search for more effective policy levers to increase civic activity. Some UK policymakers have been attracted to nudge partly because of their frustration with the limitations of the traditional tools of exhortation and legislation, particularly in an area characterised by its voluntaristic nature. This chapter describes the nudge concept and, specifically, the MINDSPACE framework, and how and if these can be used to nudge citizens towards greater civic action. The chapter discusses the concepts before examining some of the ethical and moral debates about the legitimacy of their use. It then presents the results from a series of scientific experimental trials, conducted in north-west England, to assess what happens when citizens are 'nudged' to behave in more civic ways including charitable giving and volunteering. By using evidence from the field, these experiments allow us to see what the potential and limits are of nudge-type interventions in the context of Big Society.

WHAT IS NUDGE?

The 'original' concept of nudge is most closely associated with the applied behavioural scientists Richard Thaler and Cass Sunstein (2008). In the past few years, references to the term 'nudge' have multiplied, giving it a slippery quality common to many quickly popularised and over-applied concepts. Thaler and Sunstein have subsequently refocused their work on the core underpinning principles, drawn from the work of Herbert Simon (1947) on bounded rationality. They explain nudge as being about the creation of environments, called 'choice architecture', that encourage people to make better decisions without elements of coercion. Architecture implies a choice architect, who has access to different tools and actions including: changing default settings; expecting user error; understanding mappings, giving feedback; structuring complex choices; and creating incentives. The core idea behind nudge is that human beings are not 'heroic decision makers' but that instead they use heuristics and hunches as shortcuts to making decisions. Therefore, tools to change behaviour work best when they go along with the grain of how people make choices, by assisting their heuristics in subtle ways, accepting people's selectivity in processing information, generating and weighing up options, as well as acknowledging the role of emotion and habit as constraints on true choice.

When designing and conducting the experiments described later in this chapter, we struggled to find a parsimonious solution to defining the concept in a way that could be operationalised. For example, in a thorough explication of bounded rationality, our (arguably crude) attempt to summarise what a new choice architecture might look like states: 'This is often about the provision of information, and how it may be structured or framed to achieve effects on individual behaviour' (John et al., 2011, p. 22).

The gap between theory and practice is a crucial one when nudge is used for policy purposes, as the core principles need to hang on a distinctive and deliverable framework. In our empirical work with public and voluntary sector partners, we have found that the MINDSPACE framework (Dolan et al., 2010), which is based on the core idea of bounded rationality, is an effective mnemonic that is amenable to policy thinking about how to operationalise nudge in different policy contexts. MINDSPACE was developed by a team including academics from the London School of Economics, the Institute of Government think tank and the Cabinet Office. MINDSPACE can be seen as a hybrid framework that incorporates several sets of overlapping ideas from the different debates and attempts to define nudge. MINDSPACE stands for:

Messenger: people are influenced by who communicates information.
Incentives: responses are shaped by mental shortcuts, e.g. avoiding losses.
Norms: we are strongly influenced by what others do.
Defaults: we 'go with the flow' of pre-set options.
Salience: our attention is drawn to what is novel and seems relevant to us.
Priming: our acts are often influenced by subconscious cues.
Affect: our emotional associations can powerfully shape our actions.
Commitments: people want to be consistent with their public promises, and reciprocate others' acts.
Ego: we act in ways that make us feel better about ourselves.

Nudge is not a single solution to complex and multi-faceted questions of human motivation, behaviour and social policy goals. The need for a blended approach and deliberation is also reflected in Thaler and Sunstein's work. The MINDSPACE framework includes a process model that outlines how policymakers may need to engage and debate with the public, particularly if a nudge is potentially controversial. This framework itself is set in a broader model of social change that includes context and infrastructure. Proponents of MINDSPACE argue that policy should also: enable (by removing other barriers); encourage – through including traditional tools; and, finally, exemplify by getting governments to put their money where their mouth is. Therefore, it is the MINDSPACE framework that is used in the remainder of this chapter.

MORAL AND ETHICAL DEBATES ABOUT NUDGE

Nudge has polarised opinions. Critics argue that it is an insidious, non-transparent and anti-democratic trend that risks a negative backlash from citizens, if and when they discover they are being manipulated, arguing that:

> In addition, nudge risks creating a diminished view of humans as simplistic, irrational, too busy, multi-tasking, and unwilling to participate in serious civic engagement with difficult issues underlying the behaviour(s) in question. However, despite being seen as amenable to being nudged, eventually individuals start to see through attempts to manipulate their behaviour: numerous examples of compliant game-playing abound throughout the public sector, with or without nudge. (University of Birmingham Policy Commission, 2011, p. 33)

There are perceptions that nudge strategies are necessarily covert; for example, the House of Lords Science and Technology Select Committee stated, 'Nudges prompt choices without getting people to consider their options consciously, and therefore do not include openly persuasive interventions such as media campaigns and the straightforward provision of information' (2011, p. 12). Opposition to nudge is also often premised on the idea that nudge represents a form of social engineering not seen in other, more traditional policy.

Proponents of nudge, however, argue that citizens are already instructed, exhorted, incentivised and legally obliged to behave in certain ways through traditional policy tools by central and local government, in line with their election mandates (John et al., 2010). They contend that nudge simply offers a more effective way to construct policy outcomes than legislation or taxes. Neither do they maintain that nudges necessarily suggest hidden manipulation. For example, they argue that nudging by offering citizens more transparent feedback on the results of their actions is an overt offer of an additional aid to citizen decision making. The intention of the nudger does not need to be hidden for it to be effective; many nudges require the nudgee to have the intention or desired behaviour change communicated to them. It could be the way that communications are constructed, and not the fact of communicating, that is the nudge. For example, in a campaign to reduce non-attendance at doctors' appointments, a nudge could be to change the message from stating how many other people missed their appointments, to stating how many others *did* attend.

Traditional policy tools are not always that transparent in practice, for example in many areas of legislation, taxation and regulation where there is low transparency or citizen awareness. And, in practice, many nudges are innocuous enough to suspect opponents of nudge of setting up straw men; real life examples of nudge are often things like getting people to complete tax returns on time, reduce energy consumption and stop blocking school entrances when picking up their children. Political science has explored different ways to define democratic accountability and legitimacy, one of which is that policy-makers respond to (or are seen to be in congruence with) public opinion (Miller and Stokes, 1963; Eulau and Karps, 1977, p. 234–5; Eulau, 1987, p. 171). The nudges described in this chapter, although implemented by well-meaning but unelected academics, could be seen as legitimate on this basis, as there is data showing public opinion in favour of the outcomes they tried to produce.

Apart from the criticisms listed above, there are also accusations that nudges are paternalistic, with one critic calling Richard Thaler 'a paternalist with a velvet glove' (Posner, 2009). Thaler and Sunstein are bemused by these accusations of straight paternalism and instead describe themselves as 'libertarian paternalists', arguing that this is not an oxymoronic phrase as: 'it is both possible and legitimate for private and public institutions to affect behaviour while also respecting freedom of choice' (Sunstein and Thaler, 2003, pp. 1159–202). Existing central and local government policy is designed to generate certain outcomes that are seen by the political administrations as desirable or socially beneficial. The logic that nudge is a form of social engineering, where traditional policy is not, seems like a weak line of argument because if policymakers look at changing defaults for example, a default is inevitably set in one position rather than another; there are very few wholly neutral positions. Nudge is simply a way of making policy-makers think more carefully about their implicit choice architecture.

At the core of these ethical and moral debates are questions of trust, legitimacy and accountability. More specifically, it raises questions about who decides whether and who to nudge, and towards what policy goals. These are broader issues than nudge. They are concerned with policymaking and whether it should be part of democratic and inclusive processes through which society decides how it would like to shape itself, as well as the existing levels of trust and confidence in public institutions. The empirical work described in this chapter was part of a larger programme of work, which complemented nudge strategies with what we called 'think' strategies (John et al., 2011). 'Think' strategies are deliberative processes where citizens actively engage in discussion, reflection and debate on the types of civic behaviour citizens feel are desirable, whether intervention is acceptable to create these behaviours and, if so, who should intervene and how. In 'think', differences and tensions are acknowledged, hopefully accommodated, possibly moderated or even reconciled. We present the experiments below before discussing the relevance of our findings for the Big Society agenda.

NUDGING CITIZENS TOWARDS MORE CIVIC ACTION: EVIDENCE FROM EXPERIMENTS

Moving away from the moral and ethical debates of whether or not nudges should be used, in what circumstances and to whom, we now turn to look at some technical questions of how nudge could be used to generate more civic activity as envisaged under the Big Society agenda. In doing so, we consider the effectiveness of nudges (i.e. does it work, by how much, who and what for, under what circumstances, etc.) by examining two field experiments conducted by researchers at the University of Manchester as part of the 'Re-energising the Civic' research programme, which was conducted in partnership with the University of Southampton.[1] The projects used experimental techniques including randomised controlled trials and design experiments. Experimental approaches are considered by some academics and policymakers to be the 'gold standard' of evaluation, but are relatively rare in public policy, although there are now moves by the government to use the method to assess some of its nudge policies. However, we believe that these techniques can be very useful in providing key insights to policymakers.

TURNING COMPLAINANTS INTO VOLUNTEERS

The first field experiment ran between 2008–2009, in partnership with a northwest local authority in England. It was designed to mobilise more volunteering. It focused primarily on changing the institutional **D**efault setting (D in the MINDSPACE mnemonic), but included increasing the **S**alience of volunteering opportunities in people's local areas, and in later iterations, social **N**orms. The research question was: how can a local authority, which comes into daily contact with thousands of its local residents, increase the number and range of people engaged in civic activity, and turn 'complainers' into active volunteers? The nudge intervention was that callers to the local authority customer contact centre reporting a problem or making a query were asked if they wanted to get more involved in the neighbourhood. After the query or complaint had been dealt with, citizens from those neighbourhoods who telephoned the contact centre were asked: 'We are currently promoting civic awareness in [your neighbourhood] and are looking for people to get involved in improving the area. We want to encourage people to take action on community issues in the area. Would you be interested in finding out more?' In a second iteration, for those who expressed an interest, the council would offer a creative menu of volunteering options based on individuals' skills and interests. The researchers facilitated two workshops with frontline staff on how this could be implemented and assisted in the creation of a new leaflet with a menu of existing and possible future options.

These changes were an unusual step for a local authority to take. It was a seemingly small adjustment to the contact centre script. However, this was an important nudge as it implied a fundamental shift in the institutional **D**efault setting from seeing callers as customers or service users, to seeing them also as potential citizens. The project represented an institutional redesign of the normally one-way transactional relationship between citizen and authority to a two-way reciprocal relationship.

Initial resistance and wariness from some officers in the council illustrated the significance of the shift. From the start of the research, there had been some concern from local authority staff that there would be an adverse reaction from citizens to this change of approach. In particular the contact centre managers were worried that people phoning to report problems or make complaints might be aggravated by being invited to be proactive on neighbourhood issues, or those reporting a problem with a local service would be angry at being asked to take action themselves. Members of staff were not convinced that people would welcome a change in the nature of the relationship. The research tested the assumptions about citizens' preferences and found that these concerns were not borne out by citizens' responses. The research showed that people were happy to be mobilised by public institutions and were generally supportive, with 92 per cent across both intervention and comparison groups agreeing that the council should encourage callers to get more involved.

Over two three-week periods, focused on just two neighbourhoods and two telephone lines at the contact centre, 66 people signed up.[2] There was a broad range of diversity along age, gender and ethnicity. A third of those who agreed to participate had not previously been involved in civic activity.

The nudge was in two iterations: changing the way the authority mobilised through the contact centre, with light touch follow-up using existing volunteering opportunities; then a second iteration, which also created new volunteering opportunities. The initial surge in interest, however, was not translated into activity. The fundamental initial shift in how people were dealt with at the contact centre succeeded in creating a positive citizen response. But, in the first wave, the experiment failed to capitalise on the initial expression of interest in the follow-up intervention. The menu of options offered to interested citizens was largely focused on attending public meetings or joining local community associations to help with their limited range of activities in tightly prescribed roles. There were few options that fitted people's preferences. The change in Default setting did not extend quickly enough to volunteering options. The experiment needed to go further with changing all aspects of the choice architecture and to do this more quickly.

However, the willingness and desire of the staff participating in the project was not sufficient to overcome some of the difficulties involved in designing and managing creative options for volunteers. In practice, the institution reverted to a Default setting previously hidden, which was volunteering options that suited the institution and its skill set, rather than options tailored to the citizen. Participants in the initial wave intervention were offered an arguably uninspiring menu of involvement in existing neighbourhood groups and fora – easy for the authority to understand, based on an established repertoire of engagement skills, known entities, low supervision and transaction costs. In fact, the newly engaged citizens would have preferred options that gave them a stronger voice, were more flexible, were less based on local-authority-led group activities or requiring citizens to set up new groups.

A second wave of the experiment started to correct this failure and used the things citizens said they wanted to do to develop new options, but the speed at which this happened meant that momentum was lost with the initial group recruited.

ENCOURAGING CHARITABLE DONATIONS

The second field experiment, undertaken with 12 000 households in two electoral wards in Manchester, UK, used Commitments and Ego nudges in a randomised controlled trial designed to encourage people to make a donation to a good cause. It was conducted by the same University of Manchester team, in partnership with the Community Heart voluntary organisation.[3] The main questions were: are people more or less likely to make a charitable donation if they make a pledge to do so? What happens if they are offered public recognition for doing so? We wanted to discover whether making a pledge encourages people to give because they feel they have made a promise and want to see it through. We were also interested to see whether households who are advised that their donation will be made public are encouraged to give because their generosity will be advertised to their peers. The use of a voluntary sector partner as the Messenger was critical, although this was not tested experimentally.

In the spring of 2010 a campaign was organised to collect books for use in school libraries in South Africa. One of the two wards was relatively affluent and largely made up of private housing; the other was relatively deprived, with a high proportion of social rented housing. Households were randomly assigned to one of three groups of equal size:

- a 'pledge group' which were asked to pledge;
- a 'pledge-plus-publicity group', which got the pledge and who were also told that if they donated their names would be put up in a public place;
- a 'control group' who were asked to donate in a letter, but without the pledge or the offer of publicity.

Overall, 8 per cent of households (out of a total 1000 households) donated books. While 7000 books were donated in total, the pledge campaign on its own had no statistically significant effect. That is, the 'pledge group', which consisted of asking people to make a Commitment, were not more likely to make a charitable donation, in this project. It suggests that there is still 'many a slip 'twixt cup and lip', and the intention–action gap needs additional work to be bridged. That said, the 'pledge-plus-publicity group' did achieve a statistically significant effect compared to the control group, with an effect size of 22 per cent. This was a percentage point difference of 1.6 per cent between the control group at 7.2 per cent of households donating and the pledge plus publicity group at 8.8 per cent of households donating. There were similar effects in the more and less deprived areas from different starting points, with higher levels of donations in the more affluent area as might be expected. The combination of Commitment and Ego did have a significant effect. We did not test Ego by itself, but it would be interesting to test experimentally how far civic activity could be stimulated by the simple offer of recognition or thanks for good deeds.

CONCLUSIONS

The experiments presented here show that it was possible, in these specific examples, to generate modest amounts of civic activity, or interest in civic activities, using nudges. But, as the first experiment described above demonstrated, it is difficult to change institutional Default settings and to maintain momentum. In terms of the second experiment, we found that the impacts of the campaign were modest, but positive, and generated for relatively low cost. The book donation campaign focused on a one-off activity, which also has relatively low transaction costs for the givers. While successful on a small scale, it is not clear whether this could be translated into a more intense, complex or sustained citizen contribution over a long period of time. Nudge is more likely to be most effective in specific circumstances than situations of extremely high complexity.

Yet the Big Society agenda requires sustained behaviour change and for the long term. It is not yet apparent, therefore, whether nudging has the capacity to deliver on this challenge. Big Society type activities – volunteering, regular giving to charity, giving time to run community services – require significant and sustained effort on the part of those involved and these activities are not cost free. Nudges, therefore, may be able to achieve some level of behaviour change, but in order to sustain this, repeated nudges might be required. A wide spectrum of behaviour-change approaches and policy interventions exist. The value of different approaches and interventions must be considered within specific contexts and for particular behaviours. Nudge is perhaps most useful in triggering action from pre-existing desire, as opposed to nudging people into awareness or into building a particular interest

What is striking from the two field experiments is that, where civic action involved public institutions, nudge was not only about persuading citizens to change, but it required institutions, and those acting within them, to work in a different way. In our work, even where we were able to create institutional change, this was a slow and iterative process. We found that there are many hidden institutional defaults that may act as barriers to citizens doing more. Critics of nudge are uneasy about what they see as the manipulative nature of nudge. However, it could be argued that one benefit of nudge is to make more transparent these system barriers. Some have argued that they get a deep sense in which nudge strategies grease the skids in the direction of paternalism and the undermining of democratic ideals of citizenship. It is not clear why this should be the case if the aims of a nudge intervention are in the direction that a democratically elected government has been mandated to govern, or where there are other signs of public consent, e.g. tacit consent indicated by opinion polls showing a majority in favour of promoting volunteering.

Because a healthy democracy needs to have dialogue, debate and dissension, our research not only explored nudge strategies, but also looked at think strategies. As such, nudges could be the subject of deliberation by citizens before they are chosen. However, as is widely acknowledged, there can be trade-offs between the fullest possible democracy and effective policy outcomes. Nudge should be seen within a broader governance context where policy goals are identified, deliberated and agreed through the practice of politics, however flawed this practice might be. As discussed earlier, the MINDSPACE framework indeed seeks to achieve this by examining the broader context and infrastructure.

Our experiments of specific civic activities in specific locations with particular forms of nudges do not tell the whole story. But the use of experimental methods to test out competing claims in a contested and high-profile policy area, such as Big Society, is an important scientific principle to hold onto in further debate. Nudge techniques such as MINDSPACE have the value of being based on the idea of bounded rationality, which is sympathetic to constraints on people's decision-making processes. Therefore it is worthwhile examining how these frameworks and approaches are likely to be used by UK policymakers in the context of Big Society in the years to come.

NOTES

1. This research was part of a project that ran between 2007 and 2010 called 'Rediscovering the Civic: achieving better outcomes in public policy' and was supported by the UK Economic and Social Research Council (ESRC), the Department of Communities and Local Government (DCLG) and the North West Improvement and Efficiency Partnership (NWIEP) (RES-177-25-0002).
2. Data on callers was not recorded by neighbourhood by the contact centre, and so we were unable to see what percentage of callers this represented.
3. A UK registered charity formed by anti-apartheid activist Denis Goldberg, which supports local self-help initiatives in South Africa.

12. The Big Society and volunteering: ambitions and expectations

Nick Ockenden, Matthew Hill and Joanna Stuart

INTRODUCTION

The Big Society has been variously described as 'the most important innovation in British politics for decades' (Blond, 2011), a 'fraud' (Toynbee, 2011) and a 'failed concept' (Miliband, 2011). It has been presented as a broad vision of the kind of society that Prime Minister David Cameron and his associates aspire to create in the UK. Cameron has repeatedly referred to it as his 'mission in politics' (Cameron, 2011). Taken at face value, it is expressed through a loosely grouped collection of policies that set out to achieve this vision; through social action, public service reform and community empowerment (ACEVO, 2011). Both the achievement of this vision and the implementation of its policies are connected to volunteering; some directly relate to it, many depend on it for their success, and others, while not being primarily concerned with volunteering, nonetheless have a considerable impact upon it.

Volunteering includes a wide range of activities and is defined as being given of someone's free will, unpaid and of benefit to the wider environment or other people (Home Office, 2005). This can be further categorised into formal volunteering (which takes place within a group, club or organisation) and informal volunteering (which takes place independently). The diversity encompassed within this definition – from the highly formalised and structured to the grassroots and community-based – means that there is almost no part of society untouched by volunteering. Much volunteering falls within the scope of the Big Society, but its vision also encompasses a range of activities that are not normally regarded as volunteering, including participation in civic life (for example, voting, attending protests and caring for elderly relatives).

This chapter will concentrate on two aspects of the relationship between volunteering and the Big Society: first, the level and diversity of volunteering;

second, the relationship between volunteers and paid staff in organisations. These two areas reflect the stated policy objectives of the Big Society, which include increasing participation, empowering people in new roles and expanding people's involvement in the delivery of public services. This discussion will allow us to examine what volunteering can, or should, achieve on behalf of the Big Society and more widely, and the likely impact of the Big Society on volunteering itself. In addressing these questions, this chapter draws on research undertaken by the Institute for Volunteering Research (IVR) since its formation in 1997 as well as that carried out by other organisations. Before we turn to these two areas, we will examine previous government-led attempts that were aimed at promoting and increasing levels of volunteering and civic participation to explore the extent to which the policies of the Big Society represent a new direction or a continuation of what has come before.

CONTINUITY AND CHANGE IN GOVERNMENT POLICY TOWARDS VOLUNTEERING

The current Coalition government is certainly not the first to enthusiastically encourage an increase in volunteer numbers. The Make a Difference campaign, for example, launched in 1994 under the Conservative government of John Major, has been described as 'the most ambitious and innovative programme to encourage and support volunteering before 1997 and, perhaps, since' (Rochester et al., 2010, p. 89). In spite of the ambitious nature of the programme, sufficient evidence is not available, however, to assess the impact of the Make a Difference campaign on levels of volunteering. Such enthusiasm was also seen under New Labour, who introduced a series of ambitious public service agreements to increase overall levels of volunteering. It was focused on increasing volunteering within specific hard-to-reach groups, particularly younger and older age groups.

A range of current policies under the umbrella of the Big Society similarly rely on volunteering for their achievement and represent a continued interest in encouraging this form of participation. First, the Community Organisers programme is founded on the grassroots participation of individuals in their local communities. Second, the desire to see the Civil Service become a 'civic service' is based on the promotion and uptake of employer-supported volunteering throughout central government. Third, the pilots of the National Citizen Service programme have clear targets for the number of young people to take up voluntary placements. The ambition of the Big Society to significantly increase volunteering can therefore be viewed as a continuation of previous policy rather than as something new in its own right (see Chapter 11 on government attempts to 'nudge' citizens towards more civic action including, but not limited to, volunteering).

The Coalition government is also not the first to seek greater involvement of people in public service delivery. Public services have been in the process of being 'opened up' for many years and the development of the 'contract culture' can be traced back to the 1990 National Health Service and Community Care Act (legislation.gov.uk, 1990). New Labour were seemingly just as keen to encourage the involvement of volunteers in public service delivery as are the Coalition, stating that 'if we are to realise our goal of world class public services we must ... unlock the potential of volunteers and communities across the land' (HM Treasury, 2002, p. 7).

Despite the mentioned continuities, the current approach towards volunteering does, however, also represent a significant shift away from previous administrations' policies in two ways. First, any continuity is largely overridden by the depth, breadth and rapidity of the changes that the Coalition government is attempting to implement. The *Giving White Paper* calls for a 'step change' in levels of giving time and money (Cabinet Office, 2011), while the 'Big Society Not Big Government' policy document sets out that 'we want every adult in the country to be an active member of an active neighbourhood group' (Conservative Party, 2010), an ambitious objective that, if realised, would equate to a 100 per cent rate of volunteering amongst the adult population. A further aspect of current government policy that impacts on volunteering and the environment within which it exists is the attempt to reduce public expenditure both significantly and rapidly. The reduction in the income of the voluntary and community sector alone – the sector that involves the greatest proportion of volunteers – has been estimated to be somewhere between £3.2 billion and £5.1 billion (New Philanthropy Capital, 2011). While the government has attempted to distance its deficit reduction policies from those of the Big Society (Cameron, 2010), in practice they cannot be treated separately. Indeed critics of Big Society – ranging from the trade unions to the Bishop of Oxford – have often accused the Big Society agenda as constituting a cover for the cuts in public spending (Unite the Union, 2010; Prichard, 2011).

Second, the current approach is different from previous administrations' attempts in its desire to see a state retraction underpinned by an ideological wish for the voluntary and community sector to become less directly dependent upon the state, particularly in terms of funding. For this reason, current debates in the Labour and Conservative parties illustrate a divergence in thinking. The so-called Blue Labour movement establishes Labour's strong tradition of seeing partnership with the state as the best way to achieve the 'common good' (Glasman, 2011, p. 34), while the Red Tory philosophy, as developed by Phillip Blond, argues against the welfare state and private sector monopoly, instead favouring localism and devolution of power from central government to local communities (Blond, 2009). Central to the Coalition government's current agenda is addressing the historic dominance of the state as a sole provider of public services. Cameron established his wish to see a move 'from state power to people power' (Cameron, 2010) and the *Open Services* White Paper outlined ambitions to see the role of voluntary sector organisations, social enterprises and private sector players increase. More specifically, the Localism Bill described the 'community right to challenge', in which voluntary and community sector groups have a legal right to 'express interest in taking over the running of a local service' (House of Commons, 2011). While the focus of these policies is not volunteering, they will nonetheless have a significant impact on it. Volunteers could be exposed to new roles, increased responsibility and greater accountability as they acquire and manage assets and public services. However, there is significant debate concerning the extent to which community groups will, in reality, be able to win and deliver such contracts.

LEVELS AND DIVERSITY OF VOLUNTEERING

In order to assess the appropriateness and implications of the Big Society agenda we need to look at current and historic data on the levels and diversity of volunteering (see also Chapter 6). This section will use this evidence to answer a number of key questions. Is the government's ambition to dramatically increase volunteering levels feasible? How do they plan to increase levels? Does the volunteering population match the general population and, if not, is there a danger that increasing the reliance on volunteers for public services delivery could perpetuate rather than confront inequalities of access and provision?

The best data available on national rates of volunteering are contained within the Citizenship Survey series, which ran from 2001 to 2011 (Cooper, 2010). Rates have remained remarkably stable over time; being both largely resistant to efforts to increase rates and remarkably resilient to factors that may be thought to decrease participation (such as demographic shifts or recessions). Since 2001, around 40 per cent of the adult population in England has participated in formal volunteering at least once a year, with the rate for regular formal volunteering (at least once a month) staying steady at around 25 per cent. We have generally comparable data from other previously established national surveys of volunteering reaching back to 1981, but again the rates are strikingly consistent. Data for informal volunteering tells a similar story of stability where rates for all informal volunteering are around 65 per cent and those for regular informal volunteering are around 35 per cent (although figures for informal volunteering have recently seen an unusual fall since 2007–08). These figures have come under criticism for their lack of increase (Saxton, 2009) as well as praise for their resilience (Wilson and Leach, 2011), but the consistency of the data is without dispute and suggests that attempts to increase levels of volunteering will be extremely challenging (see Chapter 13 for information on how the volunteering rates in the UK compare with other European countries).

The government has, however, proposed certain measures to encourage volunteering, including the campaign to reduce bureaucracy and red tape around volunteer involvement such as the reforming of the Vetting and Barring Scheme. It has also earmarked funding to increase participation amongst certain groups, such as an £80 million investment in Community First, and investment through programmes such as the National Citizen Service pilots and the Voluntary and Social Action Fund (Cabinet Office, 2011). However, these comparatively modestly funded measures are likely to be undermined by the severity of the public spending cuts and the amount of money being withdrawn from the voluntary and community sector. At the same time there are question marks over whether government can ever manufacture an increase in volunteering. Indeed, the National Council for Voluntary Organisations (NCVO), IVR and Involve's Pathways through Participation project found that people tended to participate independently of government and, rather than encouraging levels of involvement, official programmes and initiatives could actually act to deter people (Brodie et al., 2011). It will certainly be interesting to see whether the stability in volunteering rates continues over the next decade, although it should be stated that tracking this information will be considerably more difficult following the government's cancellation of the Citizenship Survey.

If it is unrealistic to expect levels of volunteering to increase, then perhaps the diversity of those people taking part can be broadened. Data from the Citizenship Survey, however, highlights unequal access to volunteering. Rates vary significantly depending upon gender, age, employment status, socio-economic group, education level and locality (Low et al., 2007). These differences are intensified when we look at the distribution of volunteering hours. Recent secondary analysis of the Citizenship Survey datasets has highlighted the existence of a 'civic core', revealing that as little as 8 per cent of the population gives nearly half (49 per cent) of all volunteering hours. This core is not equally distributed throughout the population; instead, as Mohan states, its members are 'more likely to live in the most prosperous areas with a steady [declining] gradient in the distribution of the core by level of deprivation' (Mohan, 2010, p. 2). As such, policies to increase the involvement of volunteers in service delivery may further compound rather than combat inequality of provision between different communities as more affluent communities have a larger pool of volunteers to draw upon. If volunteers are to be given increased power in decision-making processes, the inequality of access to volunteering could perpetuate power asymmetries within communities, with increased local power falling to the 'usual suspects'. Furthermore, if volunteers are to be given a bigger role in public service provision the 'burden' of this care may be unevenly distributed across the population. Women, for example, deliver the majority of volunteer care within society and are significantly more likely to volunteer in roles in children's education/schools and health, disability and social welfare than men (Drever, 2010).

In summary, while the survey data does not tell us about the direct impact of the Big Society's policies on volunteering – largely due to the policy's infancy – it does indicate that the Coalition's aim of dramatically increasing both the level and diversity of volunteering is unlikely to be realised and, although we know that much volunteering is unresponsive to government initiatives, the achievement of this aim is even less likely given government funding cuts to volunteering.

VOLUNTEER RELATIONSHIPS TO PAID STAFF

The Big Society's policy drive to increase volunteering in public service delivery is likely to expose increasing numbers of volunteers to new roles and new relationships with paid staff. This raises two important questions. First, how is the position and influence of volunteers in relation to paid staff changing within service-delivery organisations? Second, in cases in which volunteers are working more closely alongside paid staff, what is the impact on both groups?

Volunteers have been involved in service delivery in the public sector, predominantly through schools, hospitals and the police, for many years. It is, however, the breadth and rapidity of the changes proposed within the compass of Big Society policy that will expose ever-increasing numbers of organisations and their volunteers to new areas of work and responsibility, particularly front-line delivery roles. As organisations take on such activity, their volunteers might subsequently be expected to undertake roles that are more 'complex' and front-facing (Gaskin, 2005). In other organisations, however, a different dynamic seems to be at play. Research suggests that instead of creating new roles for volunteers, organisations may choose 'to employ paid staff to fulfil their contract obligations' (Ellis Paine et al., 2010, p.96; see also Scott and Russell, 1997). Volunteers may subsequently lose their positions within these organisations as paid staff play a more dominant role (see Chapter 4). Volunteers, in effect, can be replaced by paid staff who may be considered more 'professional' or 'reliable'. Evidence suggests that volunteers are increasingly being sidelined into more 'ancillary' and peripheral roles as paid staff take on the 'complex tasks' (Geoghegan and Powell, 2006). This kind of change is likely to become more prevalent as organisations move into new arenas such as social care and youth offending, where some organisations voice concerns about the risks of involving volunteers in front-line delivery (Gaskin, 2005; Guirguis-Younger et al., 2005).

In those cases in which volunteers do adopt new roles, they may find themselves working more closely with paid members of staff. This can lead to concerns about the boundaries between the activities performed by paid staff and those undertaken by volunteers, when it is appropriate to involve a volunteer, and what the added value of a volunteer over and above a member of paid staff is. This can be manifested through job substitution, in which volunteers directly or indirectly replace paid staff roles. Tensions between volunteers and trade unions have long been present (Sheard, 1995) and, in 1979, a working party chaired by Geoffrey Drain published guidelines to establish parameters for the appropriate involvement of volunteers (Deakin and Davis Smith, 2011). This document has recently been revised and updated as a joint publication between Volunteering England and the Trades Union Congress (TUC) (2009). Underlying tensions do, however, still exist. A study of volunteering in six NHS Trusts by IVR found that, while volunteers were reported as having a wide range of positive impacts on the Trusts, both the staff and volunteers, albeit a minority in each case, expressed concern about job substitution. Some paid staff felt, for example, that volunteers were used as cheap labour to deliver roles that should be the domain of those employed by the state or had traditionally been provided by paid staff (Teasdale, 2008).

This issue has the potential to become more commonplace as public sector bodies explore options to reduce expenditure following spending cuts. Some will inevitably consider volunteers to be a cost-saving solution. Indeed, numerous local authorities have already looked to volunteers in an attempt to keep services open: Camden Council, for instance, has used a survey to ask residents whether they would be in favour of greater volunteer involvement in libraries; Oxfordshire County Council has asked volunteers interested in running libraries to come forward; and Hampshire County Council has explored options to create new volunteer teams to keep its four museums open. Yet, as the process continues to unfold, it remains unclear what the outcomes will be and what impact it will have.

This raises questions about the nature of job substitution. In a case in which a council takes a decision to close a library or reduce its opening hours, and proactively recruits volunteers to perform the roles once carried out by paid staff, it seems a clear example of job substitution and one that will lead to conflict. In Southampton, for example, library staff went on strike on two separate occasions to protest over plans to replace paid staff with volunteers (i-volunteer, 2010). An alternative scenario could emerge under the new community rights, however, in which local residents form a group to save the library from closure and run it themselves. While the volunteers are ultimately replacing the paid staff, due to its community-led nature it is perhaps less likely to be interpreted as an undesirable situation. On the contrary, proponents of the Big Society may hail this as an example of community empowerment and local activism. It will be interesting to consider whether, in practice, the view of job substitution varies according to whether the change is led in a bottom-up way by volunteers or top-down by an organisation.

Whether appropriate or inappropriate, council-led or community-led, such examples of job substitution can nonetheless harm volunteers and volunteering. In associating volunteers with industrial disputes, even if they are acting only with the interests of the local service in mind, volunteers may be seen as behaving inappropriately or being too closely aligned with government policy. It can risk politicising volunteering and damaging its public reputation. Furthermore, as volunteers are pushed into new roles and are encouraged to take on a wider variety of activities on behalf of the state, there is also the concern that they may be perceived as being unprofessional and can even be mocked as a means to attack the policies that encourage this. The Labour Party's 2010 election video, in which a mother takes on a variety of public sector roles in the party's vision of a future society under the Coalition government, is an example of this derisory response to the increasing reliance on volunteers to take on public sector activities (Labour, 2010).

There are examples, however, which demonstrate that new delivery roles for volunteers alongside paid staff positions can be developed effectively. In 2005 the Natural History Museum's Education Volunteering Programme introduced volunteers into its galleries to perform interpretation roles alongside paid staff members. An evaluation by IVR found that tension between staff and volunteers was minimised by involving the union in continued dialogue, from the conception of the role to its implementation. The programme was observed to be a resounding success with volunteers and staff members working effectively alongside one another (Ockenden and Machin, 2008).

The Coalition government's desire to see more volunteers and voluntary and community sector organisations involved in public service delivery has the potential to move volunteers into new, stimulating and productive roles. However, it may also exclude volunteers from positions of influence as responsibility shifts towards paid staff, who may effectively act to replace volunteers. It is also possible for volunteers to replace paid staff. Job substitution can risk inflaming historic tensions, damaging volunteering as a concept and creating a negative experience for those involved, thereby undermining one of the central policies of the Big Society.

EMERGENT CONCLUSIONS

We began the chapter by asking to what extent volunteering can, and should, contribute to the achievement of the Big Society's vision and the policy objectives associated with it, and what impact the Big Society will have on volunteering.

First, if we consider the contribution of volunteering to the Big Society, it is clear that volunteers are critical to much of its vision and its policies will not be achieved without their involvement. As a result, volunteers are likely to become more involved in the delivery of public services but, as we have illustrated, they will not automatically fill the gap left by a retreating state. Evidence of stagnant rates of volunteering suggest that the government's aims to dramatically increase volunteering are, at best, overly ambitious. Even if rates were to rise, we could see an exacerbation rather than an amelioration of current inequalities amongst those who volunteer. In other words, despite efforts to encourage volunteering from all groups and communities, current policies may further compound rather than combat inequality of provision between different communities, as more affluent communities have a larger pool of volunteers to draw upon.

Second, if we turn to consider the impact of the Big Society on volunteering, it is clear that the increased publicity around the Big Society has pushed volunteering ever higher up the public agenda and considerably raised its profile. Funding has also been invested in volunteering under the umbrella of the Big Society, although it does not match the vast sums that have been withdrawn from the voluntary and community sector through the austerity measures. Volunteers and their organisations are also experiencing new opportunities for involvement, particularly around public service delivery. Some of this is to be welcomed, but the threat of job substitution and the sidelining of volunteers are likely to have negative effects on the volunteers and their organisations.

Perhaps too much has been placed at the door of volunteering in recent years. Volunteering has the potential to change lives and frequently does, but it is not a panacea for all of society's ills. Volunteering rates also remain largely unresponsive to government initiatives. But it does need to be supported. In practice, the funding cuts, a policy that the government has consistently insisted is distinct in its own right, is likely to have a far more pervasive impact on volunteering than will Cameron's vision of the Big Society.

13. European perspectives on the Big Society agenda

Markus Ketola

It's the spirit of activism, dynamism, people taking the initiative, working together to get things done. (Cameron 2010a)

From state power to people power. From big government to the big society. I
will work with others to give Britain a brand new start. (Cameron 2010b)

INTRODUCTION

Whichever way you look at it, volunteerism is a central part of David Cameron's Big Society agenda. It speaks of a 'new culture of volunteering' that
stems from action in the areas of community empowerment, redistribution of
power, social action and public service reform. Volunteering is part of the ideological impetus behind the government agenda where free markets, charities
and volunteers come together to complete the bigger picture of what constitutes
modern conservatism. Therefore, the success of Big Society depends largely on
the capacity of citizens to volunteer and participate actively in their communities, and the proponents of Big Society tend to characterize this focus on volunteering as a radical culture change for Britain. Depicting the issue like this
paves the way for an argument that suggests change is necessary because the
current culture of volunteering is lacking either in quantity or quality, or both.
In addition the problem is framed in a way that blames big government for the
dearth of volunteerism. The argument proceeds, therefore, that the Big Society
agenda with its emphasis on small government is perfectly placed to provide
the required remedy.

But is either of the above arguments at all plausible or evidence-based? Is
there indeed a crisis of volunteering in Britain, and is big government the cause
of this? One way to explore this question further is by comparing the UK case

with those of its continental cousins in order to determine how it fares in relative terms.

First, the chapter lays out the argument that David Cameron has made in support of Big Society, pointing out the central role volunteerism plays. The sections that follow compare the British case with European perspectives on volunteerism and shows that, in comparative terms, the UK has a relatively healthy tradition of volunteerism. Furthermore, the evidence from elsewhere in Europe suggests that levels of volunteerism tend to be positively correlated with the size of government. There is a strong case for taking a more nuanced approach to the discussion about Big Society and I end on some further questions for the Coalition government to consider as it moves forward with the Big Society agenda.

BIG SOCIETY AND VOLUNTEERING

> Far more may be done by entrusting to the citizens the administration of minor affairs ... Local freedom, then, which leads a great number of citizens to value the affection of their neighbours and of their kindred, perpetually brings men together and forces them to help one another in spite of the propensities that sever them. (de Tocqueville 1835 [1998], p. 212)

The concept of active citizenship, of which volunteering is a major part, is at the centre of an important debate regarding the nature of participatory democracy in modern societies (Boje, 2010). Alexis de Tocqueville's 1835 book, *Democracy in America*, continues to have a profound impact on how we think about the relationship between volunteerism and democracy today. He saw volunteerism as the 'social glue' that binds a society together, protecting it from the harmful impact of individualism and materialism, and concluding that it was the American enthusiasm for association that explained its strong democratic foundations. In the past two decades the work of the American sociologist Robert Putnam has done much to revive and popularize this style of reasoning. Tracking the volunteering trends of Americans through a number of surveys, Putnam shows the gradual decline in the number of citizens choosing to participate in a range of voluntary activities. Although the title of the book, *Bowling Alone*, is derived from the finding that people no longer join bowling leagues but choose to bowl alone, the research shows a decline in voluntary activities across the board, including volunteering. In so doing, Putnam argues, they forgo the benefits that membership in groups such as bowling leagues engenders. Since the civic skills required by participation in such activities 'inculcates democratic habits', as Putnam puts it, the diminished interest in volunteering by American citizens in turn dilutes the social glue of the society (Putnam, 2000). The act of volunteering in a local library is of course not the same thing as joining a bowling league, but in many ways Putnam's research and the Big Society rhetoric want to make the same point: it is the quality of our civic community that determines the quality of our democracy. Putnam's framing of the decline in participation and the likely social consequences is indicative of the type of concerns that underlie the Big Society agenda.

However, in explaining the decline in participation, Putnam was keen to emphasize generational differences. In other words, the differences in levels of volunteering could not be explained purely by structural factors, such as levels of education, for the elder generation with fewer educational opportunities show higher levels of volunteerism. More recent research in this area, however, challenges this conclusion by explaining such generational differences in terms of changing interests. What emerges is a shift from traditional forms of volunteering in the provision of services to more work-oriented and political groups (Rotolo and Wilson, 2004) (see Chapter 6 for other challenges). It is not completely without credit, therefore, to claim that the Big Society agenda can tap into the changing interests of volunteers and in this way makes a valuable contribution. Yet we need to be careful how far we take such claims.

For David Cameron, Big Society is about a culture change, even a paradigm shift in the way people take responsibility over affairs in their community. Instead of asking the state to change things for them, individuals are encouraged to find the answers to their problems and to help themselves and the communities they live in. On the one hand the Big Society agenda is about devolution, and goes hand in hand with the Coalition government's public reform programme, aiming at the 'redistribution of power away from the central state to local communities' (Cameron, 2010c). On the other hand, alongside this shift in power comes a shift in responsibility from the state to local communities as Cameron aspires to build 'a society where the leading force for progress is social responsibility, not state control' (Cameron, 2010d). Policies in support of these ideas include, for example, the promise to train a 'neighbourhood army' of 5000 full-time professional community organizers[1] to guide the work of volunteers, and plans to launch a national 'Big Society Day' to celebrate the work of community volunteers and to further encourage volunteering (Cameron, 2010e). Indeed, much about Big Society is about volunteering.

The rationale for these policies and for the underlying political rhetoric is one of 'mending a broken society' (Cameron, 2010c). The very choice of the words 'Big Society' offers a vivid counterpoint to 'Big Government', which is – according to what David Cameron and the Big Society proponents argue – what the previous Labour government came to represent in its latter days. Big Society has been the perfect rhetorical device to characterize the move away from high-spending and state-oriented policies that flourished under the reign of New Labour. It is an alternative vision, where the state ought to spend less and focus its efforts on unleashing the energy for volunteering, which, proponents of Big Society argue, has been so far stifled by overzealous central and local government.

The Localism Bill is the most concrete effort so far to realize the Big Society agenda in practice and yields a useful point of reference because it puts the attractive political rhetoric on one side and gives a good indication of the kind of action the government wants to take. It presents the process of decentralization as six practical steps that need to be taken in order to achieve 'a radical shift of power from the centralised state to local communities' (Department for Communities and Local Government, 2010, p. 2). The first two steps aim to lift the burden of bureaucracy and to empower communities to do things their own way. Not surprisingly, they are regarded as the most important steps as they support the key objectives behind the Big Society rationale. The next two actions focus on resources by pledging to increase local control of public finance and diversifying the availability of choice in the supply of public services. The final two goals speak to democratization in their attention to opening up government to public scrutiny by publishing more information on government spending and by strengthening accountability to local people, centring on an intention to give power away by sharing more information and decision-making muscle. These six action points raise some big questions. Where does local government fit in (see Chapter 2 specfically on this)? Is it at the heart of the Localism Bill as the actions on reduced bureaucracy and increased local empowerment suggest? Or is it something to be bypassed, as the strengthened accountability to local people suggests? Moreover, is it realistic or advisable to pass responsibilities to unelected, legally unaccountable volunteers who may well lack relevant professional knowledge to fill the gap as services are rolled back? What implications does this have for democratic legitimacy and accountability behind local level policymaking and service delivery?

The reasoning that puts volunteering to the centre of the Big Society agenda goes something like this: the UK is currently witnessing a broken society that could be mended by local social activists, but which has yet to happen because of the straitjacket of local government regulation. Furthermore, proponents of the Big Society agenda contend that it was the big government of the New Labour years that individualized society by taking over the running of local affairs and pushing local communities aside in the process. In this context Big Society is treated like an instruction manual for (re)discovering the community spirit, a guide to teaching us how to live together and to engage with each other. It is therefore necessary to move away from big government and to devolve power to neighbourhoods in order to release the resource of local volunteering. The rationale behind the current policy drive neatly links together the critiques of big state and lack of volunteering on one side and reduced government spending (reducing the size of government) and increased volunteerism on the other side of the argument.

However, the total amounts governments spend on welfare, or the size of government, tell us relatively little about the deeper workings of a welfare state. During Margaret Thatcher's Conservative government, welfare spending in fact rose, but this was due almost purely to increased unemployment. In similar fashion, the equation between big government and Big Society is not quite as neat as the one Cameron has put forward. A comparison of a range of European examples allows us to examine the particular mix of political, social and economic arrangements as an explanation for any given system of welfare and also to think about the reasons for differences. This exercise will also yield a better idea about how volunteering in the UK fares in comparative terms.

EUROPEAN PERSPECTIVES

Esping-Andersen, the Danish economist and sociologist, proposed that there are three discrete types of welfare regime that offer a useful framework in making comparisons between European welfare states (Esping-Andersen, 1990). Instead of looking at the size of the welfare state in terms of spending, his point of departure was 'decommodification' – the degree to which welfare services are provided as a matter of right, enabling each citizen to make a living without dependence on the market. Esping-Andersen proposed three ideal types.

1   The *liberal welfare regime* is characterized by low decommodification, offering means-tested discretionary welfare with strict entitlement rules that aim at a subsistence minimum. The system values high work ethic, and benefits tend to be stigmatized. It is common in the Anglo-Saxon countries including the UK.
2   The *corporatist regime* is considered of medium decommodification, being based on industrial achievement and private insurance with state support. Welfare rights are distributed more widely but in a way that preserves existing distinctions of class and status. This arrangement is found largely in continental Europe, epitomized by Germany.
3   Finally the *social democratic regime* represents a high degree of decommodification as it aspires to universal solidarity and equality amongst citizens. The state is the first line of support for all. This regime is best suited to describe the systems in place in Scandinavian countries, such as Sweden. With each regime, the level of welfare provision also increases, leaving social democratic regimes with the largest governments.

Although Esping-Andersen's analysis did not extend to the case of civil society, other researchers have shown that it is a useful way of thinking about civil society and volunteering as well. In the slipstream of the welfare regimes' model, Salamon and Anheier (1998) have developed a theory of the social origins of civil society. Alluding to the three regimes, and the varied levels of government spending on welfare, they propose:

1   A *liberal model* that reflects low government spending, large voluntary sector and high levels of volunteering.
2   A *corporatist model* that describes states where high government spending on welfare is largely invested in voluntary sector organizations, again encouraging volunteerism.
3   The *social democratic model* that refers to systems where social welfare is delivered extensively by the state and pushes out most voluntary organizations that would otherwise be involved in service delivery. However, despite a limited role in service delivery, voluntary organizations and volunteering can still have an active role elsewhere, leading to reasonably high overall levels of voluntary activism also in social democratic regimes.

This leads us to consider an important underlying point about these models: the importance of the social origins of each system in determining the final mixture of roles assigned to public, private and voluntary sector in a given society.

Esping-Andersen's analysis shows that judging the character of a welfare system simply in terms of the level of spending or size of government is a rather simplistic way to determine the benefits and shortcomings of a given system. The characteristics are firmly embedded in the existing social, political and economic arrangements, and this is where the characteristics of a civil society, or in our case Big Society, originate. Consequently, as Salamon and Anheier have argued, civil society organizations are not rootless but draw on – and depend on – the existing historical tradition of state–civil society relations, and volunteerism is part and parcel of this same gradual evolution. The extent to which volunteering can be turned into a short-term policy initiative is therefore questionable. The welfare regimes model gives us a way to make sense of the broad differences among European welfare systems and enables us to make more informed comparisons between the different types of European countries. Most importantly, the model gives us a way to think about the claims behind Big Society through a broader, European lens and in so doing, to think more critically about the assumptions underlining it. Therefore, when we look at the Cameron-led agenda on Big Society from this broader perspective, its dichotomies present a misleadingly black-and-white picture that depicts the balance between big government and Big Society as a zero-sum tussle, ignoring the deeper social and political characteristics that make up a given political system and its history.

WHO VOLUNTEERS?

Volunteerism, according to David Cameron, offers a remedy to the ailments of Britain's broken society. If this correlation holds true, we can also assume that lack of volunteerism is at least in part to blame for it being broken in the first place. So what can extant comparative research tells us about the state of volunteerism in Britain? One recent study compared the levels of volunteering across six European countries – Belgium, Ireland, the Netherlands, Sweden, Germany and the UK. This research presents the UK with the third highest overall levels of volunteering among the six countries studied, topped only by Netherlands and Sweden (Grassman and Svedberg, 2007, pp. 138–9). Although these findings are limited to the six countries studied, Sweden and the Netherlands are often regarded as the two countries with the highest levels of volunteering anywhere in Europe. Moreover, when the overall level of volunteering is broken down to its constituent parts, the UK boasts the highest levels of volunteering in the area of 'social care and welfare'. Not bad for a country with a broken society due to its supposedly nanny state and big government.

Other studies seem to corroborate these findings. A comparison of 15 developed countries (14 from Europe and the US) found the UK to have consistently high levels of volunteerism when compared against a range of factors, ranking consistently in the top four in the group of countries investigated (Sivesind, 2008). Another example can be found in the 2004 Eurobarometer survey that asked the following question regarding volunteerism: 'do you currently participate actively or do voluntary work?' The responses show that 33 per cent of UK citizens participate in formal volunteering, compared with, for example, 50 per cent in Sweden and 35 per cent in Germany and Denmark (European Commission, 2005). Whilst the UK does not top the league tables, neither does this suggest that there is a crisis of volunteering that needs the government's immediate attention. In fact, the survey respondents were asked a second question about volunteering as well: 'how important is voluntary work to your life?' Of the UK respondents, 51 per cent replied 'important' compared with 70 per cent in Sweden and 42 per cent in Germany. In other words, whilst the UK has slightly fewer volunteers than Germany, the volunteers in Britain are likely to be more committed to the voluntary work they do.

What is also extremely interesting, in addition to the UK's high ranking in these comparisons, is the discovery that Sweden comes out as the runaway winner. This raises an interesting point about the size of the state and the impact this has on volunteering. The above statistics already go a long way to illustrating this point. Instead of discouraging volunteerism, as Cameron argues, countries with high public welfare costs are able to encourage volunteerism (Sivesind, 2008). In fact, the Swedish case shows that high welfare spending costs per citizen are correlated with high levels of volunteerism. There is simply no empirical basis to suggest that a large public sector undermines civil society or volunteerism, or the Swedish case at least provides no such proof (Grassman and Svedberg, 2007). The struggle between state and society does not have to be seen as a zero-sum game where a strong state undermines popular initiative and a large public sector stifles the spirit of activism.

In explaining these comparative differences in outcomes it makes a lot of sense to look into the incentive structures that are in place in countries with different experiences of volunteerism. This is an important point to make because it illustrates how volunteering in societies with the highest participation rates is built around long-term financial incentives. As Matthew Hilton argues in Chapter 6, the UK public have chosen to trust professionally run charities to act on their behalf, distancing themselves from an active membership in these organizations. In the Swedish case voluntary organizations draw more on a tradition of popular mass movements

The Swedish and UK voluntary sectors are different in character. Where the Swedish sector is almost entirely member-based, in the UK the sector is best described as service-based (Lundström and Svedberg, 2003). The high levels of volunteerism in the UK can be largely explained through indirect incentives in the form of tax breaks for voluntary organizations (such as GiftAid), and through direct incentives that have witnessed the support of charities and non-profit organizations in providing welfare services. In the 1960s, disillusionment with state-provided public services grew and led to an increase in volunteering and in the number of charitable organizations. From the late 1970s onward, successive governments have encouraged volunteering and the voluntary sector as a cheaper and supposedly more effective alternative to state provision of services (European Commission, 2010a). In contrast, the Swedish voluntary sector supports volunteerism through direct financial support in the form of government subsidies for membership-based associations (Trägårdh, 2010) and tax breaks are available to a comparatively small subset of voluntary organizations. In this way the Swedish state deliberately supports a form of associational activity that reflects the democratic model present elsewhere in Swedish society, in the sense that voluntary activities are not purely focused on service provision or other 'output' activities, but also involve participation in the internal political decision-making processes of the organizations (European Commission, 2010b). Participation in civil society means more or less the same as being a member of an organization, illustrated by the fact that 85 per cent of those who volunteer for an organization in Sweden are at the same time members of that same organization (Lundström and Svedberg, 2003).

The different long-term incentive structures in Sweden and the UK have led to the development of very different paths to volunteering and participation in voluntary organizations. The current efforts in the UK, however, are premised on the idea that it is possible to generate volunteerism simply by providing the space (through reduced bureaucracy) and opportunity (through increased local responsibility). In practice the uptake of volunteering opportunities is going to depend on the long-term structures that are in place to motivate the organizers who commit their time to running the voluntary activities. Is it realistic to assume that, by unshackling Big Society from the putative bureaucratic burden imposed by big government and offering opportunities for volunteering, that new community volunteers will flock to fill the space made available to them? Furthermore, can we see this leading to a long-term commitment to volunteerism that amounts to a culture shift?

The conclusions that can be drawn from these comparisons are far from irrefutable. It would be naïve to suggest that the experiences of Sweden or Germany are replicable in their entirety in the UK context. Yet the examples from elsewhere in Europe do draw into question the crisis rhetoric that propels the Big Society agenda: the levels of volunteering suggest that the UK does rather well, leading Europe in social care and welfare volunteering. To me that sounds far from broken, and suggests that it is important to engage in a much more nuanced debate regarding any future policy agendas that may spin out of the idea of Big Society. For example, recent research suggests that there is a 'civic core' of volunteers in the UK whose efforts account for a significant proportion of voluntary work. These volunteers are primarily middle-aged, highly educated and live in the more prosperous areas of the country (Mohan, 2011), leading us to question how consistent volunteering levels are across regions and socio-economic groups. The assumption that there is an untapped, latent supply of volunteers that needs merely to be unleashed by government policy should therefore be unpacked further (for more on this, see Chapter 12).

CONCLUSION

The aim of liberating volunteers from regulatory restrictions and, in so doing, facilitating the growth of volunteering is commendable, and the debate about the role of civil society that Cameron's Big Society interest has generated is a very welcome breath of fresh air. However, a clearer and more nuanced picture of the issues is needed before solutions are offered. The current levels of volunteering in the UK, when compared against other European states, are encouraging. At the same time, the European countries that deliver the highest levels of volunteering are the Scandinavian social democratic welfare regimes with a large public sector and 'big governments'. This suggests that the choice between a Big Society and big government does not need to be as black and white as Cameron suggests. The 'problem' is not as clear cut as it seems to him.

Public involvement in the voluntary sector has remained fairly constant in the UK over the past 50 years (Hall, 2002) and, more recently, there has been consistent growth in the size of the sector (Moro and McKay, 2010). Should we also be asking more questions about the central role given to volunteering? This is not to devalue volunteering in any way, but to say that perhaps the UK is closer to a saturation point in terms of volunteering than the Big Society agenda suggests. The quotidian demands of commuting, work and childcare are taking up an increasing portion of the day, leaving little if any time spare for volunteering. Do we really know what the motivators for community actors are? These tend to be poorly understood (McCabe, 2011) and it seems that the Big Society agenda is missing an opportunity when it sidesteps this need to think more carefully about what motivates local action, instead relying on persuasive rhetoric.

Perhaps more questions should be asked about the appropriate partners for realizing the Big Society agenda. Dismissing the role of local government as a mere financial drain and something that is to be replaced by Big Society activism is unhelpful and potentially leaves out a critical link in the long-term success of the agenda (see also Chapter 2). There is also a danger that the good work currently being done by civil society organizations becomes cannon fodder in an ideological battle that aims to redraw the boundaries between public and private sector in the UK.

At its simplest, the argument is about democracy and democratization. Big Society, as the actions prescribed in the Localism Bill illustrate, interprets the health of society in a particular way that emphasizes the role of local, unelected volunteers. If this shift in responsibility from local government to local volunteers effectively removes the ballot box from local politics and policymaking, we need to consider the implications of this on local democracy.

NOTE

1. However, since the initial plan to train 5000 full-time professional community organizers the policy has been significantly watered down: to training up to 500 senior organizers who will receive bursaries of £20000 in the first year. An additional 4500 part-time and voluntary organizers will be trained. See http://www.cabinetoffice.gov.uk/news/government-names-new-partner-deliver-community-organisers.

14. From 'shock therapy' to Big Society: lessons from the post-socialist transitions

Armine Ishkanian

INTRODUCTION

A report titled *International examples of Big Society initiatives* published in January 2011 by the Office for Civil Society, Cabinet Office presents examples of 'how Big Society is already at work around the world' in order to 'provide inspiration' for UK policymakers (Riegert, 2011, p. 5). Among the examples cited is the Grameen Bank and its microcredit programmes in Bangladesh. Although the report's author, Arnaud Riegert, recognises that 'the impact of microcredit is still quite controversial', he nevertheless argues there is evidence that with the aid of microcredit, women in poor communities in Bangladesh are working 'without depending on usurers' (Riegert, 2011, p. 23). Whether this work the women are engaging in – or indeed their access to microcredit – is pulling them out of poverty or empowering them in any way is left unanswered but it represents the dominant narrative, which valorises microcredit, portraying it as a panacea for the problems of poverty and underdevelopment worldwide. Since the 1997 Microcredit Summit in Washington DC, enthusiasm for microcredit as a universally applicable poverty alleviation has led to its introduction across the globe. Enthusiasts, Ruth Pearson argues, have pointed to the example of Grameen Bank's microcredit programme in Bangladesh and urged other countries to follow suit as a means for diminishing the need for dependence on national and federal welfare systems (Pearson, 2000, p. 153). In spite of this enthusiasm, problems remain in theory and application of microcredit programmes. With reference to the Grameen Bank, a number of scholars have queried and critiqued the effectiveness of microcredit as a poverty alleviation and empowerment strategy (Goetz and Sen Gupta, 1996; Hashemi et al., 1996; Kabeer, 2001, 2005).

Although the link between microcredit and poverty alleviation is hotly contested, the Bangladesh example is very popular among Big Society advocates (Clark, 2010; Power, 2011; Riegert, 2011). In his speech to Parliament titled 'Growing the Big Society', the Minister for Decentralisation, Greg Clark, also cites the Grameen Bank as an example of 'a really good idea, one that could make a much wider impact'. He says,

> If this approach [microcredit] can work in Bangladesh, it can certainly work in Britain. Enjoying, as we do, the full benefits of the information age, there is every opportunity for good ideas to spread quickly. All the more so, when decentralisation is combined with government transparency and access to social finance. (Clark, 2010)

The above examples raise several important issues, which I discuss in this chapter. First, while I agree that examining the experience of communities and organisations in other countries is useful, I am very concerned by the fact that only one side of the story is being presented by Big Society advocates. I believe we must examine failures alongside reputed successes if we intend to draw useful lessons from international experiences. In the case of microcredit, not only, as I have stated above, is there much debate whether it has worked in Bangladesh, but there is also clear evidence that it has not worked in Britain. For instance, as Ruth Pearson explains, the Full Circle microcredit programme implemented in Norfolk failed to achieve its aims because it did not take into account that most of the women they were working with were decidedly risk averse, highly dependent on the benefit system and saw the traditional microcredit model of trading in home produced goods as alien and suspect (Pearson, 2000).

Second, in the neo-liberalist rhetoric of Big Society, there is a tendency to valorise non-governmental activism and initiatives as a form of empowerment. But, some critics argue, it becomes instead a safety net for those made vulnerable by the rollback of public services (Robinson and White, 1997b; Wood, 1997). For instance, another of the examples Riegert cites in his report is the Çigdemim neighbourhood association in Turkey. He identifies the work of this association, which he states has included building sidewalks, providing electricity, collecting litter and running a library, as an example of community organising in the 'spirit of the Big Society' (Riegert, 2011, p. 12). One wonders, though, whether this work of building sidewalks and collecting litter was done as Riegert suggests in the 'spirit of Big Society', or out of sheer necessity and in the face of governmental neglect.

Indeed, Riegert presents the aims of this association as intended to 'improve the quality of life in a neighbourhood without any public funding and encourage volunteering in the community'. He describes how the story begins when the 'neighbourhood is facing major lacks in infrastructure (community centres and green space mostly) and the *muhtar* requires the help of residents of the neighbourhood'. The muhtar, he claims, is an 'informal neighbourhood leader'. This is inaccurate and misleading; *muhtars*, or *mukhtars* as they are also known, are in fact *formally elected* heads of local government (i.e. representatives of the state) (ProZ, 2011). Second, Riegert presents the work of the association as involving quite a bit of infrastructure development including 'building sidewalks or providing electricity to some areas'. Upon further investigation of the Turkish language version of the Çigdemim neighbourhood association's website, one gets a different picture of the association.

According to the Turkish language website (http://www.cigdemim.org.tr/),[1] the members of the association tend to come together to sing songs, play musical instruments, organise visits to places of interest and other similar cultural activities. As for their relationship with the *muhtar*, it tends to be one in which the association presents or advocates its interests to the *muhtar* and in association to the larger local authority. A case in point is their work to stop the building of mobile phone masts in their neighbourhood. There is a big difference between people coming together to sing songs versus building sidewalks. It is highly misleading to lump all these activities together and to claim, as Riegert does, that 'all costs are covered by the residents themselves, through donations in money, materials or time. Local businesses are also involved financially. The association doesn't require any public funding.' While the association may not 'require any public funding' to organise a sing-along, there is no evidence on the association's website to suggest that they are building sidewalks or providing electricity with monies collected from individual members.

Leaving aside for the moment these inaccuracies and accepting Riegert's claim that this association is an example of empowered community-based organising, I agree that community-based self-organising can be empowering and rewarding. However, as I discuss in this chapter, there are also instances and issues where the curtailment or withdrawal of state services and support can have negative community consequences, particularly for deprived neighbourhoods and vulnerable groups. In this chapter, I examine the impact of neo-liberal reforms, often referred to as 'shock therapy', which were implemented with deliberate rapidity in the former socialist countries of Eastern Europe and the former Soviet Union in the 1990s (Wedel, 1998; Marangos, 2002). Idealistically, and apparently naïve of any historical understanding of the time required for cultural change on the scale proposed, American and European donors expected the reforms to be implemented rapidly, effectively and for the 'transition'[2] to take no more than five years (Wedel, 1998, p. 22). Twenty years on, however, donors including the European Bank for Reconstruction and Development (EBRD) continue to speak about the ongoing 'transition' (EBRD, 2011). There is now also public recognition that neo-liberal 'shock therapy' policies left much suffering in their wake (Townsend, 2002; Dudwick et al., 2003; Stiglitz, 2003).

Following a broad-based discussion about the impact of 'shock therapy', I focus on one specific area of social welfare: domestic violence. Drawing on my research on domestic violence in Armenia, I demonstrate the danger of neo-liberal reforms and cuts in public spending in this area for the UK. This issue is particularly relevant to the UK because, as I discuss later in this chapter, many charities in the UK addressing the problems of domestic violence have lost much of their government funding under the Coalition's deficit reduction programme and are subsequently having to curtail or close their programmes. Although the logic of Big Society is that volunteers or communities will or should step up to fill the gap, as the chief executive of one London charity says, 'Domestic violence victims don't go and storm the local town hall to demand more help; rape victims don't go to the local paper to complain that there isn't a good service for them. They are invisible.' (Gentleman, 2011)

Of course, the UK of today is not at the same starting point as the socialist countries in 1990. It has a strong national health system and a functioning system of social housing and unemployment and incapacity benefits. Yet the institutions of the welfare state (i.e. the statutory bodies that provide protection to citizens against major economic risks in the areas of old age, sickness, unemployment, poverty, etc.) are slowly being chipped away, dismantled and privatised. This process began under Margaret Thatcher, continued under New Labour and is intensifying under the current Coalition government. There is real danger that the current cuts will adversely affect groups in society that are already at risk including, for instance, domestic violence victims, which I discuss later in this chapter. Additionally, the assumption that communities in areas that are already suffering from levels of high deprivation, inequality and social exclusion will somehow step in and begin fending for themselves is not supported by existing evidence. Moreover, the argument made by some Big Society proponents that 'families, friends, and communities' take a more active role in addressing problems (Brown, 2010) also does not work in this instance because the family and sometimes the community (in the case of honour crimes or female genital cutting) are the sites where women encounter violence and repression.

SHOCK THERAPY: NEO-LIBERAL INSPIRED MODELS OF TRANSITION AND DEVELOPMENT

Beginning in the 1980s the welfare state came under intense and sustained attack, from neo-liberal policymakers and donor institutions such as the International Monetary Fund (IMF) and the World Bank, as one of the sources of economic failure and an obstacle to development. Government was characterised as inefficient, hampered by bureaucracy and in thrall to self-interested politicians (Robinson, 1997a, p. 61). Neo-liberal policies in the form of structural adjustment programmes (SAPs) were embraced by development agencies and international donors. In developing countries, these SAPs led to cuts in social investment and spending, the privatisation of social welfare programmes, the downsizing of the public sector and the abandonment of social planning as an integral part of policymaking. It was believed that the public sector's inflated bureaucracies and inefficiencies would be corrected through greater involvement of non-state actors – such as non-governmental organisations (NGOs) and private companies – in social service delivery, bringing greater efficiency, competition and improved services to beneficiaries. However, after two decades of these policies there is much evidence that, in many cases, far from creating efficient and effective services and empowered citizens, the withdrawal of government services under conditions dictated by the World Bank and other donors has left NGOs to 'pick up the pieces' or 'fill the gaps' (Lewis, 2009, p. 92). Time and again, NGO service provision in developing countries has been criticised for being fragmented, unsustainable and frequently characterised by problems of quality control, poor coordination and general amateurism (Robinson and White, 1997b). And although NGOs are operating in a system that demands different forms of accountability and reporting, as emphasised by Charlesworth (Chapter 3) and Fries (Chapter 7), there is no legal accountability where NGOs or volunteers fail to deliver. There is also a real danger that NGOs that begin to provide services often lose their ability to advocate and campaign on behalf of their beneficiaries (Robinson, 1997a). Geoff Wood criticises the growing provision of welfare services by NGOs and argues that, by shifting the responsibility of social welfare delivery away from the state and towards NGOs, the state in essence dilutes its responsibility and accountability towards its citizens, becoming what he calls a 'franchise state'. This, he argues, renders the purpose of democracy 'toothless and meaningless' (Wood, 1997, p. 81). Wood writes,

> Citizens become consumers though often without meaningful access to a choice
> of suppliers. The loss of rights in the state is not adequately compensated for by
> acquiring them in the market. (Wood 1997, p. 85)

In the 1990s, neo-liberal policies received greater impetus with the collapse of the socialist regimes in Eastern Europe and the former Soviet Union. A triumphalist rhetoric emerged within donor circles and, as Katherine Verdery (1996) argues, Western capitalist societies came to believe that they had a monopoly on truth and could therefore dispense wisdom. The anti-socialist backlash in these countries at that time meant that meaningful debate of any kind concerning social policy and welfare was neglected or relegated:

> In 1989 the high point of neo-liberal economic thinking in the US and Britain
> conspired with the anti-socialist sentiment of post-revolutionary Eastern Europe

to knock the careful consideration of alternative social policies almost off the agenda. (Deacon, 1995, p. 92)

The transition project was conceptualised as being comprised of two equally important components to be promoted jointly: building democratic institutions *and* a market economy. The onus was on post-socialist societies to 'catch up' rapidly with the West (Wedel, 1998). Many scholars studying the post-socialist transitions have analysed how international donors' efforts at simultaneously promoting rapid liberalisation, privatisation, and democratisation coupled with the dismantling of social service delivery and social security mechanisms led to a range of unintended negative consequences, including rising rates of poverty, social exclusion, inequality and high rates of adult working-age male mortality, leading also to dependency on foreign aid and the withdrawal of grassroots support for reforms (Hann, 2002; Townsend, 2002; Dudwick et al., 2003; Kuehnast, 2004; Luong, 2004;).

Certainly there are those who have greatly benefited from the new opportunities, but the rapid collapse in industrial production and the dismantling of the welfare system and safety nets led to a dramatic surge in poverty and weakened social cohesion. Reversing this trend has proved extremely difficult (Dudwick et al., 2003, p. 2) and, as a result, a number of the former socialist countries[3] have since been included in the World Bank and IMF's Poverty Reduction Strategy programmes (PRSP), which are part of the Heavily Indebted Poor Countries (HIPC) initiative.

A group of World Bank researchers found that respondents in the countries of the former Soviet Union were 'angry and bewildered by their governments' failure to meet traditional responsibilities' (Dudwick et al., 2003, p. 25). They write,

> ... they felt that this failure violated basic tenets of social justice they had internalized during the Soviet period ... most respondents believed their governments should and eventually would reassume their previous responsibilities of providing jobs, low-cost housing, and utilities and maintaining affordable prices for consumer goods. (Dudwick et al., 2003, p. 25)

Although citizens felt betrayed and abandoned, governments in the region were under great pressure from international donors to rapidly privatise and liberalise their economies. Governments that were slow in implementing these policies were castigated by donors who threatened to decrease or cut their amount of aid (Wedel, 1998, p. 22).

In assessing the impact, numerous studies have shown that the liberalisation and privatisation policies implemented in the transition countries under the rubric of 'shock therapy' have affected women more adversely than men (Gal, 2000; Kuehnast, 2004; UNDP, 2005; UNIFEM, 2006). Beginning in the 1990s, women were forced out of the labour market in far greater numbers than men and were pushed into lower-paying jobs in the public sector or service industry (UNIFEM, 2006, p. 9). According to the EBRD's 2011 'Life in Transition' report, despite equivalent levels of education, training and skills, women continue to face more obstacles in entering the labour market, including gender-based discrimination, the lack of affordable childcare and the burden of caring for aging parents. Statistics show that women are unemployed in greater numbers than men – nearly 50 per cent of women are unemployed compared with only 33 per cent of men (EBRD, 2011, p. 50). This is not to say that men have not been affected by rising and sustained levels of unemployment. On the contrary, the rapid socio-economic transformations associated with 'shock therapy' have led to a rise in a number of health problems among men – including very high levels of depression and coronary heart disease. While the traditional risk factors of bad diet, smoking, excessive alcohol use and other diseases all play a part, studies point to additional factors, including poverty, social dislocation and exclusion, as exacerbating the situation (Stone, 2000). Those most at risk are young and middle-aged men. In recent years, life expectancy for men in transition countries has plummeted; and there is a growing gap between the life expectancy of men and women in many countries in this region. Russia is the most extreme case, where women are expected to outlive men on average by thirteen years, whereas the average gap globally is around four to five years. Even in some of the new EU states, such as Estonia and Lithuania, rates of depression and coronary heart disease among men are quite high, and the life expectancy gap between men and women is still larger than in other EU states. These developments have serious implications for both men and women. While men are clearly under stress and require assistance, women are also suffering from these ailments and related behaviours, such as the increased incidences of abandonment and domestic violence (Tarkowska, 2002). Although domestic violence is hardly a new problem, trafficking of women and girls into sex work has emerged only since the collapse of the socialist regime (UNDP, 2005).

NEO-LIBERALISM AND VIOLENCE

Based on extensive research conducted during 2001 to 2005 on projects funded under the 2002–2004 USAID anti-domestic violence initiative, I found that NGO-led provision of services to domestic violence victims in Armenia was haphazard, fragmented, unsustainable and ineffective (Ishkanian, 2007a). I focused on this initiative because it was the largest and most high-profile programme to date. Indeed, this was the first ever direct grant USAID had made to Armenian NGOs since beginning its work in the country after independence. The grant was made under USAID's Democracy Program for a total of

$476 367 USD. This amount was divided among six local Armenian NGOs, with the largest amount going to fund four shelters.

While shelters for victims of domestic violence might be successful in developed countries where there are welfare systems that include public assistance, unemployment benefits, subsidised housing and free schooling, these provisions were not present or were inadequately funded in Armenia during the 2000s. All that an NGO-run shelter was able do in Armenia was to provide counselling and housing for up to four weeks, leaving the question of what happens to a woman when she leaves a shelter unanswered. Without viable employment, affordable housing and subsistence benefits, her options are extremely limited. In spite of this, NGO-run shelter programmes were enthusiastically supported by USAID and received the bulk of funding from the 2002–2004 anti-domestic violence grant. What would explain this?

In writing about development discourses and how those discourses are used to justify donor interventions, James Ferguson argues that development agencies are often looking for ways to 'move money' and to 'plug' themselves in. This leads them to search for technical solutions to problems, which often ignore the political and structural dimensions of a problem (Ferguson, 1994). Furthermore, since USAID had been instrumentally involved in supporting the neo-liberal reforms and the rollback of state service delivery, it would be antithetical if, in the case of domestic violence, it were to reverse this stance. By ignoring the socio-economic problems, including poverty, unemployment and multi-generational households living in cramped conditions, which exacerbate and at times provoke incidences of domestic violence, as well as the fact that Armenia has a weak social welfare system, technical solutions such as shelters were implemented in the place of more ambitious programmes that would address the structural and economic inequalities to provide more long-term and sustainable solutions. A number of the NGOs involved in the 2002–2004 USAID-funded campaign recognised the need for a more structured, comprehensive and universal approach to the problem, but they did not challenge the donor's interest in funding NGO-run shelters.

In 2011, there is only one shelter operating in Armenia and it is funded by grants from diaspora Armenian organisations. Today there are more calls for state-supported programmes for the victims of domestic violence in Armenia (UNFPA, 2010). The 2010 United Nations Population Fund (UNFPA) report on domestic violence in Armenia recommends that domestic violence should be a 'priority for the government', 'be carried out under the patronage of the state and through the establishment of necessary infrastructures' and that the 'state has the responsibility to combat all forms of violence against women' (UNFPA, 2010, pp. 20–21). These recommendations for an enhanced role for the state are in stark contrast to the approach advocated by international donors in the early 2000s, where the emphasis was on NGOs as the main service providers and advocates.

To be clear, I am not arguing that the state is necessarily going to provide better service than NGOs or that NGO provision was of poor quality. Rather, I am arguing for more structural and institutional support so that NGO provision, if it should continue, can have a chance of contributing to a policy aimed at long-term effectiveness. There should be systems and policies for supporting women and providing them with viable options, beyond simply housing them in a shelter for a fortnight. Civil society lobbying on this issue has increased in the past few years, but state agencies have yet to take a more active role. Although currently there is more awareness of domestic violence in Armenia, much remains to be done to find sustainable and appropriate solutions to addressing the problem.

BIG SOCIETY AND DOMESTIC VIOLENCE

According to the national Women's Aid charity, domestic violence is very common in the UK and affects one in four women in their lifetimes regardless of age, social class, race, disability or lifestyle. Domestic violence accounts for between 16 and 25 per cent of all recorded violent crime and, in any one year, there are 13 million separate incidents of physical violence or threats of violence against women from partners or former partners (Dobash and Dobash, 1980; Home Office, 2002; Dodd et al., 2004; Walby and Allen, 2004)

In February 2011, Devon county council wanted to save £1 million by reducing the funding for the Against Domestic Violence and Abuse charity by 100 per cent. Following a public outcry, a Facebook campaign and protests from women's groups (BBC, 2011), the council backed down and as of August 2011 the budget was cut by 34.4 per cent. This is not an isolated case; in a report published on 2 August 2011 by the anti-cuts campaign False Economy, more than 2000 charities throughout the UK are being forced to close services and sack staff as local authorities slash their funding. Domestic violence charities throughout Britain have had their budgets slashed from a minimum 6.8 per cent up to 100 per cent in some instances (False Economy, 2011).[4] A number of charities addressing poverty alleviation, and which have expertise on the UK welfare system, prepared a joint briefing for the second reading of the Welfare Reform Bill at the House of Lords on 13 September 2011. In this briefing they express serious concerns about the specific provisions of the Bill. One of the signatories of the briefing, Women's Aid, argues that in the area of domestic violence, the Welfare Reform Bill is likely to make it more difficult for victims and survivors of domestic violence to have access to benefits and money. This lack of financial support, they argue, will make it more difficult for them to leave a violent partner and resettle (Women's Aid, 2011). It is expected that domestic violence services will also be affected by the proposed 20 per cent cuts to police forces. According to the chairman of the Police Federation of England and Wales, the Coalition government's proposed cuts and the redistribution of back-office staff into communities will weaken back-office functions, which include police roles within child protection, domestic violence and surveillance units (Public Service, 2011).

Angered by the proposed cuts facing her organisation, in February 2011 Denise Marshall, the chief executive of Eaves charity in London, which specialises in helping women who have been victims of violence, announced that she was returning the OBE she received for services to disadvantaged women. Marshall stated that she was handing back the OBE because she believes government cuts will leave her unable to provide proper support to vulnerable women. 'You're not helping women to escape the broader problems they face. They may get a bed, but no help with changing their lives and moving out of situations of danger.' Criticising the Big Society rhetoric, Marshall said,

> To be told that we are all in this together and must make cuts like everyone else isn't right, because we didn't have enough money to begin with. Do we have to say to rape victims, you can only have half the counselling sessions you need because we don't have enough money? That's just wrong. It's not like there are other services we can tell them to go to instead – that's just not the case anymore. Domestic violence victims don't go and storm the local town hall to demand more help; rape victims don't go to the local paper to complain that there isn't a good service for them. They are invisible. (Gentleman, 2011)

Two issues are important to note. First, it is clear that the cuts have led and will lead to the curtailment and in some cases the closure of services. According to Big Society proponents, communities must step in and provide support, but I agree with Marshall that it is highly unlikely that domestic violence or rape victims are going to mobilise and organise their own services. It is unclear who will fill the gap in provision. Second, given that many of the victims receiving support from domestic violence charities often suffer post-traumatic stress disorder and require professional care and assistance, relying on volunteers is not feasible. Domestic violence is one area, among others, where Big Society approaches of individual responsibility and community-based organising are not going to provide solutions. Instead, the cuts will leave those who are already vulnerable in even greater risk of further harm and re-victimisation (Towers and Walby, 2012).

CONCLUSION

Neo-liberal reforms are not benign and, for all the talk of individual responsibility, choice and empowerment by proponents of Big Society, there is the darker and untold story of loss of services, marginalisation and impoverishment. The Big Society agenda is a neo-liberal agenda that valorises individual choice and responsibility alongside a critique of the big and bureaucratically bloated state. But this assumes that individuals have equal opportunities and access to resources and information. Yet as David Harvey points out, the neo-liberal presumption that everyone has access to equal levels of information and that there is a level playing field for competition is either an innocent utopian projection or a deliberate obfuscation of the existing social and economic processes (Harvey, 2007, p. 68). By discussing the impact of the neo-liberal 'shock therapy' policies implemented in the former socialist countries, I have argued that the rapid cuts and withdrawal of government funding can lead to gaps in much-needed services and support. I have demonstrated that 'shock therapy' created some winners, but also many more losers in society. Asymmetrical power relations and social and economic inequalities meant that the losers in the post-socialist countries tended to be the most weak and vulnerable in society including women, children, the elderly, disabled, and long-term unemployed men who lacked access to resources and information.

To return to my starting point, I agree with many Big Society proponents that examining international examples is a useful exercise. However, I would qualify that by adding that this is only the case when considering instances of failure alongside the success stories referenced by advocates of Big Society. Cherry-picking stories of success and grossly simplifying matters – whilst ignoring the mountains of evidence that neo-liberal reforms lead to much suffering – creates a distorted and inaccurate account. Big Society is being presented by its leading proponents as a form of universal social welfare panacea, but the international evidence from transition countries and elsewhere (e.g. Latin America, Africa, etc.) indicates the approach is most unlikely to be effective, particularly in contexts where there have been dramatic cuts to public services supporting the more vulnerable in society, such as the victims of domestic violence.

NOTES

1. I am grateful to Hakan Seckinelgin for assisting me with the translation of the Turkish language website.
2. The term 'transition' has been problematised by various scholars including Michael Buroway and Katherine Verdery (1999) who argue that 'transition' implies an evolutionary development that has a single, well-defined objective and trajectory. While I agree with this assessment, I have chosen to use the term 'transition' for the sake of simplicity and because the term continues to be applied to the region by a number of international organisations including the World Bank and the European Bank for Reconstruction and Development.
3. Of the former socialist countries, eleven have had PRSPs: Albania, Armenia, Azerbaijan, Bosnia Herzegovina, Georgia, Kyrgyzstan, Macedonia, Moldova, Serbia and Montenegro, Tajikistan and Uzbekistan.
4. The following domestic violence charities lost 100 per cent of their funding: the Nene Valley Christian Family Refuge in Northampton; the Northamptonshire Domestic Abuse Forum; Women's Aid in Northampton; Christian Family Care in Central Bedfordshire; the Nia Project in Hackney; Pakistan Women's Welfare Association in Waltham Forest; Independent Domestic Violence Initiative in Pendle; and the Women Acting in Today's Society in Birmingham (False Economy, 2011).

Conclusion: the Big Society and social policy

David Lewis

INTRODUCTION

Proponents of the Big Society idea argue that it is about giving people more control over their own lives. There seem to be three main strands. The first is concerned with the promotion of volunteerism and philanthropy, with citizens being encouraged to give up more of their time for free and to set aside more resources to help others. The second is a new emphasis on localism and community-level empowerment, based on the principle that voluntary and community groups can and should play a more central role in running public services such as sports centres, fire and rescue, and libraries. Finally, the Big Society brings a new and more aggressive approach to public sector reform that seeks to cut red tape and encourage innovation and entrepreneurship, including promotion of the ideas of 'mutualisation' and floating off parts of the public sector into 'employee-owned' John Lewis-style partnerships in the effort to improve efficiency and job satisfaction. The Big Society idea is therefore part of the government's attempt to continue the reshaping of relationships between citizens, the third sector, the state and the market. As such, and as many of the authors in this volume have explored, the Big Society idea needs to be understood against the context of longstanding historical, ideological and theoretical debates around social policy and the welfare state, both in the UK and elsewhere. Yet the Big Society idea remains nebulous, still evolving and open to multiple interpretations. Significantly, it has been introduced against the backdrop of swingeing public expenditure cuts.

Two main texts are used by the Big Society lobby to underpin the Big Society policy agenda. Phillip Blond's book *Red Tory* (2010) situates the Big Society idea within a form of 'progressive conservatism'. He argues that the post-1945 consensus around the 'market state' has been swept away by the 2008 crash and ensuing recession, requiring the development of a new orthodoxy, and suggests that the free-market conservatism of the 1980s and 1990s has been similarly undermined. A renewed, radical, social-reform agenda centred on communitarian civic conservatism based on older, pre-Thatcher traditions is required – what Blond calls 'red Toryism'. He invokes the conservative radicalism of eighteenth-century political thinker, Edmund Burke, and his description of society's reliance upon the 'little platoons of family and civic association' (Blond, 2010a). Such ideas are also reminiscent of the 'communitarian' ideas from the US that call for efforts to restore civic virtues, to persuade citizens to focus on their responsibilities as well as their rights and entitlements, and to try to shore up society's moral foundations to deal with social problems (Etzioni, 1993).

For Blond, it was both Keynesianism and Thatcherism that in their different ways squeezed out the civic 'middle' (the self-organised social, political, religious activities of citizens) in their championing of the state and the market, respectively, and unhelpfully reinforced individualism in place of community (Blond, 2010a). He suggests that the appropriate response is reform on four main fronts: (i) re-localising the banking system; (ii) developing local capital; (iii) helping more people gain new assets (through local investment trusts to run schools and hospitals, more local procurement, encouraging more employee-owned businesses, and mutuals); and (iv) breaking up big business monopolies. In short, this is a programme of 'rebasing and renewal'. The other manifesto that sets off the Big Society agenda is that written by Conservative MP, Jesse Norman (2010). He argues that the Big Society idea forms a comprehensive alternative to a discredited Fabian tradition of state-led development, and a critique of neo-liberalism that had placed 'rigor mortis economics' at its centre and caused the financial crisis. Yet Norman is at pains to distinguish between the idea itself and the label that has become attached to it in the current economic and political context of the UK (Norman, 2010a).

Critics of the Big Society idea, many from within the third sector or civil society, point out that while no one is actually opposed to giving people more control over their lives, in the hands of the Conservative-led Coalition government the reality is that this serves as a smokescreen that allows government to shift the burden of cuts in social spending onto the most vulnerable. For example, Tim Stevens, Bishop of Leicester, recently predicted that many so-called 'faith groups', though keen to help in practice, would often be unwilling in principle to step in to fill the gaps in care left by cuts in state spending. He worries that the Big Society will increasingly simply leave the care of vulnerable people in the hands of 'amateurs' (Butt, 2010). This is of course reminiscent of the experience of the 1980s Conservative idea of 'care in the community', another loosely thought-out social policy idea and an important precursor of Big Society thinking.

Trade union critics point out that the Big Society implies worsening gender inequality in the workplace, as the shift takes place from women's paid employment towards an expectation that women will provide more 'free labour' in their local communities. Critics from the charity sector, too, have been vocal. In October, Lord Wei, another thinker associated with the origins of the Big Society idea, upset Stephen Bubb of the Association of Chief Executives of Voluntary Organisations (ACEVO) by attacking what he called 'big charity', seen as self-interested, bureaucratic and unresponsive to local needs (Asthana and Helm, 2010). Some are now beginning to ask where the voluntary sector fits into the Big Society idea. And charities, many of whom receive funds from government, are facing cuts alongside the public sector. They point out that you can't cut both state *and* charities and then just expect people to do things for free. At the same time, for cooperatives and mutuals to work properly, they will need long-term financial training and support. Phillip Blond himself has subsequently been critical of the Treasury/government's readiness for 'cutting without thinking', arguing that you can't combine austerity with renewal (Blond, 2010b).

Labour's response to the Big Society idea has so far been relatively muted. The work of academic and community activist Maurice Glasman, who was made a Labour peer in 2011, has been placed at the centre of Labour's emerging alternative ideas about the 'good society'. Glasman has worked with the London Citizens group – an alliance of faith groups, universities, schools and unions – that he organised to run community projects along lines influenced by the US activist Saul Alinsky's approach to community organising. The aim is to build a new emphasis on old-fashioned, local, 'bottom up' political community activism in an attempt to counter Cameron's capture of localism. Glasman argues for an alternative to Tory-style volunteerism through revitalising extant local institutions such as churches, post offices, hospitals, schools and football clubs. Developing a vision of 'blue labour', Glasman's ideas seek to reconnect Labour with the social conservatism of 'family, faith and flag'. Influenced by Karl Polanyi, he speaks of providing a more socially embedded counterbalance to the primacy of the market and its commodification of people and environment. His vision is rooted in tradition, custom and place – that he hopes can serve as countervailing force to the market, and to the powerful interests of capital. The Big Society idea, he suggests, is too dependent on free-market economics and is essentially anti-community (Helm and Coman, 2011).

THEORETICAL AND HISTORICAL CONTRADICTIONS

States and Citizens

While much of the Big Society discussion has focused on the changing role of the third sector, the debate is really as much about the changing role of the state and the market in relation to social policy. As such, this is simply the latest instalment of longstanding discussions among economists and political theorists about the 'great society', embodied most notably in Adam Smith's ideas about mutual respect and cooperation set out in his *Theory of Moral Sentiments*. Yet many of the current Big Society ideas and policy discussions appear curiously detached from these antecedents in the history of ideas, as Jose Harris (Chapter 1) usefully outlines in her detailed overview of the Great Society perspective that looms over the current debate like a 'globally encircling presence'.

In an informative and useful effort to historicise the discussion further, Simon Szreter (Chapter 2) discusses the way that, contrary to the current ideological policy assumptions being promoted by Big Society advocates, civil society in Britain has always relied on effective and well-resourced public institutions. He argues that unless the attempt at a revival of civic activism is properly embedded within a revitalised framework of local government, it is unlikely to move beyond the level of rhetoric. He shows that local government activism based on increased investment in local government institutions and democratic accountability is the surest way to promote civic engagement, and suggests a set of policy reforms that include more progressive local land and property taxes, new revenue-raising powers for local authorities through bond-raising power, a properly funded legal aid system, and experimenting with compulsory voting. Lorie Charlesworth (Chapter 3) further interrogates the myth of a glorious voluntarist past, and examines the Poor Law and the origins of local government in England. She shows that the long history of localism in England was derived from an established legal culture of citizenship rights that made welfare services to the poor an obligation under an overarching legal framework that made these rights real.

The Third Sector

Turning to the state's relationship with citizens and third sector, Matthew Hilton's chapter (Chapter 6) focuses on the post-1945 period in Britain. It comprehensively questions the validity of the narrative of civic decline that underpins the Big Society idea, by showing the steady growth and evolution of civic participation away from earlier forms of associational social capital towards a stronger commitment to large-scale professional forms of organised civil society. In this way, citizens have built new forms of social and political engagement in dynamic ways that challenge both the crude nostalgia of the Big Society idea and the ideological notion that the voluntary sector can be seen primarily as a provider of cheap services.

The theme is further deepened by Daniel Weinbren (Chapter 4), who reminds us of an earlier unsuccessful experiment during which a Conservative-dominated government attempted to place health care services in the hands of officially sanctioned community organisations following the 1911 National Insurance Act. In a highly unequal version of what in today's policy discourse would be termed 'partnership', mutual societies faced growing levels of bureaucratisation, received less than expected levels of funding from the complex health insurance arrangements, lost their value base in the face of a strong cuts agenda and finally became increasingly party political. The failure of this initiative, Weinbren argues, set back the relationship between the state and voluntary sectors many years and laid the ground for the broad welcome subsequently given to the central state intervention ushered in during the 1940s.

Another key element contained within the Big Society idea, that of 'citizen service', is subjected to historically informed scrutiny in Kater Bradley's chapter (Chapter 5) that focuses on young peoples' engagement with charities during the first half of the twentieth century. The new National Citizen Service scheme currently being piloted in the UK is also underpinned by a highly selective vision of the past that the author suggests would benefit from a more nuanced understanding of the disruptive and coercive aspects of the earlier National Service regime, and of the long traditions of organised youth work and the selective impact on 'social capital' that followed from these traditions. Finally, Richard Fries (Chapter 7) traces the history of charity, and asks how and if the idea of charity fits into the big society idea. He concludes that despite its lack of explicit profile in David Cameron's pronouncements about the Big Society, ideas of charity are central and that recent reforms to charity legislation continue a process of opening up the campaigning and political roles of charities alongside their more familiar service delivery roles. He also warns that the independence of the charity sector is crucial to its well-being and social value, and suggests that while there is a need to ensure that the Big Society idea is not allowed to become synonymous with the cuts agenda, it is also crucial to ensure that the public funding that is attached to this agenda does not further undermine the independence of a charity sector that has long been at risk from losing its independence as public funding increased from the 1990s onwards under New Labour.

The chapter by Nick Ockenden, Matthew Hill and Joanna Stuart (Chapter 12) focuses on volunteering, another key plank of the Big Society agenda. It asks how volunteering might make a contribution to this agenda, and also what effect the new policies associated with the Big Society might have on the landscape of volunteering itself. It finds that volunteering is unlikely to fill the gaps left in public services and that government plans to stimulate higher levels of volunteering are somewhat unrealistic. It finds only a weak relationship between levels of volunteering and government efforts to promote it, and the authors worry that the government's high level of expectations that is unmatched by resources may damage the sector in the longer term. Liz Richardson (Chapter 11) also examines the claim that governments can influence citizens to become more active in their communities, and uses the newly fashionable 'nudge' concept in her discussion of the effort to prompt changes in behaviour. Based on two field experiments, she finds encouraging evidence that modest gains can be made but argues that the nudge idea needs to be seen within the broader context of political practice and governance.

The Role of the Market

The 1980s saw increased use of the voluntary sector as sub-contractor for services in a new contract culture, in which a 'mixed economy of welfare' aimed to broaden delivery away from reliance on the state to include private and voluntary providers. This was linked to the 'new public management' approach to public service reform, a set of ideas that aimed to reform the public sector by better linking incentives and performance, measuring outputs using indicators and creating a purchaser–provider split. This was also the era of the rediscovery by policymakers and academics of the concept of 'civil society', sometimes alternatively termed the 'third sector', that was seen as a space between state and market in which citizens organised in pursuit of their diverse interests. Robert Putnam's famous phrase 'bowling alone' came to symbolise a set of anxieties about the decline of civic values and participation within and across local communities, particularly in the US. At the same time, the rising international profile of non-governmental organisations (NGOs) paralleled the neo-liberal preference for exploring the contribution of non-state, private organisational actors to social policy, leading to the rise of an ideology of 'non-governmentalism' within the field of international development (Lewis, 2005).

The 1990s saw a deepening of the use of marketised language to talk about social change and the role of the private sector in social and community issues, with talk of 'social entrepreneurship', 'social capital', 'social enterprise' and 'social business', alongside appeals for increased volunteering and private philanthropy. Diana Leat's chapter (Chapter 10) explores the new centrality of philanthropy to UK social policy within the Big Society rhetoric, suggesting that this forms part of a wider trend for rethinking the relationship between policy and administration towards newer, neo-liberal 'governance' models. She concludes, on the basis of a review of the historic tensions between government and the foundations sector, that philanthropic foundations are unlikely to serve as ready-made gap fillers in relation to withdrawn public provision, as they are guided as much by their own pursuit for independence and autonomy as by public welfare goals.

Social investment is also one of the key pillars of the Big Society project. Cathy Pharoah (Chapter 9) examines the financing of social ventures in the context of the Big Society policy context. She points out that while the voluntary sector is often taken to be at the centre of the Big Society, the increased role of private capital is likely to change the nature of the sector and the focus of social welfare activities taking place. Private giving is, she argues, likely to narrow in focus rather than cater for the broader social needs required as public expenditure cuts begin to bite.

International Perspectives

The final chapters of the book move away from the UK to take a look at international policy perspectives. Markus Ketola's chapter (Chapter 13) examines the context of volunteering in Germany and Sweden and finds that, by comparison, the state of volunteering in the UK is healthy, and somewhat at odds with the 'crisis rhetoric' of the Big Society policy push being made by David Cameron and other Conservatives. Indeed, the so-called crisis of civic participation in the UK is something of a myth. Data shows that relationships between state, civil society and citizens have remained fairly stable during the past 60 years, with healthy levels of volunteering and a consistent growth in voluntary organisations (Hilton et al., 2010). Forms of participation may have changed, with membership of trade unions, political parties and churches having fallen, but newer movements, pressure groups and NGOs have all increased and received growing support.

Armine Ishkanian (Chapter 14) questions the overwhelmingly positive use of international examples, such as micro-credit services provided by non-governmental organisations in developing countries, by those promoting the Big Society idea in the UK. She suggests that lessons from the context of post-communist Armenia during the 1990s, where citizens felt abandoned by government in the wake of the collapse of the Soviet Union, do not augur well for dealing with the rapid withdrawal of public services in the UK. The shock therapy of the 1990s produced heightened social inequalities, with the 'losers' being amongst the most vulnerable sections of society. The rhetoric of 'building civil society' in such contexts, despite the high levels of spending on 'capacity building' and 'technical assistance' that could never be matched today in the UK, led to disappointing results at the organisational level.

Wider lessons from the earlier efforts within the world of international development work to promote civil society and build the capacity of NGOs through technical assistance are not particularly encouraging, and offer salutary lessons for the Big Society advocates. Evidence suggests that this is extremely difficult even with a high level of resource commitment. Furthermore, in countries such as Somalia and Afghanistan, some would argue that the dominant 'Big Society' looks distinctly 'uncivil'. Also questioned from the international evidence in many developing country contexts is the idea that civil society organisations are necessarily effective forms of service delivery agencies, as they vary widely in terms of quality and coverage and may also serve to undermine accountability between states and citizens (Lewis and Kanji, 2009; Robinson, 1997a).

The Big Society Idea as Policy: Coherence and Fragmentation

Anthropologists who study policy processes focus on the far-from-straightforward ways that policy ideas and policy outcomes are linked. Rational models of policy as decision-making and implementation as a politico-technical process fail to engage with the subtler aspects of the animating narratives that inform policy, while conventional approaches also tend to play down the social dimensions of the policymaking process itself. As Wedel et al. have put it, the key challenge is to understand policy's 'enabling discourses, mobilizing metaphors, and underlying ideologies and uses' and to focus not just on the means–ends questions of policy but to analyse what different social actors do 'in the name of policy' (Wedel et al., 2005, pp. 34–5). In order to gain traction, policy initiatives need to create a central animating idea that is simultaneously simple, appealing and most importantly open to multiple interpretations.

The Big Society idea is a good example of this complexity in action, and illustrates the ways that policymakers try to mobilise policy change through creating a narrative discourse that at one level seems straightforward and inclusive, but at another remains elusive and contested. Though vague, as a policy term the Big Society idea clearly 'works' to the extent that it has provoked political debate (particularly within the third sector) and its initial implementation has started to inform change within the social policy landscape. As a classic policy 'buzzword' (Cornwall and Brock, 2005), the term's vagueness works to its advantage, appealing to people from across many different ideological and practical terrains. Martin Albrow's chapter (Chapter 8) usefully discusses the Big Society idea as a rhetorical intervention, and as such requiring serious attention and analysis. He shows how it opens a window into the public relations machinery that underpins modern British politics. He shows how the label has been politically designed to connect David Cameron's politics with different discourses within the media, the professions and community groups, to overwrite older New Labour ideas, and to divert attention away from financial crisis. Although partly succeeding in this, Albrow's sociological analysis draws out the longer-term unsustainability of a label that nevertheless invites deeper discussion about society, class and social justice and predicts that it may still be 'the sound bite that bites back'.

While we might argue from an ethnographic perspective that the Big Society is a reasonably successful mobilising metaphor for policy, it does not provide the necessary coherence to drive a programme of change. Nor, for the same reasons, does it provide a clear rallying point for critical opposition. As a policy idea, the Big Society is beginning to fragment in more ways than it coheres. Beneath the veneer of building a more people-centred approach to social policy – which resonates, for example, with the idea of the 'human economy' agenda set out by Hart et al. (2010) – there is a less palatable, opportunistic and potentially damaging ideological agenda. Such fragmentation is also driven by the more serious problem that, while the emphasis on non-state actors and local participation is seen by some as serving to usefully counterbalance the state and the market, many others view the increasing emphasis on rolling back the state with suspicion. The attempt to turn the Big Society idea into a viable policy programme is heavily – perhaps fatally – compromised by its timing. The unprecedented level of cuts to public spending in the UK means that whatever merits the basic constellation of ideas that make up the Big Society may possess – and there is much that can be usefully debated here – these seem destined to become debased by what appears to be the political opportunism at its core. The reality is that the public investment that would necessarily underpin a major shift towards, say, the localism agenda, will not be made available. While the government has made great play of the training of 5000 community activists to carry forward the agenda in their local areas, given the scale of wholesale transformation of institutions that is being promised, at this level the overall resources that are being committed for such a task remain relatively small.

The Conservative-led Coalition government of course rejects the idea that the Big Society is merely the 'fig leaf' for the decision to cut important services (either opportunistically, or as part of a wider privatisation agenda) and argues that it offers useful mechanisms to allow cash-strapped government to operate more 'smartly' during a time of austerity by rethinking aspects of its work. For example, in Liverpool, with some of the largest local government cuts in the country, Big Society supporters say that local government will need to be 'more clever' if local facilities such as sports centres and libraries are to be kept open, arguing that this is now about to be achieved by taking them out of local authority control and placing them in the hands of a community trust (*The Big Society*, BBC Radio 4, 8 January 2010). Government supporters of the Big Society idea, such as the Minister for the Cabinet Office and Paymaster General Francis Maude, have tried to suggest that it is more than just a new label on an old idea, and that it is more than simply political expediency that has brought it into focus. He argues that while the Big Society builds on longer traditions, there are new elements – such as the emphasis on localism and the mix of different public service reform ideas. He goes so far as to suggest that the Conservatives would have wanted to go down this route regardless of whether there was a financial crisis (*The Big Society*, BBC Radio 4, January 8, 2010).

But every time the 'Big Society' idea is relaunched by the government (as it has been three or four times at the time of writing) we are reminded of the basic contradiction at its core. This makes it difficult, despite the continuing level of general interest and debate about the Big Society rhetoric, to send out a clear policy message and to secure public support for the idea – and increasingly reveals its limitations as a mobilising metaphor. One strand is the localism project that seeks to place more power in the hands of organised groups of local citizens, who can take over key resources from government. This makes it part of the vision of compassionate conservatism, embodied in the ideas of Blond and other thinkers, and in the ideas of free school activists such as Toby Young and where there is a strongly communitarian slant. The other strand of the Big Society project is a more pragmatic set of responses to the opportunities provided by the budget deficit to drive through a massive programme of cuts, and to implement a new set of managerialist partnerships, contracting relationships, marketisation and an imposed 'choice agenda' in the form of personalisation. Some critics have begun referring to this as the 'bid society' rather than the 'Big Society', where there is as much emphasis on bringing in private for-profit companies and marketisation as there is on not-for-profit citizen action.

There are, of course, important questions about how far the promotion of increased competition within the third sector is really a good idea. The Big Society idea seems likely to create further fragmentation and conflict within the sector itself. For example, it was reported last year that one of the government's flagship 'free schools' set up by journalist Toby Young is set to occupy a prime west London site that will mean it will displace more than 20 longstanding voluntary groups working on issues such as homelessness, refugees and young offenders who already use the building (Vasagar, 2011).

Some critics argue that these debates are simply two sides of the same policy programme. But there is a growing contradiction. For many in the world of voluntary and community organisations (who oppose the free marketeer approach), the Big Society idea finally offers the promise of conclusively validating their deep-rooted belief in the intrinsic value of their sector to society – as a diverse, bottom-up set of organisations and networks with authentic community-centred values and powers at its heart and strong capacities for social innovation at its core. But much of what has been learned (Kendall, 2003; Anheier, 2005) since the sector became a recognised area of social policy research 20 or so years ago is that the third sector needs a support system and capacity building if it is to rise above well-meaning but amateurish activism, or piecemeal responses to large-scale problems. Experience suggests that the voluntary sector may well offer the possibility of better services, but not necessarily cheaper ones (Robinson, 1997a).

CONCLUSION

At the start of this book, the editors' introduction raised a set of questions about how the Big Society idea operates politically, how it works at the level of rhetoric and how far it engages with realities on the ground. It is, of course, too early to answer such questions, but the writers in this volume have begun exploring them. At the level of politics, the Big Society is an attempt to roll up a set of older social policy debates about localism, the marketisation of public services and the importance to society of the third sector into a new configuration. But what is the new twist? There are two possible answers – one is primarily ideological: the Big Society idea emerges out of new thinking about progressive conservatism; the other is more pragmatic: the Big Society is a matter of political expediency for a cash-strapped government dealing with the need to cut public expenditure. The reality is a combination of both impulses, and there are emerging contradictions because of this. In terms of rhetoric, the Big Society is a mobilising metaphor that is designed to appeal across a diverse set of policy actors, from the voluntary sector to the free marketeers and, while this may cohere in the short term, it is unlikely to do so in the medium or longer terms. It engages with realities on the ground, but in a manner that brings markets further into social provision and that looks likely to damage the capacity and the diversity of the voluntary sector. The reality on the ground is that most people want to use sports centres or libraries, not run them.

The current policy debates reflect a longstanding universal social policy tension in the UK – between the top-down, funder-driven agenda of government and other donors, and the bottom-up logic of people in the third sector wanting to organise and work with people. A central principle of the voluntary or third sector is the idea that people will organise in non-directed ways, in pursuit of a set of both their own and wider public goals. When the welfare state was created after the Second World War a key motivation was the recognition that the Big Society of its day – the diverse and patchy landscape of private and charitable health care providers – was insufficient to meet the needs of the population. Passing over a set of responsibilities from citizens to state, to which the state can be held accountable, is at the heart of the contract between government and its citizens, and this is now to be undermined at our peril.

Some people in the third sector argue that the damage already being done to the range, diversity and quality of sector support or 'infrastructure' organisations in the UK will seriously weaken their capacity, at the expense of the decentralisation and localism that many activists would otherwise broadly welcome (see the boxes by Rachael McGill from the National Coalition for Independent Action [NCIA] and Jane Holgate and John Page from Hackney Unites in the Introduction to this volume). Others who support what is happening, such as Lord Nat Wei, take the view that a measure of 'de-professionalisation' in the sector, forced by the lack of resources, may actually be a blessing in disguise, as it forces a voluntary sector that has become too formalised and bloated (the unprecedented golden age experienced during the post-1997 New Labour era) to return to its voluntarist, informal roots (Plummer, 2010). For this second group, a reduction of the third sector's dependence on government is a good thing. More reliance on volunteers brings more autonomy and freedom of decision-making, and creates activist, caring values that can challenge the dominant culture of managerialism.

Yet the Big Society is undoubtedly central to the agenda for rolling back the state as part of the neo-liberal restructuring of welfare services, and there are likely to be very rough times ahead. Whether the motive is political expediency, or whether it reflects a deeper ideological project or, as seems likely, a combination of both, the Big Society idea risks undermining the integrity of both the state and civil society. One of the core aims of the government's Big Society programme is to devolve power and the provision of public services to groups of citizens and voluntary groups. But more support and capacity building for the third sector is needed if it is to be able to contribute to Big Society plans. Perhaps more promising is the prospect of more employee-owned businesses, and the reinvigoration of mutualist ideas. But the government's attempt to reshape relationships between citizens, state and market may rapidly become a political liability, burdening a wide range of both voluntary and market-based organisations with responsibilities that they may be unable to deliver on.

To conclude, three main sets of contradictions have contributed to the flawed idea of the Big Society as presently configured. First, it seeks to build a legitimacy through a largely unconvincing appeal to an idealised and essentially unreal past, while possessing all the ahistorical power of a typical policy buzzword. A historicised perspective that goes beyond the ahistorical perpetual present of policy discourse tells us that the framing of the Big Society idea is flimsy, at odds with earlier theorisations of the 'great society', and with a basic lack of clarity at its heart. Second, the Big Society idea in the UK is inextricably bound up with the practical contingencies of public expenditure cuts, whether one believes this to be the result of either design or bad timing. The ideological dimensions and political economy context of the Big Society idea therefore cannot be ignored. Finally, evidence from widespread efforts from the early 1990s onwards to build and strengthen 'third sectors' and 'civil societies' across the developing and post-Soviet worlds increasingly point to the fact that such approaches were flawed, with little today to show for outsider efforts and resources that attempted to influence or speed up the self-organising logics of citizens.

Bibliography

ACEVO (2011), *Powerful People, Responsible Society: The Report of the Commission of the Big Society*, London: ACEVO.

Achur, J. (2010), *Trade Union Membership 2009*, London: Department for Business, Information and Skills/Office of National Statistics, available at: www.bis.gov.uk/policies/employment-matters/research/trade-union-stats (accessed 30 September 2011).

Ainsworth, D. (2011), 'The mixed fortunes of the first spin-outs', available at: http://www.thirdsector.co.uk/news/1075749/ (accessed 2 February 2012).

Alborn, T.L. (2001), 'Senses of belonging: the politics of working-class insurance in Britain, 1880–1914', *Journal of Modern History*, **73** (3), 561–602.

Albrow, M. (1990), *Max Weber's Construction of Social Theory*, London: Macmillan Education.

Allen, G. (2011), *Early Intervention: The Next Steps – An Independent Report to HM Government*, London: Cabinet Office, available at: www.dwp.gov.uk/docs/early-intervention-next-steps.pdf (accessed 6 February 2012).

Andrew III, J.A. (1998), *Lyndon Johnson and the Great Society*, Chicago: Ivan R. Dee.

Anheier, H.K. (2005), *Nonprofit Organizations: Theory, Management, Policy*, London: Routledge.

Anheier, H.K. and S. Daly (2006), *The Politics of Foundation*, London and New York: Routledge.

Anheier, H.K. and S. Toepler (1999), *Private Funds, Public Purpose: Philanthropic Foundations in International Perspective*, New York: Kluwer Academic/Plenum Publishers.

Arnove, R. and N. Pinede (2007), 'Revisiting the big three foundations', *Critical Sociology*, **33**, 389–425.

Arts & Business (2010), *Private Investment in Culture*, London: Arts & Business.

Ashton, R. 'Sweeping change: riots and the Big Society', available at: http://www.civilsociety.co.uk/governance/blogs/content/10211/sweeping_change_riots_and_the_big_society (accessed 6 February 2012).

Association for Charitable Foundations (ACF) (2007), 'Grantmaking by UK trusts and charities', available from http://www.acf.org.uk/index.aspx?id=64 (accessed 20 February 2012).

Asthana, A. and T. Helm (2010), 'Big society guru sparks row with blast at bureaucratic charities', *Guardian*, 17 October, available at: www.guardian. co.uk/society/2010/oct/17/big-society-charities-lord-wei (accessed 17 May 2011).

Aston-Mansfield Papers (Canning Town Women's Settlement and Mansfield House University Settlement), Newham Local Studies Library, Stratford Library, London E15.

Atkinson, M. (1984), *Our Master's Voices: The Language and Body Language of Politics*, London and New York: Routledge.

Babajanian, B. (2008), 'Social capital and community participation in post-Soviet Armenia: implications for policy and practice', *Europe-Asia Studies*, **60** (8), 1299–319.

Balogh, T. (1968), 'The apotheosis of the dilettante', in T. Balogh (ed.), *Crisis in the Civil Service. The Great Society*, series 7, London: Anthony Blond.

Barnett, H. (1918), *Canon Barnett: His Life, Work and Friends*, 2 vols, London: John Murray.

Bathe, D. (1984), 'Oddfellows and morris dancing in a Peak District village', *Certificate in English Cultural Tradition*, Sheffield University.

BBC (2011), 'Big Society is my mission, says David Cameron', available at: http://www.bbc.co.uk/news/uk-politics-12443396 (accessed 19 August 2011).

BBC News (2010), 'Sir Michael Caine backs Tories' youth citizen service plan', available at: http://news.bbc.co.uk/1/hi/uk_politics/election_2010/8608807. stm (accessed 9 May 2011).

Beattie, J. (2011), 'Tory MPs turn on Big Society architect Steve Hilton', 25 January, available at: www.mirror.co.uk/news/politics (accessed 11 July 2011).

Beaumont, C. (2001), 'The women's movement, politics and citizenship, 1918–1950s', in I. Zweiniger-Bargielowska (ed.), *Women in Twentieth Century Britain*, Harlow: Longman, pp. 262–77.

Beaumont, C. (2009), 'Housewives, workers and citizens: voluntary women's organisations and the campaign for women's rights in England and Wales in the post-war period', in N. Crowson, M. Hilton and J. McKay (eds), *NGOs in Contemporary Britain: Non-state Actors in Society and Politics since 1945*, Basingstoke: Palgrave, pp. 59–76.

Beveridge, W. (1948), *Voluntary Action: A Report on the Methods of Social Advance*, London: G. Allen & Unwin.

Bevir, M. (2002), 'Sidney Webb: utilitarianism, positivism, and social democracy', *Journal of Modern History*, **74**, 217–52.

Blair, T. (1998), *The Third Way: New Politics for the New Century*, Fabian Pamphlet 588, London: Fabian Society.

Blond, P. (2009) 'Rise of the red Tories', *Prospect* 155, 28 February, available at: http://www.prospectmagazine.co.uk/2009/02/riseoftheredtories/ (accessed 4 August 2011).

Blond, P. (2010a), *Red Tory: How Left and Right Have Broken Britain and How We Can Fix It*, London: Faber and Faber.

Blond, P. (2010b), 'The austerity drive must not derail the winning "big society"', *The Observer*, 3 October.

Blond, P. (2011), 'The Big Society: innovation or slogan', available at: http://www.independent.co.uk/news/uk/politics/the-big-society-innovation-or-slogan-2208494.html (accessed 4 August 2011).

Boje, T.P. (2010), 'Commentary: participatory democracy, active citizenship, and civic organizations – conditions for volunteering and activism', *Journal of Civil Society*, **6** (2), 189–92.

Borsay, P. (1989), *The English Urban Renaissance. Culture and Society in the Provincial Town, 1660–1770*, Oxford: Clarendon Press.

Bowman v Secular Society Ltd [1917] AC406 (HL).

Bradley, K. (2009), *Poverty, Philanthropy and the State: Charities and the Working Classes in London, 1918–1979*, Manchester: Manchester University Press.

Brewer, J. (2011), 'What's wrong with the "Big Society"', available at: http://sociologyandthecuts.wordpress.com (accessed 20 May 2011).

Briggs, A. and A. Macartney (1984), *Toynbee Hall; The First Hundred Years*, London: Routledge Kegan Paul.

Broad, J. (2000), 'Housing the rural poor in southern England', *Agricultural History Review*, **48**, 151–70.

Brodie, E., T. Hughes, V. Jochum, S. Miller, N. Ockenden and D. Warburton (2011), *Pathways Through Participation: What Creates and Sustains Citizenship?*, London: NCVO.

Brooks, D. (2009) 'The long voyage home', *New York Times*, 4 May, available at: http://www.nytimes.com/2009/05/05/opinion/05brooks.html?_r=3&th&emc=th (accessed 10 December 2010).

Brown, A. (2010), 'Just How Big is the Big Society?', http://www.instituteforgovernment.org.uk/blog/479/just-how-big-is-the-big-society/ (accessed 15 February 2012).

Brown, G. (2000) 'Civic Society in Modern Britain: 17th Arnold Goodman Charity Lecture by Rt. Hon. Gordon Brown, Chancellor of the Exchequer', available at: http://archive.treasury.gov.uk/speech/cx200700.html (accessed 30 April 2012).

Brown, S.J. (1992), 'Thomas Chalmers and the communal ideal in Victorian Scotland', *Proceedings of the British Academy*, **78**, 61–80.

Brundage, A. (1978), *The Making of the New Poor Law. The Politics of Inquiry, Enactment and Implementation, 1832–39*, Rutgers: State University of New Jersey.

Burawoy, M. and K. Verdery (1999), 'Introduction', in M. Burawoy and K. Verdery (eds), *Uncertain Transitions: Ethnographies of Change in the Postsocialist World*, Lanham, MD: Rowman & Littlefield Publishers Inc.

Butt, R. (2010) 'Faith groups will not fill gaps left by spending cuts, warns Anglican bishop', *The Guardian*, available at: http://www.guardian.co.uk/society/2010/dec/30/bishop-big-society-faith-groups (accessed 6 February 2012).

Cabinet Office (2002), *Private action, public benefit*, http://www.btinternet.com/~akme/stratgy1.html (accessed 17 February 2012).

Cabinet Office, Office of Third Sector (2009), *Social Enterprise Summit: Next Steps*, London: HM Government.

Cabinet Office (2010), 'Building the Big Society', available at: http://www.cabinetoffice.gov.uk/news/building-big-society (accessed 20 April 2012).

Cabinet Office (2011), *Giving*, White Paper, London: HM Government.

Calmann, J. (ed.) (1967), *The Common Market. The Treaty of Rome Explained*, The Great Society Series, London: Anthony Blond.

Cameron, D. (2009), 'The Big Society', 10 November, available at: http://www.conservatives.com/News/Speeches/2009/11/David_Cameron_The_Big_Society.aspx (accessed 17 May 2011).

Cameron, D. (2010a), 'The "Big Society Spirit": It's the spirit of activism, dynamism, people taking the initiative, working together to get things done', available at: http://www.conservatives.com/News/Speeches/2010/07/David_Cameron_Our_Big_Society_Agenda.aspx/ (accessed 19 July 2010).

Cameron, D. (2010b), 'Together in the National Interest', available at: http://www.conservatives.com/News/Speeches/2010/10/ (accessed 6 October 2010).

Cameron, D. (2010c), 'Mending our Broken Society', available at: http://www.conservatives.com/News/Speeches/2010/01/David_Cameron_Mending_our_Broken_Society.aspx (accessed 22 January 2011).

Cameron, D. (2010d) 'Our "Big Society" plan', available at: http://www.conservatives.com/News/Speeches/2010/03/David_Cameron_Our_Big_Society_plan.aspx (accessed 31 March 2010).

Cameron, D. (2010e) 'David Cameron's Conservative speech in full', available at: http://www.telegraph.co.uk/news/politics/david-cameron/8046342/David-Camerons-Conservative-conference-speech-in-full.html (accessed 4 August 2011).

Cameron, D. (2011a) 'David Cameron: Big Society is here to stay', available at: http://www.politics.co.uk/comment-analysis/2011/02/14/david-cameron-big-society-is-here-to-stay (accessed 4 August 2011).

Cameron, D. (2011b), Speech on the Big Society, Milton Keynes, 23 May 2011.

CGAP/CMPO (2011), 'The new state of donation: three decades of household giving to charity 1978–2008', Cass Business School, City University, and Bristol University, available at: http://www.cgap.org.uk/uploads/reports/The new state of donation.pdf (accessed 6 February 2012).

Chapman, C. (2011), 'New rules on endowment investment unlikely to open floodgates for social funding', Philanthropy UK, 6 January, available at: http://www.philanthropyuk.org/news/2011-01-06/new-rules-endowment-investment-unlikely-open-floodgates-social-funding (accessed 15 February 2012).

Charities Aid Foundation (CAF) (2010a), *The World Giving Index 2010*, Kent: CAF.

Charities Aid Foundation (CAF) (2010b), *UK Giving 2010*, Kent: CAF and NCVO.

Charity Commission (2001), *The Independence of Charities from the State*, RR7, February, http://www.charitycommission.gov.uk/publications/rr7. aspx (accessed 15 February 2012).

Charity Commission (2011), *Charities and Investment Matters. A Guide for Trustees*, CC14. http://www.charitycommission.gov.uk/Publications/cc14. aspx (accessed 16 February 2012).

Charlesworth, L. (2009), 'Justices of the Peace', (English Common Law), in Stanley M. Katz (ed.), *Oxford International Encyclopedia of Legal History*, New York: Oxford University Press.

Charlesworth, L. (2010), *Welfare's Forgotten Past: A Socio-Legal History of the Poor Law*, Abingdon, UK, and New York: Routledge.

Clark, G. (2010), 'Growing the Big Society', speech 27 July, London: Department for Communities and Local Government.

Clotfelter, C. (1992), *Who Benefits from the Non-Profit Sector?*, Chicago: University of Chicago Press.

Cohen, R. (2011), 'Impact capital is the new venture capital', Reuters, available at: http://blogs.reuters.com/great-debate/2011/07/13/impact-capital-is-the-new-venture-capital-part-ii/ (accessed 13 July 2011).

Collins, M. (2003), *Modern Love: An Intimate History of Men and Women in Twentieth-Century Britain*, London: Atlantic Books.

Commission on Unclaimed Assets (2007), *The Social Investment Bank – Its Organisation and Role in Driving Development of the Third Sector*, London: Commission on Unclaimed Assets.

Conservative Party (2010a), *Big Society, Not Big Government*, London: Conservative Party.

Conservative Party (2010b), 'Cameron unveils "Big Society" plan', press release, 31 March, available at: http://www.conservatives.com/News/News_stories/2010/03/Plans_announced_to_help_build_a_Big_Society.aspx (accessed 10 December 2010).

Cooper, S. (2010), *Citizenship Survey 2009–10* (April 2009–March 2010), London: Department for Communities and Local Government.

Cornwall, A. and K. Brock (2005), 'Beyond buzzwords: "poverty reduction", "participation" and "empowerment" in development policy', Overarching Concerns Programme Paper 10, Geneva: UNRISD.

Corporation for National and Community Service (CNCS) (2006), *Volunteering in America 2006: National, State, and City Information*, Washington, DC: CNCS.

Corporation for National and Community Service (2010), *Volunteering in America 2010: National, State, and City Information*, Washington, DC: CNCS.

Coulter, I. (1966), 'The Trade Unions', in Gerald Kaufman (ed.), *The Left: A Symposium*, London: Anthony Blond, pp. 31–50.

Crick, B. (1964), *In Defence of Politics*, Middlesex: Pelican Books.

Dahrendorf, R. (1995), *LSE: A History of the London School of Economics and Political Science 1895–1995*, London and New York: Oxford University Press.

Das-Gupta, I. (2008), 'Volunteer schemes "not effective"', *Third Sector Online*, available at: http://www.thirdsector.co.uk/news/archive/775360/Volunteer-schemes-not-effective (accessed 16 May 2011).

Davies, G. (1996), *From Opportunity to Entitlement. The Transformation and Decline of Great Society Liberalism*, Kansas: University of Kansas Press.

Davis, J. (1988), *Reforming London. The London Government Problem 1855–1900*, Oxford: Clarendon Press.

Davis, F. and B. Strevens (2010), *The Big Society: A View from the South*, Southampton: SCA Institute of Social Enterprise.

DCMS (2010), 'Culture Secretary announces action plan to boost philanthropy', available at: http://www.culture.gov.uk/news/media_releases/7631.aspx (accessed 6 February 2012).

Deacon, B. (ed.) (1995), *Global Social Policy: International Organizations and the Future of Welfare*, London: SAGE Publications.

Deakin, N. and J. Davis Smith (2011), 'Labour, charity and voluntary action: the myth of hostility?', in M. Hilton and J. McKay (eds), *The Ages of Voluntarism: How We Got to the Big Society*, Oxford: Oxford University Press.

Department for Business, Innovation and Skills (2010), 'Community Interest Companies, Annual Report, 2009–10', available at: http://bis.ecgroup.net/Publications/CommunityInterestCompaniesRegulator/AnnualReports.aspx (accessed 6 February 2012).

Department for Communities and Local Government (2009), *Citizenship Survey: 2009–10 (April–June 2009), England Statistical Release*, 9, London: Department for Communities and Local Government.

Department for Communities and Local Government (2010), *Decentralisation and the Localism Bill: An Essential Guide*, London: Department for Communities and Local Government.

Dewey, J. (1927), *The Public and its Problems*, (1991 edn), Athens, OH: Swallow Press.

Digby A. and N. Bosanquet (1988), 'Doctors and patients in an era of national health insurance and private practice, 1913–1938', *Economic History Review*, **41** (1), 74–94.

DirectGov (2010), 'National Citizen Service pilots announced', available at: http://webarchive.nationalarchives.gov.uk/+/www.direct.gov.uk/en/Nl1/Newsroom/DG_189542 (accessed 19 September 2011).

Dobash, R.E. and R. P. Dobash (1980), *Violence Against Wives*, London: Open Books.

Dobkin Hall, P. (2006), 'A historical overview of philanthropy, voluntary associations, and nonprofit organizations in the United States 1600–2000', in W.W. Powell and R. Steinberg (eds), *The Non-profit Sector: A Research Handbook*, second edition, New Haven and London: Yale Univerity Press, pp. 32–55.

Dodd, T., S. Nicholas, D. Povey and A. Walker (2004), 'Crime in England and Wales 2003/2004', London: Home Office.

Dolan, P., M. Hallsworth, D. Halpern, D. King and I. Vlaev (2010), *MINDSPACE: Influencing Behaviour Through Public Policy*, London: Cabinet Office/ Institute of Government.

Dorling, D., J. Rigby and B. Wheeler (2007), *Poverty, Wealth and Place in Britain, 1968–2005*, Bristol: Policy Press.

Drever, E. (2010), *2008–09 Citizenship Survey: Volunteering and Charitable Giving Topic Report*, London: Department for Communities and Local Government.

Dudwick, N., E. Gomart and A. Marc, with K. Kuehnast (eds) (2003), *When Things Fall Apart: Qualitative Studies of Poverty in the Former Soviet Union*, Washington, DC: The World Bank.

Duncan Smith, I. (2007), *Breakthrough Britain: End the Costs of Social Breakdown: Overview*, London: Centre for Social Justice.

Durkheim, E. (1912), *The Elementary Forms of Religious Life*, trans. C. Cosman (2001), Oxford: Oxford University Press.

Durose, C., F. Gains, L. Richardson, R. Combs, K. Broome and C. Eason (2011), *Pathways to Politics – Research Report 65*, Manchester: Equalities and Human Rights Commission.

EBRD (2011), 'Life in transition: after the crisis', London: EBRD.

Ellis Paine, A., N. Ockenden and J. Stuart (2010), 'Volunteers in hybrid organizations. A marginalized minority?', in D. Billis (ed.), *Hybrid Organizations and the Third Sector. Challenges for Practice, Theory and Policy*, London: Palgrave Macmillan.

Escobar, A. (1995), *Encountering Development: The Making and the Unmaking of the Third World*, Princeton: Princeton University Press.

Esping-Andersen, G. (1990), *The Three Worlds of Welfare Capitalism*, Cambridge: Polity.

Etzioni, A. (1993), *The Spirit of Community*, London: Harper Collins.

Eulau, H. and P. D. Karps (1977), 'The puzzle of representation: specifying components of responsiveness', *Legislative Studies Quarterly*, **2** (3), 233–54.

Eulau, H. (1987), 'The congruence model revisited', *Legislative Studies Quarterly*, **12** (2), 171–214.

European Commission (2005), 'Special Eurobarometer Report No 223 – Social Capital', available at: http://ec.europa.eu/public_opinion/archives/ebs/ebs_223_en.pdf (accessed 15 June 2011).

European Commission (2010a), *Study on Volunteering in the European Union – Country Report United Kingdom*, Brussels: European Commission

European Commission (2010b), *Study on Volunteering in the European Union – Country Report Sweden*, Brussels: European Commission.

Evans, E., F. Gains, M. Goodwin, P. John, N. Rao and L. Richardson (2007), *Improving The Representativeness Of Councillors: Learning from Five High Performing Local Authorities in England*, London: CLG.

Ewald, F. (1986), *L'Etat Providence*, Paris: Bernard Grasset.

False Economy (2011), 'Exclusive: More than 2,000 charities and community groups face cuts', available at: http://falseeconomy.org.uk/blog/exclusive-more-than-2000-charities-and-community-groups-face-cuts (accessed 4 August 2011).

Farr, J. (2004), 'Social capital: a conceptual history', *Political Theory*, **32**, 6–33.

Ferguson, J. (1994), *The Anti-Politics Machine: 'Development', Depoliticization, and Bureaucratic Power in Lesotho*, Minneapolis, MN: University of Minnesota Press.

Finlayson, G. (1990), 'A moving frontier: voluntarism and the state in British social welfare 1911–1949, *Twentieth-Century British History*, **1** (2), 183–206.

Follett, M. (1918), *The New State. Group Organization in the Solution of Popular Government*, London and New York: Longmans, Green & Co.

Foster, P.O.P. (1955), *The Two Cities: A Study of Church-State Conflict*, London: Blackfriars Publications.

Foster, P.O.P. (1958), *The Great Society*, London: Blackfriars Publications.

Freeden, M. (1978), *The New Liberalism*, Oxford: Oxford University Press.

Gal, S. and G. Kligman (2000), *Politics of Gender after Socialism*, Princeton: Princeton University Press.

Galloway, P. (1988), 'Basic patterns in annual variations in fertility, nuptiality, mortality, and prices in pre-industrial Europe', *Population Studies*, **42**, 275–303.

Gardner, J.W. (1970), 'Taxing foundations is dangerous', in T.C. Reeves (ed.), *Foundations Under Fire*, Ithaca and London: Cornell University Press, pp. 214–18.

Gaskin, K. (2005), *Getting a Grip: Risk, Risk Management and Volunteering: A Literature Review*, London: Volunteering England and IVR.

Gentleman, A. (2011), 'Women's refuge chief returns OBE in protest over cuts', *Guardian*, Tuesday 15 February.

Geoghegan, M. and F. Powell (2006), 'Community development, partnership governance and dilemmas of professionalization: profiling and assessing the case of Ireland', *British Journal of Social Work*, **36**, 845–61.

Giddens, A. (1998), *The Third Way: The Renewal of Social Democracy*, Cambridge: Polity and Malden, MA: Blackwell.

Giddens, A. (2007*)*, *Over to You, Mr Brown*, Cambridge and Malden MA: Polity.

Gilbert, B.B. (1970), *British Social Policy, 1914–1939*, London: Batsford.

Gittell, R. and A.C. Vidal (1998), *Community Organizing: Building Social Capital as a Development Strategy*, Thousand Oaks, CA: SAGE.

Glasman, M. (2011), 'Labour as a radical tradition', in Glasman, M., J. Rutherford, M. Stears and S. White (eds), *The Labour Tradition and the Politics of Paradox*, London: The Oxford London Seminar Series/Soundings.

Glynn, S. (2010), 'Can private philanthropy fill the shortfall in UK arts budget?', *Renaissance*, The Art Market, available at: http://www.renaissanceonline. co.uk/2010/08/can-private-philanthropy-fill-the-shortfall-in-uk-arts-budget/ (accessed 16 February 2012).

Goetz, A.M. and R. Sen Gupta (1996), 'Who takes the credit? Gender, power, and control over loan use in rural credit programs in Bangladesh', *World Development*, **24** (1), 45–63.

Goodwin, R.N. (1974), *The American Condition*, New York: Doubleday.

Gramsci, A. (1957), *The Modern Prince and Other Writings*, New York: International Publishers.

Grantcraft (2010) *Working With Government: Guidance for Grantmakers*, available at: http://www.grantcraft.org/index.cfm?fuseaction=Page. ViewPage&pageId=1547 (accessed 8 March 2012).

Grassman, E.J. and L. Svedberg (2007), 'Civic participation in a Scandinavian welfare state: patterns in contemporary Sweden', in Lars Trägårdh (ed.), *State and Civil Society in Northern Europe: The Swedish Model Reconsidered*, New York: Berghahn Books, pp. 126–64.

Greening, J. (2011), Press statement to launch the *Giving White Paper*, 23 May, available at: http://www.cabinetoffice.gov.uk/news/giving-white-paper- %E2%80%93-making-it-easier-take-part-bigger-stronger-society (accessed 15 September 2011).

Gregory, D. (2011), 'How state aid rules affect the "big society" bank', available at: http://www.guardian.co.uk/public-leaders-network/2011/apr/19/big- society-bank (accessed 19 April 2011).

Grooteart, C. (ed.) (1997), *Expanding the Measure of Wealth – Indicators of Environmentally Sustainable Development*, Washington, DC: World Bank.

Guirguis-Younger, M., M. Kelley and M. Mckee (2005), 'Professionalization of hospice volunteer practices: what are the implications?', *Palliative and Supportive Care*, **3**, 143–4.

Hajer, M. and H. Wagenaar (eds) (2003), *Deliberative Policy Analysis, Understanding Governance in the Network Society*, Cambridge: Cambridge University Press, pp. 1–30.

Hall, P. (2002), 'Great Britain: the role of government and the distribution of social capital', in Robert D. Putnam (ed.), *Democracies in Flux*, Oxford: Oxford University Press, pp. 21–58.

Hall, S. (1967), 'Class and the mass media', in R. Mabey (ed.), *Class: A Symposium*, London: Anthony Blond, pp. 93–113.

Hall, S. (2011), 'The neoliberal revolution', *Soundings*, **48**, Summer, 9–27, available at: http://www.lwbooks.co.uk/ReadingRoom/Hall.pdf (accessed 20 September 2011).

Hann, C. (ed.) (2002), *Postsocialism: Ideals, Ideologies and Practices in Eurasia*, London: Routledge.

Hansard Society (2010), *Audit of Political Engagement 7: The 2010 Report*, London: Hansard Society.

Harris, J. (2003), *Civil Society in British History*, Oxford: Oxford University Press.

Harriss, J. (2002), *Depoliticizing Development: The World Bank and Social Capital*, London: Anthem Press.

Hart, K., J.L. Lavile and A.D. Cattani (eds) (2010), *The Human Economy*, Cambridge: Polity.

Harvey, D. (2007), *A Brief History of Neoliberalism*, Oxford: Oxford University Press.

Hashemi, S., S.R. Schuler and A.P. Riley (1996), 'Rural credit programs and women's empowerment in Bangladesh', *World Development*, **24** (4), 635–53.

Hassan, J.A. (1985) 'The growth and impact of the British water industry in the nineteenth century', *Economic History Review*, **38**, 531–47.

Hay, C. (2007), *Why We Hate Politics*, Cambridge: Polity Press.

Hayek, F.A. (1944), *The Road to Serfdom*, London: Routledge,

Hayek, F.A. (1973–9), 3 vols, *Law, Legislation and Liberty*, London: Routledge.

Hayek, F.A. (1983), *Knowledge, Education and Society*, London: Adam Smith Institute.

Heaney, V. (2010), *Investing in Social Enterprise: The Role of Tax Incentives*, CSFI & NESTA, London.

Helm, T. and J. Coman (2011), 'Maurice Glasman – the peer plotting Labour's new strategy from his flat', *The Guardian*, available at: http://www.guardian.

co.uk/politics/2011/jan/16/maurice-glasman-peer-labour (accessed 16 January 2011).

Hennock, E.P. (1973), *Fit and Proper Persons: Ideal and Reality in Nineteenth Century Urban Government*, London: Edwin Arnold.

Henriques, B. (1937), *The Indiscretions of a Warden*, London: Methuen.

Henriques, B. (1951), *Fratres: Club Boys in Uniform*, London: Secker and Warburg.

Hickman, T. (2004), *The Call Up: A History of National Service*, London: Headline.

Hill, C.E. (1993), 'Sidney Webb and the common good', *History of Political Thought*, **XIV**, 4, pp. 591–622.

Hilton, M. (2003), *Consumerism in Twentieth-Century Britain: The Search for a Historical Movement*, Cambridge: Cambridge University Press.

Hilton, M., J. McKay, N. Crowson and J.F. Mouhot (2010), 'The Big Society: civic participation and the state in modern Britain', *History and Policy papers*, June.

Hilton, M., N. Crowson, J.F. Mouhot and J. McKay (2012), *A History of NGOs in Britain: Charities, Civil Society and the Voluntary Sector since 1945*, Basingstoke: Palgrave.

Hilton, Steve (2010), available at: http://blogs.ft.com/westminster/2010/01/the-steve-hilton-strategy-bulletins/ Bulletin No 1, 16 October (accessed 10 December 2010).

Hindle, S. (2004), *On the Parish? The Micro-Politics of Poor Relief in Rural England, c.1550–1750*, Oxford: Clarendon Press.

HM Government (2005), Companies (Audit, Investigations and Community Enterprise) Act 2004.

HM Government (2010), *Giving Green Paper*, London: Cabinet Office.

HM Government (2011a), *Giving White Paper*, Cm 8084, London: TSO, available at: www.official-documents.gov.uk/document/cm80/8084/8084.pdf (accessed 20 April 2012).

HM Government. (2011b), *Growing the Social Investment Market: A vision and strategy*, Cabinet Office, February 2011, available at: http://www.cabinetoffice.gov.uk/resource-library/growing-social-investment-market-vision-and-strategy (accessed 9 February 2012).

HMSO (1979), *Government Expenditure Plans*, London: HMSO.

HM Treasury (2000), *Public Expenditure. Statistical Analyses 2000–01*, London: HM Treasury, Cmd 4601, Tables 1.11 and 4.1.

HM Treasury (2002), *Next Steps on Volunteering and Giving*, London: HM Treasury.

Home Office (2002), 'Crime in England and Wales 2001/2002', London: Home Office.

Home Office (2005), *The Volunteering Compact Code of Good Practice*, London: Home Office.

House of Commons (2011), 'Localism Bill', available at: http://www. publications.parliament.uk/pa/cm201011/cmbills/126/11126.i-v.html (accessed 4 August 2011).

House of Commons Communities and Local Government Committee (2011), Localism, 'Summary', Third Report of Session 2010–12, Volume 1, HC 547, available at: http://www.publications.parliament.uk/pa/cm201012/cmselect/ cmcomloc/547/547.pdf.

House of Lords Science and Technology Select Committee (2011), *2nd Report of Session 2010–12, Behaviour Change Report HL Paper 179*, London: TSO.

Howell, J. and J. Pearce (2001), *Civil Society and Development: A Critical Exploration*, Boulder, Colorado: Lynne Rienner Publishers.

Howell, J., A. Ishkanian, E. Obadare, H. Seckinelgin, and M. Glasius (2008), 'The backlash against civil society in the wake of the Long War on Terror', *Development in Practice*, **18** (1), 82–93.

Hudson, S. (2011), 'Cuts are undermining volunteering', available at: http://www.thirdsector.co.uk/news/Article/1053308/cuts-undermining-volunteering-says-dame-elisabeth-hoodless/ (accessed 9 May 2011).

Humphreys, R. (1999), *No Fixed Abode: A History of Responses to the Roofless and Rootless in Britain*, Basingstoke: Macmillan.

Hunt, J. (Secretary of State for Culture, Media and Sport) (2010), in a speech to the European Association for Philanthropy and Giving, 8 December 2010.

Hutson, S. and D. Clapham (1999), *Homelessness: Public Policies and Private Troubles*, London: Cassell.

Income Tax Special Purpose Commissioners v Pemsel [1891] AC531 (HL).

Innes, J. (2009), *Inferior Politics. Social Problems and Social Policies in Eighteenth Century Britain*, Oxford: Oxford University Press.

IPSOS MORI/Royal College of Physicians (2008), *Trust in the Professions: IPSOS MORI Veracity Index*, available at: http://www.ipsos-mori.com/ Assets/Docs/Polls/Ipsos_MORI_Veracity_Index_2008.pdf (accessed 30 September 2011).

Ishkanian, A. (2007a), 'En-gendering civil society and democracy building: the anti-domestic violence campaign in Armenia', *Social Politics: International Studies in Gender, State & Society*, **14** (4), 488.

Ishkanian, A. (2007b), 'Democracy promotion and civil society', in Martin Albrow et al. (eds), *Global Civil Society 2007/8: Communicative Power and Democracy*, London: SAGE Publications Ltd, pp. 58–85.

Ivens, M. (1967), 'Beyond the organisation man', in R. Mabey (ed.), *Class: A Symposium*, London: Anthony Blond, pp. 67–8.

i-volunteer (2010), 'Library staff strike in protest to volunteers', available at: http://www.i-volunteer.org.uk/newshound/strike-in-protest-over-volunteers/ (accessed 4 August 2011).

John, P., L. Richardson, G. Smith, G. Stoker and C. Wales (2011), *Nudge, Nudge, Think, Think: Using Experiments to Change Civic Behaviour*, London: Bloomsbury Academic.

Jones, M.G. (1938), *The Charity School Movement: A Study of Eighteenth Century Puritanism in Action*, Cambridge: Cambridge University Press.

Joy, I. (2010), *NPC Perspectives: Preparing for cuts, how funders should support charities in a world of government cuts and changing funding structures*, London: New Philanthropy Capital.

Judt, T. (2005), *Post War. A History of Europe Since 1945*, New York: Penguin.

Kabeer, N. (1994), *Reversed Realities: Gender Hierarchies in Development Thought*, London: Verson.

Kabeer, N. (2001), 'Conflict over credit: re-evaluating the empowerment potential of loans to women in rural Bangladesh', *World Development*, **29** (1), 63–84.

Kabeer, N. (2005), 'Gender equality and women's empowerment: a critical analysis of the third Millennium Development Goal', *Gender and Development*, **13**, 13–24.

Kain, E.D. (2011), 'Can David Cameron's 'Big Society' survive the London riots?', *Forbes*, 8 November, available at: http://www.forbes.com/sites/erikkain/2011/08/11/can-david-camerons-big-society-survive-the-london-riots/ (accessed 9 February 2012).

Karl, B.D. and A.W. Karl (1999), 'Foundations and the government', in C.T. Clotfelter and T. Ehrlich (eds), *Philanthropy and the Nonprofit Sector in a Changing America*, Bloomington Indiana: Bloomington University Press.

Kaufman, G. (ed.) (1966), *The Left: A Symposium*, The Great Society Series 3, London: Anthony Blond.

Kellner, P. (1998), *New Mutualism. The Third Way*, The Co-operative Party, London: The Co-operative Press.

Kendall, J. (2003), *The Voluntary Sector: Comparative Perspectives in the UK*, London: Routledge.

Korten, D. (1990), *Getting to the 21st Century: Voluntary Action and the Global Agenda*, West Hartford: Kumarian Press.

Kuehnast, K. and C. Nechemias (eds) (2004), *Post-Soviet Women Encountering Transition: Nation Building, Economic Survival and Civic Activism*, Washington, DC and Baltimore, MD: Woodrow Wilson Center Press and Johns Hopkins University Press.

Labour (2010), 'Labour finds its sense of humour in video lampooning David Cameron's "big society"', available at: http://www.guardian.co.uk/politics/wintour-and-watt/2010/may/03/general-election-2010-labour (accessed 4 August 2011).

Lady Margaret Hall Papers (1957), Lambeth Archives, Minet Library, London SE5.

LaMarche, G. (2010), 'What we're learning: the local impact of global philanthropy', speech 6 October, available at: http://www. atlanticphilanthropies.org/learning/speech-local-impact-global-philanthropy (accessed 9 February, 2012).

Leadbeater, C. (1997), *The Rise of the Social Entrepreneur*, London: Demos.

Leat, D. (1999), 'British foundations: the organisation and management of grantmaking', in H.K. Anheier and S. Toepler (eds) *Private Funds, Public Purpose*, New York: Kluwer Academic/Plenum.

Lees, L.H. (1998), *The Solidarities of Strangers: The English Poor Laws and the People, 1700–1948*, Cambridge: Cambridge University Press.

Legislation.gov.uk (1990), 'National Health Service and Community Care Act 1990', available at: http://www.legislation.gov.uk/ukpga/1990/19/contents (accessed 4 August 2011).

Levitan, S. (1969), *The Great Society's Poor Law. A New Approach to Poverty*, Baltimore: Johns Hopkins.

Lewis, D. (2005), 'Individuals, organisations and public action: trajectories of the "non-governmental" in development studies', in Uma Kothari (ed.), *A Radical History of Development Studies*, London: Zed Books.

Lewis, D. and N. Kanji (2009), *Non-Governmental Organizations and Development*, London: Macmillan.

Leymore, V. (1982), 'Structure and persuasion: the case of advertising', *Sociology*, **16** (3), 377–389.

Li, Y. and D. Marsh (2008), 'New forms of political participation: searching for expert citizens and everyday makers', *British Journal of Political Science*, **38**, 247–272.

Lindert, P.H. (1994), 'Unequal living standards', in R. Floud and D. McCloskey (eds), *The Economic History of Britain 1700–1860*, Cambridge: Cambridge University Press, p. 383.

Lippmann, W. (1927), *The Phantom Public*, New York: Macmillan.

Lippmann, W. (1937), *The Good Society*, (1943 edn), New York: Little Brown; (2005 edn), New Brunswick: Transaction Publishers.

Llewellyn Smith, H. (1935), *New Survey of London Life and Leisure. Vol. IX, Life and Leisure*, London: P.S. King.

London Voluntary Services Council (LVSC) (2011), 'The Big Squeeze: the squeeze tightens', available at: http://www.lvsc.org.uk/campaigns/big-squeeze.aspx (last accessed, 6 February 2012).

London Youth (2010), *Annual Report and Financial Statements, Year Ended 31 August 2010*, London: London Youth, available at: http://www.londonyouth. org.uk/sites/default/files/London%20Youth%20accounts%2031%2008%20 10%20signed%20copy%20with%20pictures.pdf (accessed 19 September 2011).

Lord Hodgson of Astley Abbotts (2011), 'Unshackling good neighbours: report of the task force established to consider how to cut red tape for small charities, voluntary organisations and social enterprises', Cabinet Office, available at: http://www.cabinetoffice.gov.uk/resource-library/ unshackling-good-neighbours (accessed 15 February 2012).

Lord Nathan (1952), Committee of Enquiry into the Law and Practice Relating to Charitable Trusts (Nathan Committee): Evidence and Final Report (CMND 8710), London: Her Majesty's Stationery Office.

Low, N., S. Butt and A. Paine (2007), *Helping Out. The National Survey of Volunteering and Charitable Giving*, London: Home Office.

Lowe, P. and J. Goyder (1983), *Environmental Groups in Politics*, London: Allen & Unwin.

Lumley, T., M. Brookes, R. Macdougall and P. Lomax (2011), *Ten Ways to Boost Giving: NPC Perspectives*, London: New Philanthropy Capital.

Lundström, T. and L. Svedberg (2003), 'The voluntary sector in a social democratic welfare state? The case of Sweden', *Journal of Social Policy*, **32** (2), 217–38.

Luong, P.J. (ed.) (2004), *The Transformation of Central Asia: States and Societies From Soviet Rule to Independence*, Ithaca, NY: Cornell University Press.

Luxton, P. (2001), *The Law of Charities*, Oxford: Oxford University Press.

Mabbott, J.D. (1947), *The State and the Citizen*, London: Hutchinson.

Mabey, R. (ed.) (1967), *Class: A Symposium*, Great Society Series 1, London: Anthony Blond.

Major, J. (1993), 'Speech to the Conservative Group for Europe', 22 April, available at: http://www.johnmajor.co.uk/page1086.html (accessed 17 May 2011).

Malik, S. (2011), 'Schoolboy warned by police over picket plan at David Cameron's office', available at: http://www.guardian.co.uk/uk/2010/dec/10/ schoolboy-quizzed-cameron-office-picket (accessed 9 May 2011).

Mandler, P. (1987), 'The making of the New Poor Law redivivus', *Past and Present*, **117**, 131–57.

Marangos, J. (2002), 'The political economy of shock therapy', *Journal of Economic Surveys*, **16** (1), 41–76.

Marsden, D. (1967), 'School, class and the parent's dilemma', in R. Mabey (ed.), *Class: A Symposium*, London: Anthony Blond.

Marshall, J. (2009), 'Membership of UK political parties', London: House of Commons Library, available at: http://www.parliament.uk/documents/ commons/lib/research/briefings/snsg-05125.pdf (accessed 30 September 2011).

Matheson, J. and C. Summerfield (2001), *Social Trends 30*, London: Office of National Statistics, available at: http://www.ons.gov.uk/ons/search/index. html?newquery=social+trends+30 (accessed 15 February 2012).

Mavity, J.H. and P.N. Ylvisaker (1977), 'Private philanthropy and public affairs', in *The Commission on Private Philanthropy and Public Needs, Research Papers Part 1, Vol.2*, Washington DC: Department of Treasury.

McCabe, A. (2011), *Briefing Paper 51: Below the radar in a Big Society? Reflections on community engagement, empowerment and social action in a changing policy context*, Southampton: Third Sector Research Centre.

Meacham, S. (1987), *Toynbee Hall and Social Reform, 1880–1914: the Search for Community*, New Haven: Yale University Press.

Micheletti, M. (2010), *Political Virtue and Shopping: Individuals, Consumerism, and Collective Action*, New York, NY: Palgrave Macmillan.

Miliband, E. (2011a), 'Ed Miliband: the Big Society: a cloak for the small state', available at: http://www.independent.co.uk/opinion/commentators/ed-miliband-the-big-society-a-cloak-for-the-small-state-2213011.html (accessed 4 August 2011).

Miliband, E. (2011b), 'Responsibility in the twenty-first century', available at: http://www.politics.co.uk/comment-analysis/2011/06/13/ed-miliband-responsibility-speech-in-full (accessed 9 February 2012).

Miller, W.E. and D.E. Stokes (1963), 'Constituency influence in Congress', *American Political Science Review*, **57**, 45–56.

Milton, J. (1643), 'The Doctrine and Discipline of Divorce, Restor'd, to the Good of both Sexes', reprinted in (1927), *Areopagitica and other Prose Works*, London: J.M. Dent and New York: E.P. Dutton, pp. 187–277.

Milton, J. (1644), 'Of Education', reprinted in (1927), *Areopagitica and other Prose Works*, London: J.M. Dent and New York: E.P. Dutton, pp. 42–53.

Mitchell, J. (1991), 'Public campaigning on overseas aid in the 1980s', in A. Bose and P. Burnell (eds), *Britain's Overseas Aid since 1979: Between Idealism and Self-Interest*, Manchester: Manchester University Press, pp. 146–57.

Mohan, J. (2010), 'What do volunteering statistics tell us about the prospects for the Big Society?', NCVO/TSRC Big Society Evidence Seminar, 11 October.

Mohan, J. (2011), *Mapping the Big Society: Perspectives from the Third Sector Research Centre (Working Paper 62)*, Birmingham: TSRC.

Montaigne, M. de (1842), trans. W. Hazlitt, *The Works of Montaigne*, London: John Templeman.

Moore, C. (2011), 'I'm starting to think that the Left might actually be right', available at: http://www.telegraph.co.uk/news/politics/8655106/Im-starting-to-think-that-the-Left-might-actually-be-right.html (accessed 9 February, 2012).

Moro, D. and S. McKay (2010), *Briefing Paper 28: The growing workforce in the voluntary and community sectors: analysis of the Labour Force Survey, 1993–2009*, Southampton: Third Sector Research Centre.

Mowat, C.L. (1944), 'The fall of the Labour government in Great Britain, August 1931', *Huntington Library Quarterly*, **7** (4) 353–86.

Murray, M. (1967), 'Class and the welfare state', in R. Mabey (ed.), *Class: A Symposium*, London: Anthony Blond.

National Council for Voluntary Organisations (NCVO) (1996), 'Meeting the challenge of change', report of the Commission on the future of the voluntary sector.

National Council for Voluntary Organisations (1998), 'Blurred vision: public trust in charities', *NCVO Research Quarterly*, **1**.

National Council for Voluntary Organisations (NCVO) (2001), 'For the public benefit?', a consultation document on charity law reform.

National Council for Voluntary Organisations (2010), *UK Civil Society Almanac 2010*, London: National Council of Voluntary Organisations, available at: http://www.ncvo-vol.org.uk/almanac2010 (accessed 30 September 2011).

National Council of Social Service (NCSS) (1976), 'Charity law and voluntary organisations', a report of the Goodman Committee.

New Economics Foundation/Charities Aid Foundation (2006), *Developing a Social Equity Capital Market*, West Malling: Charities Aid Foundation.

New Philanthropy Capital (2011), *NPC Perspectives: Preparing for Cuts. How Funders Should Support Charities in a World of Government Cuts and Changing Funding Structures*, London: NPC.

New Philanthropy Capital/National Endowment for Science, Technology and the Arts (NPC/NESTA) (2011), *Understanding the demand for and supply of social finance. Research to inform the Big Society Bank*, London: NESTA.

Nicholls, A and C. Pharoah (2008), *The Landscape of Social Investment: A holistic topology of opportunities and challenges*, Oxford: Said Business School Skoll Centre for Social Entrepreneurship.

Nichols, D. (1975), *The Pluralist State*, London: Macmillan.

Nielsen. W.A. (1972) *The Big Foundations*, New York: Columbia University Press.

Norman, J. and J. Ganesh (2006), *Compassionate Conservatism*, London: Policy Exchange.

Norman, J. (2010a), *The Big Society: The Anatomy of the New Politics*, Buckingham: University of Buckingham Press.

Norman, J. (2010b), 'We need not just a Spending Review, but a Full Audit of Government', available at: http://conservativehome.blogs.com/centreright/2010/06/we-need-not-just-a-spending-review-but-a-full-audit-of-government.html (accessed 20 February 2012).

Northern Rock Foundation, (2011), 'Entering the lists', and 'Beyond "flat-earth" maps of the third sector', available at: http://www.nr-foundation.org.uk/thirdsectortrends/tt_reports.html (accessed 9 February 2012).

Oborne, P. (2011), 'The moral decay of our society is as bad at the top as the bottom', available at: http://blogs.telegraph.co.uk/news/peteroborne/100100708/the-moral-decay-of-our-society-is-as-bad-at-the-top-as-the-bottom/ (accessed 9 February 2012).

Ockenden, N. and J. Machin (2008), *Volunteer Engage Learn: A New Volunteer Programme at the Natural History Museum*, London: Natural History Museum.

Office for Civil Society (2010a), *Building a Stronger Civil Society. A strategy for voluntary and community groups, charities and social enterprises*, October.

Office for Civil Society (2010b), *Supporting a Stronger Civil Society. An Office for Civil Society consultation on improving support for frontline civil society organisations*, October.

Office for Civil Society (2011a), 'Big Society – Overview', available at: http://www.cabinetoffice.gov.uk/content/big-society-overview (accessed 15 February 2012).

Office for Civil Society (2011b)'Government names new partner to deliver Community Organisers', 19 February, available at: http://www.cabinetoffice.gov.uk/news/government-names-new-partner-deliver-community-organisers (accessed 9 February 2012).

Office of National Statistics (2003), *Census 2001: Local Authority Profiles and Population Pyramids (London)*, London: Office of National Statistics.

Office of the Regulator of Community Interest Companies (2011), *Operational Report*, First Quarter 2011–2012, London: Department of Business, Innovation and Skills.

Oppenheimer, M. and N. Deakin (eds) (2011), *Beveridge and Voluntary Action in Britain and the Wider British World*, Manchester: Manchester University Press.

Outhwaite, W. (2006), *The Future of Society*, Oxford and Malden, MA: Blackwell.

Patterson, J.T. (1997), *Grand Expectations: The USA 1945–74*, Oxford: Oxford University Press.

Peacock, A.T. and J. Wiseman (1967), *The Growth of Public Expenditure in the United Kingdom*, 2nd edn, London: George Allen and Unwin.

Pearson, R. (2000), 'Think globally, act locally: translating international microcredit experience into the United Kingdom context', in David and Tina Wallace Lewis (eds), *New Roles and Relevance: Development NGOs and the Challenge of Change*, Bloomfield, CT: Kumarian Press, Inc., pp. 153–64.

Pharoah, C. (2011), *Charity Market Monitor 2011*, London: CaritasData and Cass Business School.

Philanthropy Review (2011), *A Call to Action*, available at: http://www.philanthropyreview.co.uk/Philanthropy%20Review%20Charter.pdf (accessed 9 February 2012).

Phillips, G. (1992), *The Rise of the Labour Party 1893–1931*, London: Routledge.

Phillips, L. (2011), 'National Citizen Service "too costly to last"', available at: http://www.publicfinance.co.uk/news/2010/07/national-citizen-service-too-costly-to-last/ (accessed 9 May 2011).

Pickering, M. (1993), *Auguste Comte, An Intellectual Biography*, vol. 1, Cambridge: Cambridge University Press.

Plummer, J. (2010), 'Lord Wei accuses some charities of "damaging civil society"', *Third Sector Online*, available at: http://www.thirdsector.co.uk/channels/Governance/article/1034858/Lord-Wei-accuses-charities-damaging-civil-society/ (accessed 13 October 2010).

Popper, K. (1957), *The Poverty of Historicism*, London: Routledge and Kegan Paul.

Porritt, J. (1994), 'Scientists plagued by the credibility gulf', *Daily Telegraph*, 17 December.

Posner, R. (2009), 'Treating financial consumers as consenting adults', *Wall Street Journal*, 23 July, available at: http://online.wsj.com/article/SB10001424052970203946904574302213213148166.html (accessed 15 September 2011).

Powell, J. (2010), *The New Machiavelli: How to Wield Power in the Modern World*, London: Bodley Head.

Power, A. (2011), 'International examples of decentralisation', in R. Tunstall, R. Lupton, A. Power and L. Richardson (eds), *Building the Big Society* (CASE report 67), London: Centre for Analysis of Social Exclusion, London School of Economics.

Prest, D. (2011), 'The peacetime conscripts: National Service in the post-war years', available at: http://www.bbc.co.uk/history/british/modern/peacetime_conscripts_01.shtml (accessed 9 May 2011).

Prewitt, K. (2006), 'Foundations', in W.W. Powell and R. Steinberg (eds), *The Nonprofit Sector: A Research Handbook*, New Haven: Yale University Press, pp. 355–77.

Prichard, J. (2011), cited in 'Big society "could widen gap between town and country"', http://www.guardian.co.uk/society/2011/feb/11/big-society-volunteering-north-south (accessed 21 October 2011).

Prochaska, F. (1988), *The Voluntary Impulse: Philanthropy in Modern Britain*, London: Faber.

Prochaska, F. (2006), *Christianity and Social Service in Modern Britain: The Disinherited Spirit*, Oxford: Oxford University Press.

ProZ (2011), 'Definition of muhtar', available at: http://www.proz.com/kudoz/turkish_to_english/law_general/966802-muhtar.html#2347291 (accessed 8 February 2012).

Public Administration Select Committee (PASC) (2011a), 'Funding of the Voluntary Sector', committee meeting on 16 February, available at: http://

www.parliamentlive.tv/Main/Player.aspx?meetingId=7704 (accessed 9 February 2012).

Public Administration Select Committee (PASC) (2011b), Public Administration Committee - 902-I, Seventeenth Report *The Big Society*, House of Commons, available at: http://www.publications. parliament.uk/pa/cm201012/cmselect/cmpubadm/902/90202.htm (accessed 16 February 2012).

Public Service (2011), 'PM '"wrong about effect of police cuts"', available at: http://www.publicservice.co.uk/print_news.asp?type=news&id=17162 (accessed 19 August 2011).

Putnam, R. (2000), *Bowling Alone: The Collapse and Revival of American Community*, New York: Simon & Schuster.

Qualter, T.H. (1980), *Graham Wallas and the Great Society*, London and Basingstoke: Macmillan.

Ramesh, R. (2010), 'Interview with Mr Big Society', *The Guardian*, 22 June, available at: http://www.guardian.co.uk/society/2010/jun/22/nat-wei-big-society-adviser-conservatives (accessed 9 February 2012).

Reich, R. (2005), 'A failure of philanthropy: American charity short-changes the poor, and public policy is partly to blame', *Stanford Social Innovation Review*, **3** (4) 23–33.

Richardson, L. (2005), 'Social and political participation and inclusion', in J.K Hills, and K. Stewart (eds), *A More Equal Society? New Labour, Poverty, Inequality and Exclusion*, Bristol: Policy Press.

Riegert, A. (2011), 'International examples of Big Society initiatives', London: Office for Civil Society, Cabinet Office.

Robinson, M.(1997a), 'Privatising the voluntary sector: NGOs as public service contractors', in David Hulme and Michael Edwards (eds), *NGOs, States and Donors*, London: Macmillan, pp. 59–78.

Robinson, M. and G. White (1997b), 'The role of civic organizations in the provision of social services', *Research for Action Papers 37*, Helsinki: United Nations University/World Institute for Development Economics Research.

Rochester, C., A. Ellis Paine and S. Howlett with M. Zimmeck (2010), *Volunteering and Society in the 21st Century*, London: Palgrave Macmillan.

Rootes, C. (2007), 'Nature protection organizations in England', in C.S.A. van Koppen and W. Markham (eds), *Protecting Nature: Organizations and Networks in Europe and the United States*, Cheltenham, UK and Northampton, MA, USA: Edward Elgar Publishing, pp. 34–62.

Rootes, C. (2009), 'Environmental NGOs and the environmental movement in England', in N. Crowson, M. Hilton and J. McKay (eds), *NGOs in Contemporary Britain: Non-state Actors in Society and Politics since 1945*, Basingstoke: Palgrave, pp. 201–21.

Rotolo, T. and J. Wilson (2004), 'What happened to the "Long Civic Generation"? Explaining cohort differences in volunteerism', *Social Forces*, **82** (3): 1091–121.

Royal National Lifeboat Institution (RNLI) (2011), Paul Boissier, Chief Executive, quoted in *The Times*, 6 September.

Rushton, N.S. (2001), 'Monastic charitable provision in Tudor England,' *Continuity and Change*, **16** (1), 9–44.

Russell, L. and D. Scott (1997), *Very Active Citizens? The Impact of Contracts on Volunteers*, Manchester: University of Manchester.

Salamon, L.M. and H.K. Anheier (1998), 'Social origins of civil society: explaining the nonprofit sector cross-nationally', *Voluntas: International Journal of Voluntary and Nonprofit Organizations*, **9** (3), 213–48.

Saxton, J. (2009), 'Fewer volunteers than a year ago', available at: http://www.thirdsector.co.uk/channels/Volunteering/Article/920756/Fewer-volunteers-year-ago/ (accessed 4 August 2011).

Schluter, A., V. Then and P. Walkenhorst (2001), *Foundations in Europe: Society, Management and Law*, London: Directory of Social Change.

Scottish Burial Reform and Cremation Society v Glasgow Corporation [1968] AC138 (HL).

Seers, D. (1968), 'The structure of power', in T. Balogh (ed.), *Crisis in the Civil Service. The Great Society*, series 7, London: Anthony Blond.

Sheard, J. (1995), 'From Lady Bountiful to Active Citizen' in J.D. Smith, C. Rochester and R. Hedley (eds), *An Introduction to the Voluntary Sector*, London: Routledge.

Simon, H. (1947), *Administrative Behavior*, New York: Free Press.

Simpson, A.B.W. (2004), *Human Rights and the End of Empire*, Oxford: Oxford University Press.

Sivesind, K.H. (2008), 'Comparative studies on volunteering – the crowding out hypothesis revisited', paper presented at the CINEFOGO Conference on Contemporary European Perspectives on Volunteering: Civic Virtue vs. Social Movement Activism, Ersta Sköndal University College, Stockholm, Sweden, 10 September.

Slack, P. (1990), *The English Poor Law 1531–1782*, Basingstoke: Macmillan.

Slack, P. (1998), *Poverty and Policy in Tudor and Stuart England*, London: Longman.

Smith, A. (1759), *The Theory of Moral Sentiments* (1979 edn), Oxford: Oxford University Press.

Smith, A. (1776), *The Wealth of Nations* (1976 edn), Chicago: University of Chicago.

Smith, R.M. (1996), 'Charity, self-interest and welfare: reflections from demographic and family history', in M.J. Daunton (ed.), *Charity, Self-Interest and Welfare in the English Past*, London: UCL Press, pp. 23–49.

Sokoll, T. (2001), *Essex Pauper Letters 1731–1837*, Oxford: The British Academy and Oxford University Press.

Stamp, T. (1987), *Stamp Album*, London: Bloomsbury.

Stedman Jones, S. (2001), *Durkheim Reconsidered*, London: Polity.

Stein, P. (1988), *The Character and Influence of the Roman Civil Law: Historical Essays*, London: Hambledon.

Stein, P. (1999), *Roman Law in European history*, Cambridge: Cambridge University Press.

Stiglitz, J. (2003), *Globalization and it Discontents*, New York: W.W. Norton & Company.

Stoker, G. (2006), *Why Politics Matters: Making Democracy Work*, Basingstoke: Palgrave Macmillan.

Stone, R. (2000), 'Stress: the invisible hand in Eastern Europe's death rates', *Science*, **288** (5472), 1732–3.

Sunstein, C.R. and R.H. Thaler (2003), 'Libertarian paternalism is not an oxymoron', *University of Chicago Law Review*, **70** (4), 1159–202.

Sutherland, G. (1973), 'Social policy in the inter-war years', *Historical Journal*, **16** (2) 420–31.

de Swaan, A. (1988), *In the Care of the State. Health Care, Education and Welfare in Europe and the USA in the Modern Era*, Oxford: Oxford University Press.

Swithinbank, T. (2001), *Coming Up from the Streets: The Story of the Big Issue*, London: Earthscan.

Szreter, S. (2002), 'The state of social capital: bringing back in power, politics, and history', *Theory and Society*, **31** (5), 573–621.

Szreter, S. and M. Woolcock (2004), 'Health by association? Social capital, social theory and the political economy of public health', *International Journal of Epidemiology*, **33** (4), 650–67.

Szreter, S. (2005), *Health and Wealth. Studies in History and Policy*, New York: University of Rochester Press.

Tarkowska, E. (2002), 'Intra household gender inequality: hidden dimensions of poverty among Polish women', *Communist and Post Communist Studies*, **35** (4), 411–32.

Teasdale, S. (2008), *In Good Health. Assessing the Impact of Volunteering in the NHS*, London: IVR.

Thaler, R. and C. Sunstein (2008), *Nudge: Improving Decisions about Health, Wealth and Happiness*, New Haven, CT, and London: Yale University Press (2009 edn, London: Penguin Books).

Thatcher, M. (1987), 'No such thing as society', interview for *Woman's Own*, available at http://www.margaretthatcher.org/document/106689 (accessed 30 April 2012).

de Tocqueville, A. (1835 and 1840), *Democracy in America*, 2 vols, reprinted in J.P. Mayer and Max Lerner (eds) (1968), London: Collins and Fontana.

Tonkiss, F. and A. Passey (1999), 'Trust, confidence and voluntary organisations: between values and institutions', *Sociology*, **33** (2), 257–74.

Towers, J. and S. Walby (2012), 'Measuring the impact of cuts in public expenditure on the provision of services to prevent violence against women and girls', report for Northern Rock Foundation and Trust for London.

Townsend, P. (2002), 'Poverty, social exclusion and social polarization: the need to construct an international welfare state', in Peter Townsend and David Gordon (eds), *World Poverty: New Policies to Defeat an Old Enemy*, Bristol: Policy Press, pp. 153–64.

Toynbee, P. (2011), 'Big society's a busted flush, but who will admit it first?', available at: http://www.guardian.co.uk/commentisfree/2011/feb/07/big-society-is-not-working, (accessed 4 August 2011).

Trägårdh, L. (2010), 'Commentary: incentives and conditions shaping civil society', *Journal of Civil Society*, **6** (2), 185–7.

Tunstall, R., R. Lupton, A. Power and L. Richardson (2011), *Building the Big Society*, CASEreport 67, London: LSE.

UNDP (2005), 'Central Asia Human Development Report', in UNDP (ed.), Bratislava: UNDP Regional Bureau for Europe and the Commonwealth of Independent States.

UNFPA (2010), 'Nationwide survey on domestic violence agaist women in Armenia 2008–2009', in UNFPA (ed.), *UNFPA Combating Gender-Based Violence in the South Caucasus Project*, Yerevan: UNFPA.

UNIFEM (2006), 'The story behind the numbers: women and employment in Central and Eastern Europe and the Western Commonwealth of Independent States', Bratislava: UNIFEM.

Unite the Union (2010), 'The "Big Society" localism bill is smokescreen for thousands of job cuts, says Unite', available at: http://www.unitetheunion.org/news__events/latest_news/the__big_society__localism_bil.aspx (accessed 19 October 2011).

University of Birmingham Policy Commission (2011), *When Tomorrow Comes: The Future of Local Public Services*, Birmingham: University of Birmingham.

Urry, J. (2000), *Sociology Beyond Societies: Mobilities for the Twenty-First Century*, London and New York: Routledge.

USAID (US Agency for International Development) (1999), *Lessons in Implementation: The NGO Story – Building Civil Society in Central and Eastern Europe and the New Independent States*, Washington, DC: USAID Bureau for Europe and Eurasia, Office of Democracy and Governance.

Vasagar, J. (2011), 'Free school plan comes at a price for voluntary groups', *Guardian*, available at: http://www.guardian.co.uk/education/2011/jan/17/young-free-school-groups-refugees (accessed 17 January 2011).

Verdery, K. (1996), *What Was Socialism, and What Comes Next?*, Princeton, NJ: Princeton University Press.

Volunteering England and the TUC (2009), 'A charter for strengthening relations between paid staff and volunteers', available at: http://www.tuc.org.uk/workplace/tuc-17329-f0.pdf (accessed 21 September 2011).

Walby, S. and J. Allen (2004), 'Domestic violence, sexual assault and stalking: findings from the British Crime Survey', *Home Office Research Study* 276, London: Home Office.

Waldman, M. (2000), *Potus Speaks: Finding the Words that Defined the Clinton Presidency*, New York: Simon and Schuster.

Walker, C. and C. Pharoah (eds) (2011), *A Lot of Give*, London: Hodder and Stoughton.

Wallas, G. (1908), *Human Nature in Politics*, reprinted 1948, London: Constable.

Wallas, G. (1914), *The Great Society: A Psychological Analysis*, London, New York and Toronto: Macmillan.

Washbourne, N. (2010), *Mediating Politics*, Maidenhead and New York: Open University.

Wedel, J.R. (1998), *Collision and Collusion: The Strange Case of Western Aid to Eastern Europe*, (hardback 1st edn) New York: St. Martin's Press.

Wedel, J.R., C. Shore, G. Feldman and S. Lathrop (2005), 'Towards an anthropology of public policy', *Annals of the American Academy of Political and Social Science*, **600** (1), 30–51.

Weinbren, D. (2010), *The Oddfellows, 1810–2010. Two Hundred Years of Making Friends and Helping People*, Lancaster: Carnegie.

Wells, P., T. Chadwick-Coule, C. Dayson and G.Morgan (2010), 'Futurebuilders Evaluation: Final Report', Report to Cabinet Office, CRESR, Sheffield: Hallam University, March.

Westall, A. (2010), 'UK government policy and social investment', *Voluntary Sector Review*, **1** (3), 119–24.

White, J. (2003), *Rothschild Buildings: Life in an East End Tenement Block 1887–1920*, London: Pimlico [1st edn 1980: Routledge].

Whiteside, N. (1983), 'Private agencies for public purposes: some new perspectives on policy making in health insurance between the wars', *Journal of Social Policy*, **12** (2), 165–93.

Whiteside, N. (1987), 'Counting the cost: sickness and disability among working people in an era of industrial recession, 1920–39', *Economic History Review*, **40** (2), 228–46.

Whiteside, N. (1997), 'Regulating markets: the real costs of poly-centric administration under the National Health Insurance scheme (1912–46)', *Public Administration*, **75** (3), 467–85.

Whiteside, N. (1999), 'Private provision and public welfare: health insurance between the wars', in D. Green (ed.), *Before Beveridge: Welfare before the Welfare State*, London: IEA Health and Welfare Unit, pp. 26–42.

Who's Who 2011 (2011), available at: http://www.ukwhoswho.com/view/article/oupww/whoswho/U40219/WILSON_Des (accessed 24 February 2011).

Wiener, M. (1971), *Between Two Worlds. The Political Thought of Graham Wallas*, Oxford: Clarendon Press.

Williams, Z. (2011), 'UK riots: This vigilantism is the very embodiment of "big society"', *Guardian*, 10 August.

Wilson, A. (1966), 'Conflict, consensus and charity: politics and the provincial voluntary hospitals in the eighteenth century', *English Historical Review* CXI, 599–619.

Wilson, R. and M. Leach (2011), *Civic Limits. How Much More Involved Can People Get?*, London: ResPublica.

Wind-Cowie, M. (2010), *Civic Streets: The Big Society in Action*, London: Demos.

Windsor, J. (1967), 'Oxbridge and redbrick: the great divide', in R. Mabey (ed.), *Class: A Symposium*, London: Anthony Blond, pp. 53–63.

Women's Aid (2011), 'Government proposals to introduce universal benefits – the implications for domestic violence survivors', available at: http://womensaid.org.uk/domestic-violence-articles.asp?section=0001000100 2200430001&sectionTitle=Articles%3A+government+initiatives&itemid=2682 (accessed 19 August 2011).

Wood, G.D. (1997), 'States without citizens: the problem of the franchise state', in David Hulme and Michael Edwards (eds), *NGOs, States and Donors: Too Close for Comfort?*, London: Macmillan, pp. 79–92.

Woodin, T, D. Crook and V. Carpentier (2010), *Community and Mutual Ownership: A Historical Review*, York: Joseph Rowntree Foundation.

Yeo, S. (1976), *Religion and Voluntary Organisations in Crisis*, London: Croom Helm.

Ylvisaker, P. (1990), 'Family foundations: high risk, high reward', *Family Business Review*, **3** (4) Winter, 331–5.

Youngs, I. (2011), 'Can philanthropy bail out the arts', *BBC News*, available at: http://www.bbc.co.uk/news/entertainment-arts-12694082 (accessed 16 February 2012).

Index